Radio Jockeying and News Anchoring

RADIO JOCKEYING AND NEWS ANCHORING

Aruna Zachariah

KANISHKA PUBLISHERS, DISTRIBUTORS
NEW DELHI-110 002

KANISHKA PUBLISHERS, DISTRIBUTORS
4697/5-21A, Ansari Road, Daryaganj
New Delhi-110 002
Phones : 2327 0497, 2328 8285
Fax : 011-2328 8285
e-mail: kanishka_publishing@yahoo.co.in

First Published 2009

ISBN 978-81-8457-168-4

PRINTED IN INDIA

Published by Madan Sachdeva for Kanishka Publishers, Distributors, 4697/5-21A, Ansari Road, Daryaganj, New Delhi-110 002; Typeset by Sunshine Graphics, Delhi, and Printed at Rajdhani Printers, Delhi.

Preface

This book entitled "Radio Jockeying and News Anchoring: Job Requirements and Processes" promises readers a complete overview of the subject areas under discussion. An introduction is provided to the roles and responsibilities of "News Presenter", "News Reader" and "Anchor" with select case study and listing of prominent news presenters around the world. Elements and dimensions of newsroom, news programme and news hole are described. Focus also lies on headline, news ticker and current events. An overview of news broadcasting, news analysts and infotainment is provided herein with the help of select case study. The subject areas of radio broadcast, talk show and sound recording are also covered with additional highlights regarding radio format, music radio format, campus radio, community radio, pirate radio, internet radio, public broadcasting, commercial broadcasting, radio comedy and radio documentary. This book also discusses news writing and news style in detail. The basic characteristics of feature writing, article writing and column writing are also analyzed. Focus also lies on news style guide, narrative hook, nut graf and obelism. A brief reflection is also presented as far as news interview, news conference and news management are concerned.

Select case study to further illustrate the theme under discussion is also made. An elaborate description of major global news agencies and news bureaus is presented along with select case studies to further understand the involved elements and dimensions. Most popular international news channels and networks have been critically evaluated on a selective leases. Similarly, important Indian news channels in particular and news media in general are covered for discussion. In sum, this book serves the purpose of a complete reference book on the subject area of radio jockeying and news anchoring. Besides, an elaborate annulated bibliography is given to further the research interests of readers. The book also provides an index.

Aruna Zachariah

Contents

1

News Presenter, News Reader and Anchor: An Introduction

NEWS PRESENTER

A news presenter is, broadly speaking, a person that presents a news show on television, radio or the Internet. The term is not commonly used by people in the industry as they tend to use more descriptive—and sometimes country-specific—terms. Examples include "newsreader", "newscaster", and "news anchor."

Different Roles

Newscaster

A newscaster is a presenter of a news bulletin who is himself or herself a working journalist and news gatherer as well as a participant in compiling the script to be delivered in a news bulletin. Prior to the television era, radio-news broadcasts often mixed news with opinion and each presenter strove for a distinctive style. These presenters were referred to as commentators. The last remaining news presenter of this type is Paul Harvey. The term newscaster came into common use to distinguish presenters of straight news broadcasts from commentators. However, in the UK, ITN's presenters are referred to as newscasters (and have been since the 1950s), whilst those working at the BBC are called newsreaders.

News Anchor

In the United States and Canada, presenters of news broadcasts are referred to as news anchors (sometimes anchorperson, anchorman, or anchorwoman) instead of "newscasters." An anchor traditionally is a television personality who presents material prepared for a news programme and, at times, must improvise commentary for live presentation. Many news anchors are also involved in writing and/or editing the news for their programmes.

The term "anchor" was coined by producer Don Hewitt. PBS cites its first usage as being on July 7, 1952, to describe Walter Cronkite's role at the Democratic and Republican National Conventions. According to Hewitt, the term was in reference to the "anchor leg" of a relay race.

CASE STUDY: NBC EVENING NEWS ANCHORS

This is a list of the people who have acted as the principal news anchors for the American NBC network's flagship weekday evening news programme, currently known as *NBC Nightly News*.

- John Cameron Swayze, 1949-56 (*Camel News Caravan*)
- Chet Huntley and David Brinkley, 1956-70 (*Huntley-Brinkley Report*)
- John Chancellor, Frank McGee, and David Brinkley, 1970-71
- John Chancellor, 1971-76
- John Chancellor and David Brinkley, 1976-79
- John Chancellor, 1979-82
- Tom Brokaw and Roger Mudd, 1982-83
- Tom Brokaw, 1983-2004
- Brian Williams, 2004-present

LIST OF NEWS PRESENTERS BY NATIONALITY

This is a list of news presenters by nationality:

American News Anchors

- Ernie Anastos, WNYW Former WABC-TV and WCBS-TV
- Christiane Amanpour, CNN
- Sade Baderinwa, WABC-TV

- Rudi Bakhtiar, formerly at CNN and last seen as Fox News as a correspondent
- Bill Bonds, formerly of WXYZ-TV, WABC-TV and KABC-TV
- Bill Beutel (deceased), WABC-TV formerly ABC News
- Wolf Blitzer, CNN
- Ed Bradley (deceased), CBS News
- David Brinkley (deceased), *The Huntley-Brinkley Report* (NBC)
- Tom Brokaw (semi-retired), NBC News
- Aaron Brown, formerly at CNN and ABC News
- Dara Brown, MSNBC
- Neil Cavuto, FOX News
- John Chancellor (deceased), *NBC Nightly News*
- Liz Cho, WABC-TV, formerly ABC News
- Connie Chung, formerly of CBS News, NBC News, CNN, and MSNBC
- Casey Coleman (deceased), WJW-TV
- Amanda Congdon, Rocketboom
- Anderson Cooper, CNN
- Katie Couric, CBS News, formerly of NBC's Today Show
- Walter Cronkite (retired), CBS News
- John Charles Daly (deceased) ABC News
- Ann Curry, The Today Show, Dateline NBC
- Chet Curtis, NECN
- Sam Donaldson, ABC News
- Lou Dobbs, CNN
- Hugh Downs (retired), ABC News' 20/20, formerly at NBC News
- Douglas Edwards (deceased), CBS News, 1950s
- Harris Faulkner
- Hal Fishman (deceased), KTLA-TV
- Charlie Gaddy (retired), WRAL-TV
- Jim Gardner, WPVI-TV
- Dave Garroway (deceased), "Today Show" NBC
- Charles Gibson, ABC News
- John Gibson, FOX News
- Calvin Hughes, WPLG Local 10
- Nancy Grace, CNN
- Enrique Gratas, Univision

- Roger Grimsby (deceased), formerly of WABC-TV, KGO-TV and WNBC
- Bryant Gumbel, former anchor of NBC's Today Show and CBS' The Early Show
- John Hambrick. Formerly WEWS-TV, KRON-TV, KABC-TV, WNBC, WTVJ and WCIX
- Judd Hambrick
- Mike Hambrick
- Lester Holt, weekend edition of NBC Nightly News and MSNBC
- Brit Hume, FOX News, formerly ABC News
- Chet Huntley (deceased), *The Huntley-Brinkley Report* (NBC)
- Natalie Jacobson (retired), WCVB-TV
- Chris Jansing, MSNBC
- Peter Jennings (deceased), ABC News
- Jim Jensen (deceased), Former WCBS-TV
- Larry Kane (retired), WPVI-TV, WCAU-TV and KYW-TV
- Ted Koppel, ABC News, *Nightline*, Discovery Channel
- Nicole Lapin (News Anchor), CNN, CNN Pipeline, Headline News
- Matt Lauer, Today Show
- Jim Lehrer, *The Newshour with Jim Lehrer* (PBS)
- Dan Lewis, KOMO-TV News
- Nancy Loo, WFLD Former WABC-TV
- Carol Marin, WBBM-TV
- Frank McGee (deceased), NBC News
- Robert MacNeil (retired), *The MacNeil/Lehrer Newshour* (PBS)
- Paul Moyer, KNBC Former KABC-TV
- Roger Mudd, CBS News, NBC News, History Channel
- Edward R. Murrow (deceased)
- Kent Ninomiya
- Keith Olbermann, MSNBC
- Miles O'Brien (Journalist), CNN
- Bill O'Reilly, FOX News
- Jane Pauley (retired), NBC News
- Julie Pearce, KBJR KDLH Northland's News Center
- Stone Phillips, Dateline NBC
- Becky Quick, CNBC Squawk Box
- Dan Rather (retired), CBS News

- Harry Reasoner (deceased), CBS News and ABC News
- Ralph Renick (deceased), WTVJ
- Frank Reynolds (deceased), ABC News
- Dennis Richmond (retired), KTVU
- Bill Ritter, WABC-TV
- Geraldo Rivera, FOX News
- John Roberts (television reporter), CBS News, CNN
- Robin Roberts, ABC News
- Max Robinson (deceased), ABC News
- Tim Russert (deceased), NBC News
- Al Sanders (deceased), WJZ-TV
- Jessica Savitch (deceased), NBC News and *Frontline (PBS)*
- Diane Sawyer, ABC News
- Chuck Scarborough, WNBC
- Bob Schieffer, *CBS News*
- Bernard Shaw (retired), CNN
- Tina Tyus-Shaw, WSAV
- Kent Shocknek, KCBS-TV
- Maria Shriver (on leave of absence), NBC News
- Sue Simmons, WNBC
- Howard K. Smith (deceased), ABC News previously at CBS News
- Shepard Smith, FOX News
- Lori Stokes, WABC-TV
- John Stossel, ABC News' 20/20
- Mark Thompson (TV)
- Marie Torre
- Jerry Turner (deceased), WJZ-TV
- Garrick Utley, CNN, formerly NBC News and later ABC News
- Greta Van Susteren, Fox News
- Elizabeth Vargas, ABC News
- Meredith Vieira, NBC News
- Chris Wallace, Fox News, formerly at NBC News and later ABC News
- Mike Wallace (retired), "60 Minutes" CBS
- Bree Walker-Former KGTV KCBS-TV AND WCBS-TV
- Barbara Walters, ABC News
- Dave Ward, KTRK-TV
- Bob Weaver, WTVJ

- Lee Webb, Christian Broadcasting Network
- Brian Williams, *NBC Nightly News*
- Cindy Williams, WCSH
- Diana Williams, WABC-TV, formerly WNEV-TV (now WHDH-TV)
- Jack Williams, WBZ-TV
- Mary Alice Williams
- Pete Williams
- Steve Wilson (Reporter)
- Al Wiman
- Bob Woodruff (on extended absence), ABC News (Bob Woodruff and Judy Woodruff are not related)
- Judy Woodruff (retired), *Frontline (PBS)* and CNN
- Chris Wragge
- Kareen Wynter
- Gideon Yago
- Toni Yates
- Bob Young
- Paula Zahn, formerly of CNN
- Arnold Zenker
- Marvin Zindler (deceased), KTRK-TV

Australian Newsreaders

- Tony Jones—ABC
- Sandra Sully—Network Ten
- Natarsha Belling—Network Ten
- Bill Woods—Network Ten
- Kathryn Robinson—Network Ten
- Natalie Barr—Seven Network
- Ann Sanders—Seven Network
- Samantha Armytage—Seven Network
- Rebecca Maddern—Seven Network
- Georgie Gardner—Nine Network
- Michael Usher—Nine Network
- Juanita Phillips—ABC
- Mark Ferguson—Nine Network
- Brian Henderson (Retired)—Nine Network
- Jim Waley (Retired)—Nine Network
- James Dibble (Retired)—ABC
- Ron Wilson—Network Ten

- Deborah Knight—Network Ten
- Ian Ross—Seven Network
- Chris Bath—Seven Network
- Sir Eric Pearce (retired and deceased)—Nine Network
- Brian Naylor (retired)—Nine Network
- Peter Hitchener—Nine Network
- Ian Henderson—ABC
- Kathy Bowlen—ABC
- Mal Walden—Network Ten
- Helen Kapalos—Network Ten
- Jennifer Keyte—Seven Network
- Peter Mitchell—Seven Network
- David Johnston (retired)—Seven Network/Network Ten
- Bruce Paige—Nine Network
- Heather Foord—Nine Network
- Bill McDonald—Network Ten
- Marie-Louise Theile—Network Ten (Retired)
- Rod Young—Seven Network
- Kay McGrath—Seven Network
- Sharyn Ghidella—Seven Network
- Kevin Crease (deceased)—Nine Network
- Rob Kelvin—Nine Network
- Michael Smyth—ABC
- Rebecca Morse—Network Ten
- George Donikian—Network Ten
- John Riddell—Seven Network
- Jane Doyle—Seven Network
- Dixie Marshall—Nine Network
- Sonia Vinci—Nine Network
- Tim Webster—Network Ten
- Charmaine Dragun (deceased)—Network Ten
- Rick Ardon—Seven Network
- Susannah Carr—Seven Network

Brazilian Newsreaders

- Sandra Annenberg
- Fátima Bernardes
- William Bonner (Journalist)
- Zeca Camargo
- Boris Casoy

- Evaristo Costa
- Hermano Henning
- Glória Maria
- Carlos Nascimento (journalist)
- Ana Paula Padrao

British Newsreaders and Newscasters

- George Alagiah, BBC *Six O'Clock News.*
- Michael Aspel, BBC *Nine O'Clock News* in the 1960s.
- Mark Austin, ITN *ITV Evening News* and *ITV News at 10.30.*
- Zeinab Badawi, BBC *World News Today.*
- Richard Baker, BBC *Nine O'Clock News* co-presenter in the 1960s and 1970s.
- Reginald Bosanquet, ITN presenter.
- Fiona Bruce, *BBC Ten O'Clock News.*
- Michael Buerk, BBC, Today Programme and previously BBC Nine O'Clock News.
- Sir Alastair Burnet, ITN longtime presenter of *News at Ten.*
- Jill Dando (deceased), Ex-BBC presenter.
- Sir Robin Day, ITN presenter in the 1950s and 1960s.
- Alan Dedicoat, BBC Radio 2 Newsreader (Also National Lottery's "Voice of the Balls").
- Katie Derham, ITN, presenting the *ITV Lunchtime News.*
- Peter Donaldson, BBC Radio 4.
- Huw Edwards, *BBC Ten O'Clock News.*
- Anna Ford, ITN *News at Ten,* retired from BBC in 2006, where she presented the *BBC One O'Clock News.*
- Sandy Gall, ITN 1963 to 1992, part of the original team of News at Ten in 1967.
- Andrew Gardner, one of the original team of News at Ten when it started in 1967.
- Krishnan Guru-Murthy, *Channel 4 News.*
- Darren Jordon, Al-Jazeera (from November 2006).
- Natasha Kaplinsky, Previous *BBC Six O'Clock News,* now Five News.
- Kenneth Kendall, BBC *Nine O'Clock News* co-presenter in the 1960s and 1970s.
- Sheena McDonald, *Channel 4 News* presenter in the 1990s.
- Sir Trevor McDonald, ITN, *Tonight.*

- John "Boggy" Marsh, BBC Radio 2 Newsreader, frequently on Wake Up to Wogan.
- Cliff Michelmore, Presenter, *Tonight*.
- Leonard Parkin, ITN Newsreader in the 1970s and 1980s.
- Jeremy Paxman, BBC, now presenter of *Newsnight*.
- Fiona Phillips, *GMTV*.
- Sophie Raworth, *BBC One O'Clock News*.
- Angela Rippon, BBC, then the (now defunct) *ITV News Channel*.
- Moira Stuart, Previously of *BBC Nine O'Clock News* and BBC Breakfast.
- Jon Snow, *Channel 4 News*.
- Peter Sissons, *Channel 4 News*, later BBC *Nine O'Clock News*. Now BBC News.
- Justin Webb, Ex-BBC Six O'Clock News and BBC One O'Clock News.
- Jonathan Wheatley, BBC World Service.
- Richard Whitmore (retired), BBC.
- Peter Woods, former newsreader on BBC 1 and BBC 2.
- Kirsty Young, Ex-*Five News*.

Canadian News Anchors

- Earl Cameron (deceased), *The National News* (CBC)
- Bernard Derome, *Le Téléjournal* (SRC)
- Barbara Frum (deceased), *The Journal* (CBC)
- Ian Hanomansing, *Canada Now* (CBC)
- Peter Kent, *The National* (CBC) and *First National* (Global)
- Harvey Kirck (deceased), *CTV National News* (CTV)
- Peter Mansbridge, *The National* (CBC)
- Knowlton Nash (retired), *The National* (CBC)
- Tara Nelson, *Global National* (Global)
- Kevin Newman, *Global National* (Global)
- Tony Parsons, *Canada Tonight*
- Sandie Rinaldo, *CTV National News* (CTV)
- Lloyd Robertson, *CTV National News* (CTV)
- Mutsumi Takahashi, *CTV News Montreal* (CTV)
- Sophie Thibault, *Les Nouvelles TVA*, first North American solo national news anchorwoman (in 2002)
- Pamela Wallin, *Canada AM* (CTV) and *Prime Time News* (CBC)

Chinese News Anchors

The following are announcers on CCTV's *Xinwen Lianbo*, the official national news programme in mainland China:

- Kang Hui
- Li Ruiying
- Li Zimeng
- Luo Jing
- Wang Ning
- Xing Zhibin
- Zhang Hongmin

Colombian Newsreaders

- Silvia Corzo, *Caracol TV*
- María Lucía Fernández, *Caracol TV*
- Ángela Patricia Janiot, *CNN en Español*
- Claudia Palacios, *CNN en Español*

Finnish Newsreaders

- Arvi Lind, *YLE*

Egyptian Newsreaders

- Shaheera Amin, *Nile TV*
- Yousef Gamal El Din, *Nile TV*
- Bassel Sabri, *Nile TV*

French Newsreaders

- Patrick Poivre d'Arvor, TF1
- Arlette Chabot, France 2
- Claire Chazal, TF1
- David Pujadas, France 2
- Béatrice Schönberg, France 2
- Jean-Pierre Pernaut, TF1
- Melissa Theuriau, La Chaîne Info then M6
- Christine Ockrent, France 2 and France 3
- Marie Drucker, France 3
- Audrey Pulvar, France 3
- Léon Zitrone, TF1
- Elise Lucet, France 3

Greek Newsreaders

- Maria Houkli, NET, ERT
- Nikos Hadjinikolaou, Alpha TV
- Elli Stai, ANT1 (known as Antenna)
- Eva Kaili, Weekends Mega Channel

Hong Kong News Anchors

- Lavender Cheung, *Cable News Hong Kong*
- Joanne Yung, *Cable News Hong Kong*
- Jolly Wong, *Cable News Hong Kong*
- Cheung Wai Tsz, *ATV News*
- Kaman Lee, *TVB News*

Indian Newsreaders

- Abul Nasr Iqbal, INDIA NEWS, formerly with INDIA TV
- Munawwar Alam [DD & AIR NEWS (URDU)]
- Nidhi Razdan, NDTV
- Sukanya Balakrishnan, All India Radio
- Prannoy Roy, NDTV
- Barkha Dutt, NDTV
- Rajdeep Sardesai, CNN-IBN, formerly with NDTV
- Vikram Chandra, NDTV
- Paritosh Vasireddy, NTV-Telugu
- Naveen Soni, Zee Business, formerly with CNBC
- Sumit Awasthi, IBN 7
- Shivendra Srivastava, Star News
- Arnab Goswami, Times Now
- Adarsh Jha, INDIA NEWS
- Ravi K Vaish, INDIA NEWS, formerly with Zee News and IBN-7
- Rashid Hashmi, INDIA NEWS
- Kanthi Suresh, Doordarshan
- Azam Azmi, ETV urdu
- Ravi Prakash, TV9 Telugu

Irish Newscasters

- Bryan Dobson, *RTÉ*
- Anne Doyle, *RTÉ*

- Brian Jennings
- Sharon Ní Bheoláin
- Gráinne Seoige, *TnaG, TV3* and *Sky News Ireland*
- Mary Kennedy, *RTÉ*

Irish Newsreaders

- Eileen Dunne, *RTÉ*
- Charles Mitchel, *RTÉ*

Israeli Newsreaders

- Haim Yavin, *Channel 1*

Japanese Newscasters

- Hiroko Kuniya (f.), *NHK (Japan Broadcasting Corporation)*
- Hideo Yanagisawa (m.), *NHK (Japan Broadcasting Corporation)*
- Masako Usui (f.), *NTV (Nippon Television Network Corporation)*
- Tetsuya Chikushi (m.), *TBS (Tokyo Broadcasting System)*
- Yûko Andō (f.), *FNN (Fuji Television Network)*
- Ichirô Furutachi (m.), *EX (TV Asahi Corporation)*

Latin American Newsreaders

- Enrique Gratas, Univision
- Joaquin Lopez Doriga, Televisa
- Neyda Sandoval, Univision
- Ilana Sod, MTV Latin America

New Zealand Newsreaders

- Judy Bailey, ONE News (retired)
- Greg Boyed, ONE News and TVNZ News At 8
- Tom Bradley, ONE News (retired)
- Angela D'Audney, ONE News (deceased)
- Corin Dann, ONE News
- Simon Dallow, ONE News
- Liz Gunn, ONE News (retired)
- John Hawkesby, ONE News (moved from 3 News) (retired)

- Kate Hawkesby, ONE News (retired)
- April Ieremia, ONE News
- Richard Long, ONE News (retired)
- Alison Mau, ONE News
- Bernadine Oliver-Kirby, ONE News
- Wendy Petrie, ONE News
- Andrew Saville, ONE News
- Tony Veitch, ONE News (retired)
- Neil Waka, ONE News
- Peter Williams, ONE News
- Geraline Knox, TVNZ News At 8
- Sonia Voigt, TVNZ News At 8
- Simon Mercep, TVNZ News at 8
- Hilary Barry, 3 News
- Mike McRoberts, 3 News (moved from ONE News)
- Carolyn Robinson, 3 News
- Rebecca Singh, 3 News
- Alistair Wilkinson, 3 News
- Suzy Clarkson, Prime News
- Eric Young, Prime News (moved from ONE News)

Pakistani Newsreaders

- Summiya Rizwan, PTV, ARY One World
- Asma Iqbal, Geo News
- Muhammad Khalid, Geo News
- Rehman Azhar, Express News
- Nida Sameer, Geo News
- Sajjad Waqar Khan, TeleBiz, CNBC, ARY One World, Geo News
- Iqrar ul Hassan Syed, ARY One World
- Ashar Zaidi, Geo News
- Najia Ashar, Geo News
- Salman Hasan, Geo News
- Faeza Dawood, ARY One World
- Jehan Ara Saeed, Radio Pakistan
- Tariq Mateen, Geo News
- Javed Iqbal, Geo News
- Masood Raza, Geo News
- Wajih Sani, Geo News
- Saud Zafar, Geo News

- Shehzad Hasan, Geo News
- Sarah Alfred, Geo News
- Waris Khan, Apna Channel
- Ghulam Murtaza, Dunya News
- Adil Abbasi, Samaa
- Rizwan Zaidi, FM-105
- Mukhtar Ahmed, UniPress
- Syed Monis Raza, CNBC Pakistan
- Myeda Syed, CNBC Pakistan
- Saadia Shaikh, CNBC Pakistan
- Zobia Zaman, CNBC Pakistan

Philippine Newscasters

- Angelo Castro Jr., *The World Tonight*, ABS-CBN, since 1986
- Noli De Castro, *TV Patrol*, ABS-CBN, up to 1998
- Arnold Clavio, *Saksi*, GMA Network
- Mike Enriquez, *24 Oras*, GMA Network
- Ted Failon
- Mari Kaimo, *News Central*, Studio 23
- Rey Langit
- Loren Legarda, *The World Tonight*, ABS-CBN, up to 1998
- Ivan Mayrina, *News on Q*
- Vicky Morales, *Saksi*, GMA Network
- Tina Monzon-Palma, *The World Tonight*, ABS-CBN
- Daniel Razon, *Hataw Balita*, UNTV-37
- Maria Ressa, ABS-CBN and former CNN Southeast Asia News Bureau Chief
- Korina Sanchez, *TV Patrol* (up to 2004) and *Bandila*, ABS-CBN
- Rhea Santos, *News on Q*
- Mel Tiangco, *24 Oras*, GMA Network

Romanian Newsreaders

- Dana Macsim, *N24*

Singaporean Newsreaders

- Glenda Chong, *News 5 Tonight*
- Genevieve Woo, *Channel NewsAsia*

Soviet and Russian Newsreaders

Tatar Newsreaders

- Abdulla Dubin, *Tatarstan Television and Radio Broadcasting*

Spanish Newsreaders

- Iñaki Gabilondo, Cuatro
- Lorenzo Milá, TVE
- Letizia Ortiz (Princess of Asturias), former TVE
- Matías Prats Luque, Antena 3

Sri Lankan Newsreaders

- Vernon Corea, *Radio Ceylon* (deceased)
- Jimmy Bharucha, *Radio Ceylon* (deceased)
- Ravi Gamage, *Sri Lanka Rupavahini Corporation 1998-2002 and Derana TV 2005-07*
- Dominic Kellar, *ABC Radio Network; 2005-07 and Colombo Communications 2007-08*
- Ruveen Dias, *ABC Radio Network; 2006-07 and Colombo Communications 2007-08*

Swedish Newsreaders

- Lars Adaktusson (retired), *Aktuellt*, Sveriges Television
- Jarl Alfredius, *Aktuellt*, Sveriges Television
- Olle Björklund (deceased), *Aktuellt*, Sveriges Television
- Claes Elfsberg, *Rapport*, Sveriges Television
- Anna Hedenmo, *Aktuellt*, Sveriges Television
- Gun Hägglund (retired), *Aktuellt*, Sveriges Television
- Anna Lindmarker, *TV4Nyheterna*, TV4
- Ulla-Carin Lindquist (deceased), *Rapport*, Sveriges Television
- Bengt Magnusson, *TV4Nyheterna*, TV4
- Ulrika Nilsson, *TV4Nyheterna*, TV4
- Petra Nordlund McGahan, TV4Nyheterna, TV4
- Morgan Olofsson, *Rapport*, Sveriges Television
- Lars Orup (deceased), *Aktuellt*, Sveriges Television
- Ann-Britt Ryd Pettersson, *Aktuellt*, Sveriges Television
- Katarina Sandström, *Rapport*, Sveriges Television
- Lisbeth Åkerman, *Rapport*, Sveriges Television

Trinidad and Europe Newsreaders

- Shelly Dass, *CNC3*
- Francesca Hawkins, *CNC3*
- Colleen Holder, *TV6 News*
- Samantha John, *TV6 News*
- Dominic Kallipersad, formerly at Panorama and TV6 News
- Paolo Kernahan, *Gayelle News*
- Roger Sant, *CNC3 Sports*

Turkish News Anchors

- Ali Kýrca, SHOW, formerly at TRT 1, ATV, Star, NTV and later ATV
- Mehmet Ali Birand, Kanal D, formerly at TRT 1, SHOW and later CNN Türk
- Uður Dündar, Star, formerly at TRT 1, SHOW, Kanal D and later CNN Türk
- Mehmet Barlas, ATV, formerly at TRT 1 and later NTV
- Nermin Tuğ uslu, TRT 2, formerly at TRT 1, Kanal 6 and later TRT 1
- Özlem Gürses, Kanal 1, formerly at ATV, Star and later HaberTürk
- Fulin Arikan, TRT 1

2

Newsroom and News Programmes: Elements and Dimensions

NEWSROOM

A newsroom is the place where journalists—reporters, editors, and producers, along with other staffers—work to gather news to be published in a newspaper or magazine or broadcast on television, cable or radio. Some journalism organizations refer to the newsroom as the city room.

Print Publication Newsrooms

In a print publication's newsroom, reporters sit at desks, gather information, and write articles or stories, in the past on typewriters, then after the early 1980s, on computers. These stories are submitted to editors, who usually sit together at one large desk, where the stories are reviewed and possibly rewritten. Reporters generally used the inverted pyramid method for writing their stories, although some of the best journalistic writing used other methods; some of the work of Tom Wolfe is an example of reporting that did not follow that style. Once finished, editors write a headline for the story and lay it out on a newspaper or magazine page. Editors also review photographs, maps, charts or other graphics to be used with a story. At many newspapers, copy editors who review stories for publication work together at what is called a copy desk, supervised by a copy desk chief, night editor, or news editor. Assignment editors, including the city editor, who supervise reporters' work, may or may not work with the copy desk.

How a newsroom is structured and functions depends in part on the size of the publication and when it is published, especially if it is a daily newspaper, which can either be published in the morning (an a.m. cycle) or the evening (a p.m. cycle). Most daily newspapers follow the a.m. cycle.

In almost all newspaper newsrooms, editors customarily meet daily with the chief editor to discuss which stories will be placed on the front page, section front pages, and other pages. This is commonly called a "budget meeting" due to the fact that the main topic of the meeting is the budgeting or allocation of space in the next issue. Newsrooms often have an assignment desk where staffers monitor emergency scanners, answer telephone calls, faxes and e-mails from the public and reporters. The assignment desk is also responsible for assigning reporters to stories or deciding what is covered and what is not. In many newsrooms, the assignment desk is raised a step or two above the rest of the newsroom, allowing staffers who work at the desk to see everyone in the newsroom.

Broadcast Newsrooms

Broadcast newsrooms are very similar to newspaper newsrooms. The major difference is these newsrooms include small rooms to edit video or audio.

Misconceptions

The popular but dated conception of an American newsroom is a large room filled with desks, typewriters and teletype terminals, where many men and few women work loudly and furiously, reading their notes from reporters' notebooks, talking on the telephone, typing out their stories, arguing with each other, smoking and even drinking alcoholic beverages openly.

The denizens of an American newsroom are portrayed as hard-nosed, world-weary cynics with little sympathy for the subjects of their stories, although some are portrayed as caring people who developed thick skins as a reaction to having reported so many depressing stories. They also are portrayed as committed to telling the truth as they found it, no matter the cost. Some consider the ethic of journalism akin to a moral philosophy in how journalists struggle to live by its principles.

Changes in Newsrooms

The modern American newsroom has gone through several changes in the last 50 years, with computers replacing typewriters and the Internet replacing teletype terminals, and more from ethnic minority groups as well as women are working as reporters and editors, including many managerial positions. Many newspapers have internet editions, and at some reporters are required to meet tighter deadlines to have their stories posted on the newspaper website, even before the print edition is printed and circulated. However, some things have not changed; many reporters still use reporter's notebooks and the telephone to gather information, although the computer has become another essential tool for reporting.

Newsrooms in Popular Culture

- The American newsroom has been a location of many books, movies and television shows about the newspaper and magazine business, especially movies like *His Girl Friday, All the President's Men* or *The Paper*, and television shows like *Lou Grant* and *Murphy Brown*.
- A Canadian newsroom is the location of the CBC Television comedy *The Newsroom*. It is also shown on some public television stations in the United States.
- *The 2004 Film Anchorman*: The Legend of Ron Burgundy, is set around a newsroom.

Other Uses

Newsroom is also the name of a Web site based in New Zealand which mostly supplies news to corporate intranets.

- *Newsroom Website*: Newsroom was the name of a computer software programme published by Springboard Software in the 1980s, considered to be among the first WYSIWYG desktop publishing programmes for the Apple II personal computer.

NEWS PROGRAMME

A news programme, news show, or newscast is a regularly

scheduled radio or television programme that reports current events. News is typically reported in a series of individual stories that are presented by one or more anchors. A news programme can include live or recorded interviews by field reporters, expert opinions, opinion poll results, and occasional editorial content. A special category of news programmes are entirely editorial in format. These host polemic debates between pundits of various ideological philosophies

HEADLINE

A headline (sometimes termed a news *hed*) is text at the top of a newspaper article, indicating the nature of the article below it.

Format

Headlines are usually written in bold and in a much larger size than the article text. Front page headlines are often in upper case so that they can be easily read by the passing potential customer. Headlines in other parts of the paper are more commonly in sentence case though title case is often used in the USA. Headline conventions include normally using present tense, omitting forms of the verb "to be" in certain contexts, and removing short articles like "a" and "the." Most newspapers feature a very large headline on their front page, dramatically describing the biggest news of the day. A headline may also be followed by a smaller secondary headline which gives a bit more information or a subhead (also called a deck or nutgraf in some areas). Words chosen for headlines are often short, giving rise to headlines.

According to Russ Willison Headlines are the *"barb on the hook."*

Production of Headlines within the Editorial Environment

Headlines are generally written by copy editors, but may also be written by the writer, the page layout designer or a news editor or managing editor. The film *The Shipping News* has an illustrative exchange between the protagonist, who is learning how to write for a local newspaper, and his publisher.

- *Publisher*: It is finding the centre of your story, the beating heart of it, that is what makes a reporter. You have to start by making up some headlines. You know: short, punchy, dramatic headlines. Now, have a look [*pointing at dark clouds gathering in the sky over the ocean*] what do you see? Tell me the headline.
- *Protagonist*: HORIZON FILLS WITH DARK CLOUDS?
- *Publisher*: IMMINENT STORM THREATENS VILLAGE.
- *Protagonist*: But what if no storm comes?
- *Publisher*: VILLAGE SPARED FROM DEADLY STORM.

In the United States, headline contests are sponsored by the American Copy Editors Society, the National Federation of Press Women, and many state press associations.

Unusual Headlines

Occasionally, the need to keep headlines brief leads to unintentional double meanings, if not double entendres. For example, if the story is about the president of Iraq trying to acquire weapons, the headline might be IRAQI HEAD SEEKS ARMS. Or if some agricultural legislation is defeated in the United States House of Representatives, the title could read FARMER BILL DIES IN HOUSE.

- WALL ST. LAYS AN EGG—*Variety* on Black Monday (1929).
- STICKS NIX HICK PIX—*Variety* writing that rural moviegoers preferred urbane films (1935).
- DEWEY DEFEATS TRUMAN—The *Chicago Tribune* reporting the wrong election winner (1948).
- FORD TO CITY: DROP DEAD—*New York Daily News* reporting the denial of a federal bailout (1975).
- SICK TRANSIT'S GLORIOUS MONDAY—*New York Daily News* reporting a state transit bailout (1980).
- GOTCHA!—The UK *Sun* on the sinking of the *Belgrano* during the Falklands War (1981).

- HEADLESS BODY IN TOPLESS BAR—*New York Post* on a local murder (1983).
- HICKS NIX KNICKS IN SIX—*New York Daily News* on an NBA Conference Finals win by Indiana Pacers (2000).
- GREAT SATAN SITS DOWN WITH THE AXIS OF EVIL—The UK *The Times* on US-Iran talks (2007).
- SUPER CALEY GO BALLISTIC CELTIC ARE ATROCIOUS—*Sun* on Inverness Caledonian Thistle beating Celtic in the Scottish Cup.
- FREDDIE STARR ATE MY HAMSTER—*Sun* on Lea La Salle's claim that the comedian had eaten her pet in a sandwich. Max Clifford later admitted that the story was a fabrication.
- ICE CREAM MAN HAS ASSETS FROZEN—*BBC News*: An ice cream salesman has his assets frozen for suspectedly smuggling tobacco.

NEWS TICKER

A news ticker (sometimes referred to as a "crawler") is a small screen space on news television networks dedicated to presenting headlines or minor pieces of news. It may also refer to a long, thin scoreboard-style display seen around the front of some offices or public buildings.

TV News Tickers

History

Though modern and efficient news tickers were not popularized in the United States until September 11, 2001, the first record of a news ticker as part of a regular broadcast is from *NBC's Today* show on its debut edition, January 14, 1952. Without the benefit of computer-generated headlines and graphics, the ticker was vastly different than the one we would know today. The *Today* ticker was an actual piece of paper with typewritten headlines superimposed on the lower third of the screen. The ticker was never very successful as a communications tool, and was dropped not long thereafter.

By the 1980s, in northern parts of the United States, many local television stations used a ticker placed over morning local and network newscasts to pass along information on school closings due to weather. Severe weather watch and warning information was also commonly run on local station tickers. In both cases, the start of the ticker's cycle was often accompanied by an attention signal, such as warning tones, a small jingle from the station's news theme or network (such as the NBC Chimes), or either the station's calls or channel number in Morse code.

One of the first networks to regularly utilize a ticker was CNN Headline News. During the late 1980s and early 1990s, the ticker featured stock prices during the daytime, and sports scores during the evening and weekend. CNBC and forerunner network Financial News Network also debuted a ticker featuring stock prices during business hours. By the mid-1980s, ESPN featured an update ticker at the top and bottom of each hour, scrolling up-to-the-minute sports scores and news. By 1996, spin-off network ESPN2 debuted a ticker, dubbed the "BottomLine," which featured non-stop sports scores and news nearly twenty-four hours a day. ESPNEWS, after a 2000 redesign of their on-air look became the first network to keep their ticker going during commercial breaks.

Several European news channels have used tickers as part of their on-air design for years. For example, German news channel n-tv has had a news ticker since its launch in 1992. While tickers had been used occasionally by other networks over the years, it was the September 11 attacks of 2001 that made the ticker a ubiquitous part of the television news experience. Needing a way to provide a continuous stream of vital but repetitive emergency information to viewers, Fox News Channel placed a ticker on-screen at 10:49 a.m. CNN launched its own ticker at 11:11 a.m., and MSNBC started one at approximately 2:00 p.m. Although the need for attack-related tickers lasted only a few weeks, the management at all three major U.S. news channels quickly decided that news tickers would help increase viewership amongst viewers with the ability to process multiple simultaneous streams of information. As a result, the tickers have been permanent features on all three channels ever since, except during some documentary programming, presidential speeches, or select other programmes.

In Australia, the first major use of news tickers also occurred in the aftermath of the September 11 attacks. Since the initial introduction, morning programmes Sunrise and Today have kept tickers. While visible on other channels, tickers are rarer and more specific: ABC TV News at Midday has a stock ticker while Sky News Australia normally features a stream of weather information.

The use of news tickers has also been parodied on a number of programmes, including an episode of *The Simpsons* from 2003 (*Mr. Spritz Goes to Washington*), as well as a sketch on *Saturday Night Live*. Films such as *Austin Powers in Goldmember* sometimes place jokes within news crawls seen on screen. The Onion News Network uses a parody ticker to offer jokes in its online newscasts. The Australian show CNNNN went a step further: although it featured a joke news ticker throughout the show, one episode had a news ticker summarizing the initial news ticker, as well as one for the sight impaired, which covered the whole screen.

Current Uses

The presentation of headlines or other information in a news ticker has become a common element of many different news networks. The use of the ticker has been different on a number of different channels, financial news channels using two or more tickers progressing at different speeds, displaying stock prices and business headlines. Networks with a focus on sports often use a slightly different system, where scores and status of current and finished games are displaced one by one, along with minor sports highlights. News networks commonly use a setup in which news headlines are scrolled across the bottom half of the screen, though some variations have formed, such as CNN International presenting them without a scrolling effect. Usage of the scroller has also grown in a number of local news stations, used during hours of severe weather to provide information about storms and areas effected by them, in addition to other uses, such as presented school delays and cancellations during winter weather in some regions, and the presentation of headlines alike to the general news networks.

Due to their prevalence currently, they have been occasionally been made targets of pranks and vandalism. For example, a North Carolina station used a ticker where viewers could submit relevant information such as school closings or traffic delays via telephone or Internet, which would be displayed automatically without human screening and intervention. In February of 2004, a news ticker on News 14 Carolina was exploited to display humorous messages, including the infamous "All your base are belong to us."

Building News Tickers

The most famous news ticker display is the "zipper" that circles One Times Square in New York City. *The New York Times* erected the first such display in 1928, and now several buildings in midtown Manhattan feature such a display. A similar display appears on the exterior of the Fox News/News Corporation headquarters in the west extension of Manhattan's Rockefeller Centre. Another ticker, displaying the latest stock details, is also located in Times Square.

The Reuters buildings at Canary Wharf and in Toronto have news tickers and stock tickers for the NYSE, NASDAQ and LSE. The Toronto building's ticker also shows TSX quotes. When NBC renovated 10 Rockefeller Centre to accommodate the *Today* show in 1994, a red-LED ticker was added to the perimeter of the building at the juncture of the first and second floors. The ticker is visible to spectators in Rockefeller Plaza and passersby on West 49th Street and updates continuously, even when the show is off the air.

NEWS HOLE

The news hole is the amount of content a news provider needs to create in every publishing cycle. For example, a news broadcast on radio or TV has a certain amount of air time it needs to fill. Likewise, a newspaper, magazine, newsletter, or website, has a news hole of a certain number of printed pages, dependent in part on how many advertisements are sold to advertisers.

CURRENT EVENTS

Current events are contemporary happenings of significance. The phrase may also refer to the following:

- *Current Events*: A journal published by Weekly Reader Publishing.
- *Portal*: Current events, a Wikipedia introduction to ongoing global news stories

3

News Broadcasting, News Analysts and Infotainment: An Overview

BROADCASTING

Broadcasting is the distribution of audio and/or video signals which transmit programmes to an audience. The audience may be the general public or a relatively large sub-audience, such as children or young adults.

Fig. 3.1: A TV Studio Broadcast Center in Olympia, Washington.

There is a wide variety of broadcasting systems, all of which have different capabilities. The smallest broadcasting systems are institutional public address systems, which transmit spoken messages and music within, for example, a school or hospital, and low-powered radio or television stations transmitting programmes to a small local area. National radio and television broadcasters have nationwide coverage, using retransmitter towers, satellite systems, and cable distribution. Satellite radio and television broadcasting can cover areas as wide as entire continents, while internet channels can distribute text or streamed music and speech worldwide. Individuals can also use make use of internet services to stream or podcast sound or video.

The sequencing of content in a broadcast is called a schedule. As with all technological endeavours, a number of technical terms and slang have developed. A list of these terms can be found at list of broadcasting terms. Television and radio programmes are distributed through radio broadcasting or cable, often both simultaneously. By coding signals and having decoding equipment in homes, the latter also enables subscription-based channels and pay-per-view services.

The term "broadcast" originally referred to the sowing of seeds by scattering them over a wide field. It was adopted by early radio engineers from the midwestern United States to refer to the analogous dissemenation of radio signals. Broadcasting forms a very large segment of the mass media. Broadcasting to a very narrow range of audience is called narrowcasting.

Economically there are a few ways in which stations are able to continually broadcast. Each differs in the method by which stations are funded:

- In-kind donations of time and skills by volunteers (common with community broadcasters);
- Direct government payments or operation of public broadcasters;
- Indirect government payments, such as radio and television licenses;
- Grants from foundations or business entities;
- Selling advertising or sponsorships; and
- Public subscription or membership.

Broadcasters may rely on a combination of these business models. For example, National Public Radio, a non-commercial network within the United States, receives grants from the Corporation for Public Broadcasting (which in turn receives funding from the U.S. government), by public membership, and by selling "extended credits" to corporations.

Recorded Broadcasts and Live Broadcasts

The first regular television broadcasts began in 1937. One can record and produce live broadcasts. The former allows correcting errors, and removing superfluous or undesired material, rearranging it, applying slow-motion and repetitions, and other techniques to enhance the programme. However, some live events like sports telecasts can include some of the aspects including slow motion clips of important goals/hits etc. in between the live telecast.

Fig. 3.2: A TV Studio Control Room in Olympia, Washington.

American radio network broadcasters habitually forbade prerecorded broadcasts in the 1930s and 1940s requiring radio programmes played for the Eastern and Central time zones to be repeated three hours later for the Pacific time zone. This restriction was dropped for special occasions, as in the case of the German dirigible airship *Hindenburg* at Lakehurst, New Jersey in 1937. During World War II, prerecorded broadcasts from war correspondents were allowed on U.S. radio. In addition, American radio programme were recorded for playback by Armed Forces Radio stations around the world.

A disadvantage of recording first is that the public may know the outcome of an event from another source, which may be a spoiler. In addition, prerecording prevents live announcers from deviating from an officially-approved script, as occurred with propaganda broadcasts from Germany in the 1940s and with Radio Moscow in the 1980s.

Many events are advertised as being live, although they are often "recorded live" (sometimes called "live-to-tape"). This is particularly true of performances of musical artists on radio when they visit for an in-studio concert performance. This intentional blurring of the distinction between live and recorded media is viewed with chagrin among many music lovers. Similar situations have sometimes appeared in television ("*The Cosby Show* is recorded in front of a live studio audience"). A broadcast may be distributed through several physical means. If coming directly from the studio at a single radio or TV station, it is simply sent through the air chain to the transmitter and thence from the antenna on the tower out to the world. Programming may also come through a communications satellite, played either live or recorded for later transmission. Networks of stations may simulcast the same programming at the same time, originally via microwave link, now usually by satellite.

Distribution to stations or networks may also be through physical media, such as analog or digital videotape, CD, DVD, and sometimes other formats. Usually these are included in another broadcast, such as when electronic news gathering returns a story to the station for inclusion on a news programme. The final leg of broadcast distribution is how the signal gets to the listener or viewer. It may come over the air as with a radio station or TV station to an antenna and receiver, or may come through cable TV or cable radio (or "wireless cable") via the station or directly from a network. The Internet may also bring either radio or TV to the recipient, especially with multicasting allowing the signal and bandwidth to be shared.

The term "broadcast network" is often used to distinguish networks that broadcast an over-the-air television signal that can be received using a television antenna from so-called networks that are broadcast only via cable or satellite television. The term "broadcast television" can refer to the programming of such networks.

Legal Definitions

UK

The Copyright, Designs and Patents Act, 1988 defines a

broadcast as *a transmission by wireless telegraphy of visual images, sounds, or other information which is capable of lawful reception by the public or which is made for presentation to the public*. It thus covers radio, television, teletext *et al*.

NEWS BROADCASTING

News broadcasting (also known as *newscast* or *newsbreak*) is the broadcasting of various news events and other information via television or radio. The content is usually either produced locally in a newsroom, or by a broadcast network. It may also include such additional material as sports coverage, weather forecasts, traffic reports, commentary and other material that the broadcaster feels is relevant to their audience.

Television News

Television news refers to disseminating current events via the medium of television. "News bulletins" or "newscasts" are programmes lasting from seconds to hours that provide updates on world, national, regional or local news events. Television news is very image-based, showing video of many of the events that are reported. Television channels may provide news bulletins as part of a regularly scheduled news programme. Less often, television shows may be interrupted or replaced by "news flashes" to provide news updates on current events of great importance or sudden events of great importance.

Cable News

Cable news refers to channels which are devoted to current events 24-hours a day. The originator of this format from which the name derives is CNN (as well as CNN International), which originally stood for cable news network in reference to the then-new phenomenon of cable television. As satellite and other forms have evolved, the term *cable news* has become something of an anachronism but is still in common use; many other channels have since been established, such as BBC World News, BBC News, Sky News, Al Jazeera, France 24, STAR News, Fox News Channel, MSNBC and ABC News Now. Some news channels specialize even further, such as ESPNEWS (sports from ESPN), CNBC, and Fox Business Network (Financial).

A term which has entered common parlance to differentiate cable news from traditional news broadcasts is network news, in reference to the traditional television networks on which such broadcasts air. A classic example is the cable news channel MSNBC, which overlaps with (and, in the case of breaking world-changing events, pre-empts) its network counterpart NBC News.

Television News Channel

Television news channels are television specialty channels which focus on presenting news content. The world's first dedicated 24-hour news channels were CNN and BBC World News.

Radio News

Radio news is the same as television news but is transmitted through the medium of the radio. It is more based on the audio aspect rather than the visual aspect. Sound bites are captured through various reporters and played back through the radio. News updates occur more often on the radio than on the television—usually about once or twice an hour.

At most news/talk radio stations, newscasts run from: 00-06 minutes after the top of each hour. Some stations produce the entire six minutes on their own. Others begin with a network newscast, which covers national and world news, followed by a 2- or 3-minute local newscast. Most of the time, time is taken out of the news "window" for commercials and a weather forecast. In larger cities, traffic reports are also included. Some stations do traffic only during rush hour while others cover traffic around the clock.

Newscasts

Local TV news stations normally broadcast 3-4 times a day: 5:00 and 6:00 in the morning, Noon, 5:00 and 6:00 in the evening, and 10:00 or 11:00 at night. Many stations title their newscasts with catchy names like "Daybreak," "Good Morning (insert city here)," "Live at Five," "Eleven @ 11:00," or "Nightcast." These names are intended to set one station apart from the rest, especially for viewers who are chosen for audience measurement surveys. If the respondent was unable to provide a channel number or call letters, the newscast title is often enough for the appropriate station to receive Nielsen ratings credit.

Radio station newscasts can range from as little as a minute to as much as the station's entire schedule, such as the case of all-news radio.

- More often, AM stations will air a 6½ minute newscast on the top of the hour, which can be either a local report, a national report from a radio network such as CBS Radio or ABC Radio, or a mix of both local and national content, including weather and traffic reports. Some stations also air a two minute report at the bottom of the hour.
- FM stations, unless they feature a talk radio format, usually only air minute-long news capsules featuring a quick review of events and an abbreviated weather forecast, and usually only in drive time periods or in critical emergencies, since FM stations usually focus more on playing music. Traffic reports also air on FM stations, depending on the market

In some parts of the world there are 'rolling news' TV channels that broadcast news 24 hours a day, such as CNN in the United States or BBC News in the United Kingdom. Many news reports presented on the Internet are updated 24 hours a day. Newscasts consist of several different elements, introduced by a news presenter or presenters. The presenters read 'links' and do interviews.

Most news stories come in the form of short 'packages'. These are pre-recorded reports usually lasting from one to five minutes. News reporters gather and edit together interview clips, pictures and their own 'pieces to camera' to tell a story. They script and record a 'voice-over' to explain the pictures and link the elements together.

Some stories are done as live reports. This can be a reporter on the scene of a story either being interviewed by a studio presenter (sometimes known as a 'two-way'), a reporter interviewing one or more other people, or simply live pictures and sound of an event. The sound and pictures are sent back to the TV station via fixed cable links, bounced off a satellite through a satellite truck, or sent through microwave radio transmissions from a vehicle carrying a microwave transmitter.

With the growth of "rolling news" channels the use of live material has increased enormously and TV reporters are now often judged as much on their ability to perform live in front of a camera as on their package-making or writing skills.

TV news programmes are put together by producers, who decide what goes in and what gets left out, and how long and in what form each story is presented. They put together 'running orders'—a list of the stories in what they decide is the right order. A separate news editor or assignment editor is often responsible for co-ordinating the gathering of material.

A director puts the show together, with help of the technical director, floor director and a crew of people running audio, graphics, teleprompter, and cameras. Most news shows are broadcast live.

Effects on Society

The invention of telecommunications and broadcasting has resulted in "the uncoupling of space and time." Spatial distanciation no longer required temporal distanciation. Information can be transmitted over long distances with hardly any delay. Broadcasting, especially news programmes, have changed the way we perceive many people, ideas, jobs, etc. At one time, the leadership and authority of politicians were in awe with everybody. Now that their speeches, actions and decisions are all recorded and broadcast on news programmes, people realized they make mistakes too, and are just like any other person. Not only does TV decrease our awe, it also increases the politician's self-doubt and lowers self-esteem. When giving a speech, we can see the speech-givers nerves and anxiety up close.

CASE STUDY: MAJOR AMERICAN BROADCAST NEWS ANALYSTS

- Imran Anwar
- Sonia Baghdady
- Rudi Bakhtiar
- Jay Barbree
- Bobbie Battista
- Willow Bay

- Jason Bellini
- J.J. Bittenbinder
- Wolf Blitzer
- Jim Bohannon
- Eric Bolling
- David Brinkley
- Beverly Broadman
- Tom Brokaw
- Aaron Brown
- Campbell Brown
- Wally Bruner
- Conrad Burns
- Eric Burns
- Jack Cafferty
- Tucker Carlson
- Boake Carter
- Neil Cavuto
- John Chancellor
- Julie Chen
- Connie Chung
- Liz Claman
- Charles Collingwood (Journalist)
- Alan Colmes
- Ann Compton
- Anderson Cooper
- Marc Cooper
- Mort Crim
- Walter Cronkite
- John Charles Daly
- Elmer Davis
- Andy Dominianni
- Sam Donaldson
- Steve Doocy
- Wayne A. Downing
- Alex Dreier
- Edward P. Morgan
- Bob Edwards
- John Facenda
- Karen Finerman
- Fulton Lewis

- Delia Gallagher
- John Gibson (Media Host)
- Amy Goodman
- Gordon Graham
- Roger Grimsby
- Terry Gross
- Eric L. Haney
- Sean Hannity
- Aaron Harber
- Thom Hartmann
- Paul Harvey
- John Harwood
- Gabriel Heatter
- Bill Hemmer
- Hope Hines
- Brit Hume
- Chet Huntley
- Carol Iovanna
- Larry C. Johnson
- Daryn Kagan
- Hans von Kaltenborn
- Sara Lee Kessler
- Patrice King Brown
- Sam Kouvaris
- Lawrence Kudlow
- Victoria Langley
- Jim Lehrer
- Robert C. Maynard
- Thomas McInerney
- Dana Milbank
- Edward R. Murrow
- Kent Ninomiya
- Michele Norris
- Monica Novotny
- Soledad O'Brien
- Bill O'Reilly (Commentator)
- Charles Osgood
- Drew Pearson (Journalist)
- Dan Rather
- Dylan Ratigan

- Jacque Reid
- Ken Rice
- Cokie Roberts
- Max Robinson
- Susan Rook
- Dave Ross
- Luke Russert
- Tim Russert
- Bill Ryan
- Donna Savarese
- Diane Sawyer
- Michael Scheuer
- Bob Schieffer
- David Schoenbrun
- Jon Scott
- John Seigenthaler, Jr.
- Eric Sevareid
- Maria Shriver
- John Shumway
- Howard K. Smith
- Stacy Smith
- Nancy Snyderman
- Susan Stamberg
- Raymond Gram Swing
- Lowell Thomas
- Paul E. Vallely
- Roger Wilkins
- George Will
- Walter Winchell
- Richard Wolffe
- Brian Wood (Journalist)
- Paula Zahn

INFOTAINMENT

Infotainment (a portmanteau of information and entertainment) refers to a general type of broadcast programme which provides a combination of current events news and "feature news", or "features stories." Infotainment also refers to the segments of programming in television news programmes which overall consist of both "hard news" segments and interviews, along with celebrity interviews and human drama stories. Critics have claimed the combination of the two aspects is a conflict of interest by corporate news outlets—focusing on marketing, not journalism. The term "infotainment" thus may be a pejorative among those who hold professional journalistic values in esteem. Infotainment should not be confused with documentaries, educational television, or hard news programming. These go more in depth of the subjects they cover and can even provide classroom level instruction in areas such as mathematics, science, biology, or writing, etc.

Infotainment may also be found, not only in broadcast media, but also in retail environments whereby display material containing information about the features and benefits of various products on display is combined with style, colour, even sound, to provide a shopping "experience"—such "retail infotainment" is often referred to as retailtainment.

Infotainment usually covers a long-term change or point of interest, or a general trend—an aspect of the zeitgeist. Many such stories as those cover topics such as health tips or gardening tips, exploring television show genres, travel, shopping, yachting or exploring new wines—topics that are not actually "news" at all, in the sense of things that are currently happening. Other stories deal with something that is happening, but is gradual, rather than tied to a single event—a new music genre coming into prominence, a shift in tide in the political views of the nation, a new turn in teen attitudes about sexuality, a commonality among political candidates, the returning appeal of the retro styles and memories of a past decade, crazes like Tamagotchi or Furby, or a common thread among current events that reveals something about the times.

Criticism

Adding to the distinction between journalists and anchors and reporters are "human interest", personality, or celebrity news stories, which typically are directed by marketing departments based on a demographic appeal and audience share. It is commonly accepted that anchors are also media personalities, who may even be considered celebrities. The very nature of corporate network news requires its media personalities to use their public appeal to promote the networks investments, just as network broadcasts themselves (morning shows, TV news magazines) schedule self-promotional stories, in addition to advertising. Critics might go so far as to view anchors as a weak link in the news trade, representing the misplacement of both the credit and the accountability of a news journalism organization—hence adding to a perceived erosion of journalistic standards throughout the news business.

Most infotainment, especially television programmes on the networks or broadcast cable, only contain general factual information on the subjects they cover, and should not be considered as formal learning or instruction. For example, you may learn that a motorcycle contains an engine, or how fast one can travel, on American Chopper, but you will not learn the inner-workings of the engine, the physics and chemistry involved when it is running, or how to customize a motorcycle on your own using schematics.

Hard News, Soft News and Infotainment

Hard news and soft news are terms for describing a relative difference between poles in a spectrum within the broader news trade—with "hard" journalism at the professional end and "soft" infotainment at the other. Because the term "news" is quite broad, the terms "hard" and "soft" denote both a difference in respective standards for news value, as well as for standards of conduct, relative to the professional ideals of journalistic integrity.

The idea of hard news embodies two orthogonal concepts:

- *Seriousness:* Politics, economics, crime, war, and disasters are considered serious topics, as are certain aspects of law, science, and technology.
- *Timeliness:* Stories that cover current events—the progress of a war, the results of a vote, the breaking out of a fire, a significant public statement, the freeing of a prisoner, an economic report of note.

The logical opposite, soft news is sometimes referred to in a derogatory fashion as infotainment. Defining features catching the most criticism include:

- *The least serious subjects:* Arts and entertainment, sports, lifestyles, "human interest", and celebrities.
- *Not timely:* There is no precipitating event triggering the story, other than a reporter's curiosity.

Timely events happen in less serious subjects—sporting matches, celebrity misadventures, movie releases, art exhibits, and so on. There may also be serious reports which are not event-driven—coverage of important social, economic, legal, or technological trends; investigative reports which uncover ongoing corruption, waste, or immorality; or discussion of unsettled political issues without any special reason. Anniversaries, holidays, the end of a year or season, or the end of the first 100 days of an administration, can make some stories time-sensitive, but provide more of an opportunity for reflection and analysis than any actual "news" to report.

The spectrum of "seriousness" and "importance" is not well-defined, and different media organizations make different tradeoffs. "News you can use", a common marketing phrase highlighting a specific genre of journalism, spans the gray area. Gardening tips and hobby "news" pretty clearly fall at the entertainment end. Warnings about imminent natural disasters or acute domestic security threats (such as air raids or terrorist attacks) are considered so important that broadcast media (even non-news channels) usually interrupt other programming to announce them. A medical story about a new treatment for breast cancer, or a report about local ground water pollution might fall in between. So might book reviews, or coverage of religion. On the other hand, people frequently find hobbies and entertainment to be worthwhile parts of their lives and so "importance" on a personal level is rather subjective.

Concerns and Criticisms

The label "infotainment" is emblematic of concern and criticism that journalism is devolving from a medium which conveys serious information about issues that affect the public interest, into a form of entertainment which happens to have fresh "facts" in the mix. The criteria by which reporters and editors judge news value—whether something is worth putting on the front page, the bottom of the hour, or is worth commenting on at all—is an integral part of this debate.

Some blame the media for this perceived phenomenon, for failing to live up to ideals of civic journalistic responsibility. Others blame the commercial nature of many media organizations, the need for higher ratings, combined with a preference among the public for feel-good content and "unimportant" topics (like celebrity gossip or sports).

A specialization process has also occurred, beginning with the rise of mass market special-interest magazines, moving into broadcast with the advent of cable television, and continuing into new media, like the Internet and satellite radio. An increasing number of media outlets are available to the public that focus exclusively on one topic such as current events, home improvement, history, movies, women and Christianity. This means that consumers have more choice over whether they receive a general feed of the most "important" information of the day, or whether they get a highly customized presentation that contains only one type of content, which need not be newsworthy, and which need not come from a neutral point of view. Some publications and channels have found a sizable audience in the "niche" of featuring hard news. But controversy continues over whether the size of that audience is too small, and whether those outlets are diluting content with too much "soft" news.

What Counts as Journalism?

Some journalists define "journalism" to include only report on "serious" subjects, where common journalistic standards are upheld by the reporter. The larger "news business" or news trade encompasses everything from professional journalism to so-called "soft news" and "infotainment", and support activities such as marketing, advertising sales, finance and delivery. Professional journalism is supposed to place more emphasis on research, fact-checking, and the public interest than its "non-journalistic" counterparts.

Entertainment and News Crossovers

Infotainers are entertainers in infotainment media, such as news anchors or "news personalities" who cross the line between journalism (quasi-journalism) and entertainment within the broader news trade. Notable examples in the U.S. media are Barbara Walters, Katie Couric, Bill O'Reilly, Maury Povich, Deborah Norville, and Geraldo Rivera among others. Barbara Walters, though not the first to cross the line between news and personality stories, is for many the quintessential news-media icon. Her career dates back to the 1950s, and her current prominence at ABC is largely celebrity interviews, with a long running co-anchorship on *20/20* with Hugh Downs and, later, John Stossel until 2004 and her overlapping morning infotainment show The View.

When Geraldo Rivera became the host of his own news-oriented talk show on CNBC, others within the NBC organization voiced their protest, including Tom Brokaw who was reported to have threatened to quit. Rivera had a notorious history as a "sleaze reporter" and daytime talk show host, where he and one or two others were representative of "trash TV"; television seen to have little social value or redeeming intelligence, but still popular with viewers. A particular example is of the career of Andrea Thompson, formerly an actress on *Babylon 5* and *NYPD Blue*, who quit acting to become a reporter for KRQE News in Albuquerque, New Mexico, and was later hired by CNN Headline News. She later quit CNN, citing a desire to spend more time with her son. Some speculated that others at CNN resented the presence of the former actress, and had some degree of influence on her decision to quit.

Infomercials

The infotainment concept is taken to its logical extreme by the increasingly ubiquitous "infomercial", which is blatant, thinly disguised advertising presented as though it were infotainment. This is not the same thing as Home Shopping, which does not attempt to disguise its real purpose. This technique can be quite insidious, depending on the skill of the presenter, and his/her ability to seamlessly transfer focus from the lead topic to the advertising. Other disguised advertising techniques, aside from infotainment, include Subliminal Message advertising and Product Placement (also known as embedded marketing).

The terms "Infotainment" and "Infotainer" were first used in September 1980 at the Joint Conference of Aslib, the Institute of Information Scientists and the Library Association in Sheffield, UK. The Infotainers were a group of British information scientists who put on comedy shows at their professional conferences between 1980 and 1990.

4

Radio Broadcast, Talk Shows and Sound Recording

RADIO FORMAT

A radio format or programming format describes the overall content broadcast on a radio station. Radio formats are frequently employed as a marketing tool, and constantly evolve. Music radio; Old Time Radio, All-news radio; Sports radio; Talk radio and Weather radio describe the operation of different genres of radio format and each format can often be sub-divided into many speciality formats.

RADIO BROADCASTING

Radio broadcasting is an audio (sound) broadcasting service, traditionally broadcast through the air as radio waves (a form of electromagnetic radiation) from a transmitter to an antenna and thus to a receiving device. Stations can be linked in radio networks to broadcast common programming, either in syndication or simulcast or both. Audio broadcasting also can be done via cable FM, local wire networks, satellite and the Internet.

History

The earliest radio stations were simply radiotelegraphy systems and did not carry audio. The first claimed audio transmission that could be termed a *broadcast* occurred on Christmas Eve in 1906, and was made by Reginald Fessenden. While many early experimenters attempted to create systems similar to radiotelephone devices where only two parties were meant to communicate, there were others who intended to transmit to larger audiences. Charles Herrold started broadcasting in California in 1909 and was carrying audio by the next year. For the next decade, radio tinkerers had to build their own radio receivers. Dr. Frank Conrad began broadcasting from his Wilkinsburg, Pennsylvania garage with the call letters KDKA. Later, the equipment was moved to the top of an office building in Pittsburgh, Pennsylvania and purchased by Westinghouse. KDKA of Pittsburgh, under Westinghouse's ownership, started broadcasting as the first licensed "commercial" radio station on November 2, 1920. The commercial designation came from the type of license; advertisements did not air until years later. The first broadcast was the results of the U.S. presidential election, 1920. The Montreal station that became CFCF began programme broadcasts on May 20, 1920, and the Detroit station that became WWJ began programme broadcasts beginning on August 20, 1920, although neither held a license at the time.

Radio Argentina began regularly scheduled transmissions from the Teatro Coliseo in Buenos Aires on August 27, 1920, making its own priority claim. The station got its license on November 19, 1923. The delay was due to the lack of official Argentine licensing procedures before that date. This station continued regular broadcasting of entertainment and cultural fare for several decades.

Internet Radio

When Internet-based radio became feasible in the mid-1990s, the new medium required no licensing and stations could broadcast from anywhere in the world without the need for over the air transmitters. This greatly reduced the overhead for establishing a station, and in 1996, George Maat started 'A' Net Station (ANET) under the now defunct domain Advice-Net.com, and began broadcasting commercial-free from Antarctica. MIT developed the "Radio Locator" List of Radio Stations. After stations started streaming audio on the Internet, Radio-Locator added this to their search engine so anyone could locate a station's website and listen to a station offering a worldwide stream. This list also tracks "terrestrial" radio stations who may not have live audio on the net, or even a website, but are able to find station information by various other search queries.

Types

The best known type of radio station are the ones that broadcast via radiowaves. These include foremost AM and FM stations. There are several sub-types, namely commercial, public and non-profit varieties as well as student-run campus radio stations and hospital radio stations can be found throughout the developed world. Although now being eclipsed by internet-distributed radio, there are many stations that broadcast on shortwave bands using AM technology that can be received over thousands of miles (especially at night). For example, the BBC has a full schedule transmitted via shortwave. These broadcasts are very sensitive to atmospheric conditions and solar activity.

Also, many other non-broadcast types of radio stations exist. These include base stations for police, fire and ambulance networks, military base stations, dispatch base stations for taxis, trucks, and couriers, emergency broadcast systems, and amateur radio stations. Arbitron, the United States based company which reports on radio audiences defines a "radio station" as one of: government-licensed AM or FM station a HD Radio (primary or multicast) station, an internet stream of an existing government-licensed station or one of the satellite radio channels from XM Satellite Radio or Sirius Satellite Radio.

Over Radiowaves

Shortwave

See shortwave for the differences between shortwave, medium wave and long wave spectra. Used largely for international broadcasts by organs of state propaganda, religious organizations, militaries and others.

AM

AM stations were the earliest broadcasting stations to be developed. AM refers to amplitude modulation, a mode of broadcasting radio waves by varying the amplitude of the carrier signal in response to the amplitude of the signal to be transmitted. Many countries outside of the U.S. use a similar frequency band for AM transmissions. Europe also uses the long wave band. In response to the growing popularity of FM radio, stereo radio stations in the late 1980s and early 1990s, some North American stations began broadcasting in AM stereo, though this never gained popularity, and very few receivers were ever sold.

Advantages. One of the advantages of AM is that its unsophisticated signal can be detected (turned into sound) with simple equipment. If a signal is strong enough, not even a power source is needed; building an unpowered crystal radio receiver was a common childhood project in the early years of radio.

AM broadcasts occur on North American airwaves in the medium wave frequency range of 530 to 1700 kHz (known as the "standard broadcast band"). The band was expanded in the 1990s by adding nine channels from 1620 to 1700 kHz. Channels are spaced every 10 kHz in the Americas, and generally every 9 kHz everywhere else.

Disadvantages. The signal is subject to interference from electrical storms (lightning) and other EMI. AM transmissions cannot be ionospherically propagated during the day due to strong absorption in the D-layer of the ionosphere. In a crowded channel environment this means that the power of regional channels which share a frequency must be reduced at night or directionally beamed in order to avoid interference, which reduces the potential night-time audience. Some stations have frequencies unshared with other stations in North America; these are called clear-channel stations. Many of them can be heard across much of the country at night. *(This is not to be confused with Clear Channel Communications, merely a brand name, which currently owns many U.S. radio stations)*. During the night, this absorption largely disappears and permits signals to travel to much more distant locations via ionospheric reflections. However, fading of the signal can be severe at night.

AM radio transmitters can transmit audio frequencies up to 15 kHz (now limited to 10 kHz in the U.S. due to FCC rules designed to reduce interference), but most receivers are only capable of reproducing frequencies up to 5 kHz or less. At the time that AM broadcasting began in the 1920s, this provided adequate fidelity for existing microphones, 78 rpm recordings, and loudspeakers. The fidelity of sound equipment subsequently improved considerably, but the receivers did not. Reducing the bandwidth of the receivers reduces the cost of manufacturing and makes them less prone to interference. AM stations are never assigned adjacent channels in the same service area. This prevents the sideband power generated by two stations from interferring with each other. Bob Carver created an AM stereo tuner employing notch filtering that demonstrated that an AM broadcast can meet or exceed the 15 kHz baseband bandwidth allocted to FM stations without objectionable interference. After several years, the tuner was discontinued. Bob Carver had left the company and the Carver Corporation later cut the number of models produced before discontinuing production completely. AM stereo broadcasts declined with the advent of HD Radio.

FM

FM refers to frequency modulation, and occurs on VHF airwaves in the frequency range of 88 to 108 MHz everywhere (except Japan and Russia). Japan uses the 76 to 90 MHz band. FM stations are much more popular in economically developed regions, such as Europe and the United States, especially since higher sound fidelity and stereo broadcasting became common in this format.

FM radio was invented by Edwin H. Armstrong in the 1930s for the specific purpose of overcoming the interference (static) problem of AM radio, to which it is relatively immune. At the same time, greater fidelity was made possible by spacing stations further apart. Instead of 10 kHz apart, they are 200 kHz apart. For example, the difference between the lowest current FM frequency in the U.S., 88.1 MHz, and the next lowest, 88.3 MHz. This was far in advance of the audio equipment of the 1940s, but wide interchannel spacing was chosen to take advantage of the noise-suppressing feature of wideband FM.

In fact, 200 kHz is not needed to accommodate an audio signal—20 kHz to 30 kHz is all that is necessary for a narrowband FM signal. The 200 kHz bandwidth allowed room for ±75 kHz signal deviation from the assigned frequency plus a 20 kHz guardband to eliminate adjacent channel interference. The larger bandwidth allows for broadcasting a 15 kHz bandwidth audio signal plus a 38 kHz stereo "subcarrier"—a piggyback signal that rides on the main signal. Additional unused capacity is used by some broadcasters to transmit utility functions such as background music for public areas, GPS auxiliary signals, or financial market data.

The AM radio problem of interference at night was addressed in a different way. At the time FM was set up, the available frequencies were far higher in the spectrum than those used for AM radio—by a factor of approximately 100. Using these frequencies meant that even at far higher power, the range of a given FM signal was much lower, thus its market was more local than for AM radio. The reception range at night is the same as at daytime. The original FM radio service in the U.S. was the Yankee Network, located in New England. Regular FM broadcasting began in 1939, but did not pose a significant threat to the AM broadcasting industry. It required purchase of a special receiver. The frequencies used, 42 to 50 MHz, were not those used today. The change to the current frequencies, 88 to 108 MHz, began after the end of World War II, and it was to some extent imposed by AM radio owners so as to attempt to cripple what was by now realized to be a potentially serious threat.

FM radio on the new band had to begin from the ground floor. As a commercial venture it remained a little-used audio enthusiasts' medium until the 1960s. The more prosperous AM stations, or their owners, acquired FM licenses and often broadcast the same programming on the FM station as on the AM station ("simulcasting"). The FCC limited this practice in the 1970s. By the 1980s, since almost all new radios included both AM and FM tuners (without any government mandate), FM became the dominant medium, especially in cities. Because of its greater range, AM remained more common in rural environments.

Amateur Radio

Independent "ham" radio operators, largely hobbyists,

licensed by respective national bodies and assigned callsigns. See Amateur Radio.

Citizens Band Radio

Citizens band radio or CB is usually unlicensed broadcasting over frequencies set aside for that purpose.

Other Types of Radio Communication Over Radiowaves

Radio communications have been and are used for all variety of data transmissions. The earliest radio application, Morse code, can still be heard today. Experiments in sending pictures and text date back to the early days of radio. A variety of clock signals are also broadcast. Another early use of radio was coded transmission of information by national governments in peace and war. During the Cold War the USSR and allied governments had national programmes to block shortwave and other frequency transmissions by using jamming techniques. One signal known as Russian woodpecker suddenly appeared on July 4, 1976 and just as suddenly disappeared at the end of 1989, and is still something of a mystery. More and more radio frequencies are being used to send digital packets of information of varying degrees of complexity.

An early form of digital radio broadcasting was packet radio, which combines digital information with traditional radio broadcasting over the air. Digital radio broadcasting has emerged, first in Europe (the UK in 1995 and Germany in 1999), and later in the United States, France, the Netherlands, South Africa and many other countries worldwide. The most simple system is named DAB Digital Radio, for Digital Audio Broadcasting, and uses the public domain EUREKA 147 (Band III) system. DAB is used mainly in the UK and South Africa. Germany and Holland use the DAB and DAB+ systems, and France use the L-Band system of DAB Digital Radio.

In the United States digital radio is not used in the same way as Europe and South Africa—instead the IBOC system is named HD Radio and owned by a consortium of private companies called iBiquity. An international non-profit consortium Digital Radio Mondiale (DRM) has introduced the public domain DRM system.

Satellite

Satellite radiobroadcasters are slowly emerging, but the enormous entry costs of space-based satellite transmitters, and restrictions on available radio spectrum licenses has restricted growth of this market. In the USA and Canada, just two services, XM Satellite Radio and Sirius Satellite Radio exist.

Programme Formats

Radio programme formats differ by country, regulation and markets. For instance, the U.S. Federal Communications Commission designates the 88–92 megahertz band in the U.S. for non-profit or educational programming, with advertising prohibited. In addition, formats change in popularity as time passes and technology improves. Early radio equipment only allowed programme material to be broadcast in real time, known as *live* broadcasting. As technology for sound recording improved, an increasing proportion of broadcast programming used pre-recorded material. A current trend is the automation of radio stations. Some stations now operate without direct human intervention by using entirely pre-recorded material sequenced by computer control.

LIST OF MUSIC RADIO FORMATS

Music radio formats constantly evolve and each format can often be sub-divided into many speciality formats. Many of the following radio formats are available only regionally or through specialized venues such as satellite radio or Internet radio.

List of Music Radio Speciality Formats

- Active rock
- Adult contemporary music (AC)
- Adult standards/Nostalgia-pre-rock
- Adult album alternative (or just Adult alternative) (AAA or Triple-A)
- Adult hits
- Album rock
- Alternative rock/Modern rock

- Big band
- Bluegrass
- Caribbean (reggae, soca, merengue, cumbia, salsa, etc.)
- Contemporary rock
- Classic hits
- Classic rock
- College radio
- Comedy
- Contemporary hit radio (CHR), occasionally still informally known as Top 40
- Contemporary Christian (which is also known as CCM)
- Country Music:
    - New country/Young country
- Dance (Dance Top 40)
- Educational
- Full Service
- Radio format (Disc jockey-selected)
- General service
- Hot adult contemporary (Hot AC)
- Hot hits (a form of Hot 100; Top 40; Top 30; Top 20; Top 10)
- Hispanic Rhythmic
- Indian Music
- Mainstream rock
- Middle of the road (MOR)
- Modern adult contemporary (Modern AC)
- Music radio
- New adult contemporary/Smooth Jazz (New AC)
- Oldies-Primarily 1940s, 1950s, and 1960s
- Progressive rock
- Psychedelic rock
- Quiet Storm (most often a "day-part" format at Urban Stations, *i.e.* 7p-12 midnight)
- Radio documentary
- Ranchera
- Regional Mexican (Banda, corridos, ranchera, conjunto, mariachi, norteño, etc.)
- Revolution CHR

- Rhythmic adult contemporary
- Rhythmic contemporary (Rhythmic Top 40)
- Rock
- Rock en español
- Romántica (Spanish AC)
- Smooth jazz
- Soft adult contemporary (Soft AC)
- Soft rock
- Soul music
- Space music
- Tejano (Texas/Mexican music)
- Top 40
- Traditional pop music
- Tropical (salsa, merengue, cumbia, etc.)
- Urban contemporary (mostly rap, hip hop, soul, and R&B artists)
- Urban adult contemporary (Urban AC) (R&B, soul and sometimes gospel music, without rap)
- Variety

CAMPUS RADIO

Campus radio (also known as *college radio, university radio* or *student radio*) is a type of radio station that is run by the students of a college, university or other educational institution. Programming may be exclusively by students, or may include programmers from the wider community in which the station is based. Sometimes campus stations are operated for the purpose of training professional radio personnel, sometimes with the aim of broadcasting educational programming, while other stations exist to provide an alternative to commercial or government broadcasters.

Campus radio stations are generally licensed and regulated by national governments, and so have very different characteristics from one country to the next. One commonality between many stations regardless of their physical location is a willingness or, in some countries, even a licensing requirement—to broadcast musical selections that are not categorized as commercial hits. Because of this, campus radio has come to be associated with emerging musical trends, including genres such as alternative rock in the latter portion of the 20th century, and hip hop before that genre had become part of the musical mainstream. Campus radio stations also often provide airplay and promotional exposure to new and emerging local artists.

Despite this, many campus radio stations carry a variety of programming including news (often local), sports (often relating to the campus), and spoken word programming as well as general music. Often the format is best described as a free form radio format, with a lot of creativity and individualism among the disc jockeys and show hosts. A number of these stations have gained critical acclaim for their programming and are considered by the community in which they are embedded to be an essential media outlet.

Although the term *campus radio* implies full-power AM or FM transmission over the air, many stations experiment with low-power broadcasting, closed circuit or carrier current systems, often to on-campus listeners only. Some stations are distributed through the cable television network on cable FM or the second audio programme of a TV station. Some universities and colleges broadcast one or more Internet radio feeds—either instead of, or in addition to a campus radio station—which may differ in format significantly from licensed traditional campus radio.

Campus Radio Around the World

Canada

In Canada, radio stations are regulated by the Canadian Radio-television and Telecommunications Commission (CRTC) which provides that "a campus radio station is a station owned or controlled by a not-for-profit organization associated with a post-secondary educational institution." The CRTC distinguishes two types of campus radio: *instructional* (for training of professional broadcasters) and *community-based campus* (programming provided by volunteers who are not training to be professionals). The community-based format is the predominant one, colloquially known as "campus-community radio." In recent years, some community-based campus radio stations, including CFFF-FM in Peterborough and CJMQ-FM in Sherbrooke, have in fact had their CRTC licenses formally reclassified from campus radio to community radio. Campus radio stations broadcasting at full power are assigned a permanent frequency and call letters and, aside from a requirement not to compete directly with commercial stations, are full players in the Canadian broadcasting spectrum. Campus radio stations in Canada are more commonly associated with universities than with colleges, although some colleges also have licensed campus radio stations. As well, some institutions maintain unlicensed campus radio operations which broadcast only by closed circuit, cable FM or Internet streaming.

The first licensed community-based campus radio station was CKCU-FM, based at Carleton University in Ottawa, which first broadcast on November 14, 1975. Prior to this date, some developmental university radio projects had previously produced and aired programmes on commercial radio stations, and CJRT-FM, a campus radio station of the instructional type, had been on air since 1949. CFRC at Queen's University in Kingston has been on the air since 1923; however, until the 1940s it was a commercial radio station and even a Canadian Broadcasting Corporation affiliate. Unlike most campus radio stations, however, CFRC was owned for much of its history by the university itself, rather than by the student government.

The CRTC places responsibilities upon campus radio stations in Canada through the use of *conditions of license* that stations must follow in order to keep broadcasting. Campus stations, for example, are expected to be leaders in the Canadian content system which mandates a minimum number of Canadian musical selections throughout the day. In early 2005, Humber College's radio station CKHC-FM became the first broadcast station in Canada to air 100 per cent; Canadian content. Other requirements generally made of campus stations include quotas of non-hit, folk and ethnic musical selections as well as spoken word programming. Most campus radio stations in Canada are members of the National Campus and Community Radio Association.

India

Community groups in India, and non-governmental

organizations (NGOs) have been campaigning for permission to set up *community radio* (CR) stations since the late nineties. But the government, particularly under the earlier Bharatiya Janata Party (BJP), allowed the setting up of campus radio stations by educational institutions.

News, as of November 2006, has it that the India cabinet decided to grant permission to non-profit organizations and educational institutions to set up community radio stations. The cabinet decision will allow civil society and voluntary organizations, state agriculture universities and institutions, Krishi Vigyan Kendras or agricultural science centres, registered societies and autonomous boards and public trusts registered under Societies Act to start community radio stations. Ravi Shankar Prasad, the then Minister for Information and Broadcasting in the BJP-lead National Democratic Alliance government, told India's upper house of parliament the Rajya Sabha on December 22, 2003, that four organizations including Jammu University and Kashmir University were found ineligible for grant of license as per the laid down guidelines. The minister also ruled out any review of the policy despite limited response to the non-commercial, low-powered FM radio scheme which former information and broadcasting minister Sushma Swaraj had said would "revolutionize" radio broadcast in the country.

Radio enthusiast Alokesh Gupta saying: "The announcement of the Government was to have seen 1000 radio stations by December 2003. Instead administrative wrangling came in the way of implementing the project as colleges spent time running around for licenses and approval from four ministries—Home Affairs, Communications and Information and Broadcasting—as they took their time processing applications."

On February 2, 2004, Anna University in Chennai unveiled the country's first campus radio station, Anna FM. Radio Ujjas in Kutch (in the western state of Gujarat) is one such CR and gets its funding from the United Nations Development Programme (UNDP) and the Central Government. Similarly a community based radio programme titled Panchayat Vani (People's Voice) was recently broadcast on All India Radio (AIR), Darbhanga, Bihar. The campus station Gyanvaani has also been licensed.

Pune University is the first University in the State of Maharashtra to have an FM station. The University of Pune's FM Radio inaugurated on May 1, 2005, has been named as Vidyavani. It covers a wide range of subjects, focusing specifically on the requirements of students of various departments and affiliated colleges. It reaches an area around the campus within eight kilometres radius.

Unsuccessful attempts have been also made to start CR without obtaining any permission. The small village of Orvakal in Kurnool district of Andhra Pradesh (South India) launched "Mana Radio" (Our Radio) in November 2002. This project run under the aegis of the Society for Elimination of Rural Poverty used a tiny transmitter that covered a radius of half a kilometer to enable rural women members of self-help groups. Four months later, officials from the Central Government brought in police to seize the equipment and declared the broadcasts illegal. The Government policy to permit educational institutions to have their own FM Channels at low frequency levels emerged in mid December 2002, as a result of years of campaigning by activists and a strongly-worded Supreme Court judgement directing the opening up of the airwaves.

A unique experiment in using media technologies, especially radio, for development and empowerment of marginalized, rural communities is the community radio initiative "*Chalo Ho Gaon Mein*" a programme that is broadcast once a week on AIR Daltonganj in the Palamu district of Jharkhand, eastern India. This radio programme is supported by the National Foundation for India and produced by Community representatives, of Alternative for India Development (AID), a non-governmental organization.

According to the terms of the campus broad license, a number of aspects are disallowed from broadcasts. This includes anything that offends good taste or decency, contains criticism of friendly countries, contains an attack on religion, contains anything obscene, defamatory, false and suggestive innuendos and half truths, likely to encourage or incite violence, contains anything affecting the integrity of the nation, criticizes, maligns or slanders any individual in person, encourages superstition or blind belief, denigrates women, denigrates children, or presents or depicts or suggests as desirable the misuse of drugs, alcohol, narcotics, and tobacco.

Israel

Campus radio also exists in Israel, where several colleges, universities and high schools have successful programmes. One of the most famous is Kol Ha Campus (Voice of the Campus/ Campus Voice), broadcast out of Tel Aviv on 106 MHz. More information can be found with the Israeli Broadcasting Authority. Another college radio station is the Hebrew University's in Jerusalem, broadcasting mostly indie and alternative music.

Pakistan

- *[radio.lums.edu.pk RadioLUMS—Gal Sunn Oye]* (Lahore University of Management Sciences)
- *Karachi university campus radio FM 90.6* (University of Karachi)

Poland

- *Students Radio Zak* (Technical University of Lodz)
- *Akademickie Radio LUZ* (Wroclaw University of Technology)

Portugal

In Portugal, there are several college and university radio stations continuously broadcasting programmes. *Rádio Universidade de Coimbra* and *Rádio Universidade Marão,* founded in 1986, are the oldest university student radio stations in the country still in operation. There are also many online-only radio sites belonging to higher education institutions.

Portugal's major college and university radio stations include:

- *Rádio Universidade de Coimbra* (University of Coimbra)
- *Rádio Universidade Marão* (Trás-os-Montes and Alto-Douro University)
- *Rádio Universitária da Beira Interior* (University of Beira Interior)

- *Rádio Universitária do Algarve* (University of the Algarve)
- *Rádio Universitária do Minho* (Minho University)

Switzerland

Fréquence Banane is the student radio in Lausanne on EPFL and UNIL campus. It exists since 1993 and is broadcasting on the Internet and CATV network on FM 94.55 MHz in Lausanne and region. In the past Frequence Banane has broadcast with former Radio Acidule from 1992 to 1996 and then had its independent FM transmitter operating on 92.4 MHz from 1998 to 2005. In 2005, Swiss frequency regulation authority (BAKOM) decided to end the low power FM licence.

Radio Radius is an uprising campus radio in Zurich on ETHZ and UNIZH campus. It is broadcasting on the Internet only. Radius is trying to get a permanent licence to broadcast on FM but it is very hard in Zurich. Right now Radius is negotiating with BAKOM.

United Kingdom

In the United Kingdom, campus radio is generally referred to as Student Radio. University Radio York, founded in 1967, became the first student radio station in the country, followed by Swansea University's station Action Radio (today called Xtreme Radio) in 1968. Some student radio stations operate on the FM waveband for short periods at a time under the Restricted Service Licence scheme, while others choose to broadcast full-time on the AM waveband using an LPAM licence. There are only three UK student radio stations permitted to broadcast all year on LPFM. These are Xpression FM (Exeter), Storm FM (Bangor) and Bailrigg FM (Lancaster). None of these licences provides for a reception area greater than four kilometres from the point of transmission. To counteract these licence restrictions and, in the case of AM broadcasts, poor quality audio, many stations simulcast on the Internet.

The Student Radio Association works on behalf of more than fifty UK-based member stations to further their development, encourage and facilitate communication between member stations and links to the commercial radio industry, and lobby for the membership's interests on both a regional and national level. The association organizes and hosts the annual Student Radio Awards in conjunction with BBC Radio 1.

United States

College radio (as it is generally known in the United States) began in the 1960s when the FCC began issuing class D licenses for ten - watt stations to further the development of the then new FM band. Some colleges had already been broadcasting for decades on the AM band, often originating in physics experiments in the early 20th century. Most of the FM stations received higher-class licenses, typically a few hundred watts. A few got several kilowatts, and a small handful got licenses in the range of tens of thousands sometimes reaching up to full-power 100 kilowatt outlets. Still, due to strict class D regulations, some stations were prohibited from a wattage upgrade for possible signal interference with adjacent stations, such as KWUR 90.3 FM interfering with KWMU 90.7 FM in St. Louis, Missouri.

The earliest college radio stations carried news, sports, and music along with educational shows and sometimes distance learning courses. In the latter portion of the 20th century, many U.S. stations played what came to be known as "college rock" (later known as alternative rock), a type of rock music that had not yet hit the mainstream. Most stations have now diversified, with many following a very commercial-like music rotation during the weekdays, and having specialty shows on evenings and weekends. A few stations really go out on a limb, occasionally being described as a cacophony of randomness. College stations are typically considered to be public radio stations.

By the late 1970s, FM had taken off, and competition for channels for new stations was intensifying. The National Association of Broadcasters (NAB) and the newly-founded National Public Radio (NPR) convinced the FCC that the low-power stations were detrimental to broadcasting, and class D licenses were no longer issued for applications made after 1979. Making matters worse, the stations were demoted to a second-class status, meaning that they would be forced off the air if any full-power station wanted their space.

Many stations were forced to upgrade their facilities at considerable expense to the students. Many other stations were eventually (and still continue to be) forced off the air, because they could not afford the upgrades at all, or not in time to avoid being locked-in by other expanding stations.

There have also been situations where some college radio stations have actually been forced off the air by a school administration. In one instance, the student media director of WUSC-FM in Columbia, South Carolina implied that the station's license had been flagged by the FCC due to an out of control staff and inappropriate songs being played on public airwaves. This serious charge proved to be false, but it led directly to WUSC, which had been named as 1992 Spin Magazine College Radio Station of the Year, being shut down in 1995. The entire executive board of the station (students elected by their peers) was fired for promoting a culture of irresponsibility. This caused most student DJs to quit in protest. After silence for 45 days, WUSC came back—but it had abandoned its popular alternative format, playing songs it never allowed before. As a result, College Music Journal and the now-defunct Gavin Report dropped WUSC as a reporter of new music they played on air.

Many college stations in the U.S. also carry syndicated programming, such as that of National Public Radio and affiliated regional networks. A very few stations have been added to the airwaves in very isolated cities with the return of the LPFM license to the U.S. The restrictions that U.S. Congress placed on LPFM stations as a result of the NAB's lobbying have seriously limited the effectiveness of this however. One of the first college radio stations in the country is WRUC from Union College in Schenectady, New York. Their first experimental broadcasts under the call sign 2ADD were in 1920. A number of college stations have abandoned traditional broadcasting methods and are available as streaming audio.

Sweden

- Radio AF
- Radio UPF
- Radio AFB

Norway

- Radio Nova, Oslo
- Studentradioen-*normal*-Bergen, Bergen
- Studentradion-*normal*-Trondheim, Trondheim

COMMUNITY RADIO

Community radio is a type of radio service that caters to the interests of a certain area, broadcasting material that is popular to a local audience but is overlooked by more powerful broadcast groups. The term has somewhat different meanings in the United Kingdom, the United States, Canada, and Australia. In the UK, the idea for originating community radio came in part from the situation of many illegal pirate radio stations having been established by the influx of Afro-Caribbean immigrants in cities such as London, Birmingham, Bristol, and Manchester in the 1970s. Therefore, "community radio" remains synonymous with "pirate radio" for many people there, but despite the intentions being similar, the results are vastly different. In America, community radio is more commonly non-profit and non-commercial, often using licensed class D FM band transmitters, although pirate radio outlets have been operated in many places. Canadian and Australian community stations operate somewhat similarly to their American counterparts. Pirate radio is virtually unknown in Australia because of the strictly controlled allocation of broadcasting frequencies, and the likely application of severe, legislated penalties, including jail, for offenders.

Vision, Philosophy, and Status

Modern-day community radio stations often serve their listeners by offering a variety of content that is not necessarily provided by the larger commercial radio stations. Community radio outlets may carry news and information programming geared toward the local area, particularly immigrant or minority groups that are poorly served by other major media outlets. More specialized musical shows are also often a feature of many community radio stations. Community stations and pirate stations (where they are tolerated) can be valuable assets for a region. Community radio stations typically avoid content found on commercial outlets, such as Top 40 music, sports, and "drive-time" personalities.

Conceptions of Community in the Literature

Communities are complex entities and so what constitutes "community" in Community radio is often a contentious and tricky debate and will vary from country to country. Community may also often be replaced by a range of terms like "alternative", "radical", or "citizen" radio. Traditionally in sociology, a "community" has been defined as a group of interacting people living in a common location. Community radio is often built around concepts of access and participation and so the term community may be thought of as often referring to geographical communities based around the possible reach of the radio's signal, *i.e.* the people who can receive the message, and their potential to participate in the creation of such messages. This is of course problematized by the fact that many radio stations now broadcast over the internet as well, thereby reaching potentially global audiences and communities.

Models of Community Radio

Philosophically two distinct approaches to community radio can be discerned, though the models are not necessarily mutually exclusive. One stresses service or community-mindedness, a focus on what the station can do for the community. The other stresses involvement and participation by the listener. Within the service model localism is often prized, as community radio, as a third tier, can provide content focused on a more local or particular community than larger operations. Sometimes, though, the provision of syndicated content that is not already available within the station's service area, is seen as a desirable form of service. Within the United States, for example, many stations syndicate content from groups such as Pacifica Radio, such as *Democracy Now!*, on the basis that it provides a form of content not otherwise available, because of such a programme's lack of appeal to advertisers or (especially in Pacifica's case) politically controversial nature.

Within the access or participatory model, the participation of community members in producing content is seen as a good in itself. While this model does not necessarily exclude a service approach, there is a tension between the two, as outlined, for example, in Jon Bekken's *Community Radio at the Crossroads.*

Growth in the Area (Examples by Geographic Area)

Australia

Community Broadcasting is Australia's third media sector. As at June 2005 there were 442 fully-licensed community radio stations (including remote Indigenous services). The community radio sector in Australia fulfills a broad, but largely unacknowledged role in the Australian media landscape, particularly as a source of local content.

A 2002 report, found that 20,000 (or 0.1%; of all Australians) are involved as volunteers in the community radio sector on a regular basis and volunteers equate for more than $145 million in unpaid work each year; Nationally more than 7 million Australians (or 45 of people over 15) listen to community radio in each month (source: McNair Ingenuity).

The role of community broadcasting in Australia, according to the Community Broadcasting Association of Australia is to provide a diverse range of services meeting community needs in ways that are not met by other sectors. Community broadcasting is sustained by the principles of access and participation, volunteerism, diversity, independence and localism. Community radio stations are sometimes specialist music stations, or they might strongly represent local music and arts. Others might broadcast talks and current affairs programmes representing alternative, Indigenous Australian, environmental, feminist or gay and lesbian interests, filling perceived gaps in commercial or government radio content.

Although community radio has grown considerably over the years, both in terms of the number of listener and the number of stations, the sector is largely under funded with individual stations having to spend much of their time financing their community service activities. 53 per cent of community radio stations serve an array of different communities of interest including: Indigenous and Ethnic, people with a print disability, young people, older people, arts/ fine music, religious, gay and lesbian.

The remaining stations provide service which may be described as generalist, which address the interests of communities in particular geographic locations but will still address a range of diverse specialty interests. Community broadcasting more than any other form of media in this country shapes and reflects the national character in all its diversity. The sector is unique in its capacity to provide fresh programming by and for Indigenous, Ethnic and RPH communities. Community broadcasting stations also have a strong commitment to local news, information; the promotion of local and Australian music, arts and culture; and to providing training in media skills.

When a not-for-profit community group applies to the regulator, the Australia Communications and Media Authority, for a community broadcasting licence they specify what community interest they intend to serve. Licensees are selected by the regulator on the basis of suitability and on the merits of the licence application and the capacity to serve identified community interests. Upon grant of a 5 year renewable licence each station is then required to continue to serve the community interest for which the licence was granted.

Bolivia

One of the most famous examples of community radio was miners' radio in Bolivia. Funded by trade union dues and operated mainly at local and regional levels, there were more than 25 such radio stations during the period from about 1960 to 1985. Changes in government policy eliminated many unionized mining jobs after 1985 and some radios were sold or ceased to exist. In spite of many difficulties five stations continue to broadcast.

La Voz del Minero Radio Pío XII RadioVanguardia de Colquiri Radio Animas Radio 21 de Diciembre Radio Nacional deHuanuni... these were some of the most important radio stations created, funded and managed by Bolivian mining workers. It all started in 1949, with one radio station in the mining district of Catavi. During the next 15 years, other districts followed: they bought the equipment, they trained young people from their villages, and the workers themselves funded the experience by giving a percentage of their salary to sustain their radio stations.

Most of the radio stations started small and precariously, only equipped by very simple means. A few of them managed to get foreign support and evolved into more sophisticated radio stations, with better equipment and installations. A few, even built a theatre next to the premises, so union meetings would take place and be transmitted live through the radio. Radio Vanguardia for example, had a beautiful theatre decorated with large murals narrating the story of the Colquiri mining centre. One particular scene on the mural depicts the attack by Bolivian Air Force planes in 1967, when the country was under military rule.

In the early 1970s, 26 radio stations were in operation, all in the mining districts of the highlands of Bolivia. At that time miners' unions in Bolivia were still very powerful and considered among the most important and politically advanced in Latin America. In times of peace and democracy miners' radio stations were integrated into the daily life of the community. They became the closest and most effective replacement for telephone and postal services.

People would get their mail through the stations and post messages of all kinds, which were read several times during the day: calls for a meeting of women from the Comité de Amas de Casa (Housewives Committee); messages from the union leaders about their negotiations with the government in the capital; messages of love among youngsters; announcing a new play by Nuevos Horizontes drama group (often staged on the platform of a big truck, with workers illuminating the scene with their own lamps); announcements of sport activities, burials, births and festivities.

In times of political upheaval the union radio stations would become the only trustworthy source of information. As the military captured newspapers, radio and TV stations in the capital and other cities, the only information available would come from the miner's radio stations. All of them would join the cadena minera until the army would penetrate the mining camps and assault the stations, which were usually defended to the death by the workers. A film by Bolivian filmmaker Jorge Sanjinés, The Courage of the People, re-enacts the attack on the mining district of Siglo XX by the army in June 1967. Another film, a documentary, by Alfonso Gumucio Dagron and Eduardo Barrios, titled *Voices of the Mine* and produced by UNESCO, describes their political and social importance. In times of political and social crisis the miners' radio stations would air reports on the political situation; they would also link for live transmissions when an important sporting or cultural event took place in the mining district. Other than that, each station had full independence from the next.

Certainly, miners' radio stations were important because miners were important. But also, Bolivian miners were more influential than ever because during several decades they had powerful means to communicate their ideas. As the importance of mining in Bolivia declined in the 1980s, the unions were weakened and some of the radio stations disappeared along with the mining districts.

Canada

Community radio stations in Canada most commonly target commercially underserved minority language communities such as Franco-Ontarians, Acadians or the First Nations, although some communities also have English language community stations. These stations are often volunteer-run and operated by cooperatives or other not-for-profit corporations.

In larger cities, community-oriented programming more commonly airs on campus radio stations. Some cities do, however, have community radio stations as well. Most community stations in Canada are members of the National Campus and Community Radio Association, or NCRA. Most of Canada's French language community radio stations are members of either l'Association des Radiodiffuseurs Communitaire du Quebec (ARCQ) or l'Alliance des radios communautaires du Canada inc (l'ARC). The province with the largest number of community radio stations in Canada is Saskatchewan. The majority of those stations are affiliated with Missinipi Broadcasting Corporation, an aboriginal public radio network. Community stations are subject to the Canadian Radio-television and Telecommunications Commission's (CRTC) community radio policy.

In this policy, the CRTC requires community stations to:

- Facilitate community access to programming;
- Promote the availability of training throughout the community; and
- Provide for the ongoing training and supervision of those within the community wishing to participate in programming.

It also requires stations to offer diverse programming that reflects the needs and interests of the community including:

- Music by new and local talent;
- Music not generally broadcast by commercial stations;
- Spoken word programming; and
- Local information.

The CRTC maintains a list of community stations. In Canada, call letters and frequencies are regulated by Industry Canada's Spectrum Management.

Ecuador

In Ecuador many community radio stations are operated by religious groups. They include Catholic, Protestant and Bahá'í stations. The amount of community participation and self-management varies. Radio Latacunga was associated with a project in which indigenous organizations were supplied with simple equipment to record weekly programmes for broadcast in the early morning. Also in Ecuador some indigenous groups operate their own radios. This is the case for the Shuar Federation in the tropical rainforest, and the community of Simiatug in Bolívar Province. Unlike Bolivia, trade- union radio has historically been weak in Ecuador.

Hungary

The first community station started as pirates, broadcasting politically free speech and music programmes after the change from Socialist system. Tilos Rádió in 1991 was the first such station, followed by Fiksz Rádió and Civil Rádió. Since 2004 a new category arose, kisközösségi or small community station which are low-power stations. By 2008 more than 60 such microstations have started broadcasting throughout the country. There are village-stations, small town-stations, university stations, subcultural and religious stations as well. In Budapest Cool FM, Elsö Pesti Egyetemi Rádió, Fúzió Rádió are the small community stations.

India

In India, the campaign to legitimize community radio began in the mid-1990s, soon after the Supreme Court of India ruled in its judgement of February 1995 that "airwaves are public property." This came as an inspiration to groups across the country, but to begin with, only educational (campus) radio stations were allowed, under somewhat stringent conditions.

Anna FM is India's first campus 'community' radio, launched on 1 February 2004, which is run by Education and Multimedia Research Centre (EMRC), and all programmes are produced by the students of Media Sciences at Anna University. On 16 November 2006, the government of India notified new Community Radio Guidelines which permit NGOs and other civil society organizations to own and operate community radio stations. About 4,000 community radio licenses are on offer across India, according to government sources. By 30 November 2008, the Ministry of Information and Broadcasting, Government of India, had received 297 applications for community radio licenses, including 141 from NGOs and other civil society organizations, 105 from educational institutions and 51 for 'farm radio' stations to be run by agricultural universities and agricultural extension centres ('Krishi Vigyan Kendras'). Of these, 107 community radio stations have been cleared for licensing through the issue of Letters of Intent. 13 Grant of Permission Agreements (GOPA) have been signed with license applicants under the new scheme. By 30 November 2008, there were 38 operational community radio stations in the country. Of these, two are run by NGOs and the rest by educational institutions. The first community-based radio station, licensed to an NGO (as distinct from campus-based radio) was launched on 15 October 2008, when 'Sangham Radio' in Pastapur village, Medak district, Andhra Pradesh state, was switched on at 11.00 a.m. Sangham Radio, which broadcasts on 90.4 MHz, is licensed to Deccan Development Society (DDS), an NGO that works with women's groups in about 75 villages of Andhra Pradesh. The community radio station is managed by 'General' Narsamma and Algole Narsamma. The second NGO-led community radio station in India was launched on 23 October 2008 at 'TARAgram' in Orchha, Madhya Pradesh state. Named 'Radio Bundelkhand' after the Bundelkhand region of central India where it is located, the radio station is licensed to the Society for Development Alternatives (DA), a Delhi-based NGO.

Under the new community radio policy, any not-for-profit 'legal entity'—except individuals, political parties and their affiliates, criminal and banned organizations—can apply for a CR license. Central funding is not available for such stations, and there are stringent restrictions on fundraising from other sources. Only organizations that are registered for a minimum of three years old and with a 'proven' track record of local community service can apply. License conditions implicitly favour well-funded stations as against inexpensive low power operations, several of which (*e.g.* Mana Radio in Andhra Pradesh and Raghav FM in Bihar) ran successfully on shoe-string budgets before the imposition of any community radio policy.

The licence entitles them to operate a 100 watt (ERP) radio station, with a coverage area of approximately 12 kilometres radius. A maximum antenna height of 30 meters is allowed. Community radio stations are expected to produce at least 50 per cent; of their programmes locally, as far as possible in the local language or dialect. The stress is on developmental programming, though there is no explicit ban on entertainment. News programmes are banned on community radio in India, as also on commercial FM radio. However, the government recently clarified that certain categories of news are permitted on radio, including sports news and commentaries, information on traffic and weather conditions, coverage of cultural events and festivals, information on academic events, public announcements pertaining to utilities like electricity and water supply, disaster warnings and health alerts.

Five minutes of advertising per hour is allowed on community radio. Sponsored programmes are not allowed except when the programme is sponsored by the Government at the Centre or State.

Activists and community workers from across the country have banded together under the aegis of the 'Community Radio Forum' in order to coordinate training and support for community radio stations, as well as to continue to petition for a more proactive community radio policy. The Community Radio Forum, India, was registered as a 'Society' and 'Trust' on 26 February 2008. In the meantime, mobile telephone operators have begun to offer commercial broadcast services over GSM, evading completely government restrictions built around traditional concepts of broadcasting technology.

Ireland

Ireland has had self-described community radio stations since the late 1970s, though it was not until 1995 that the first 11 licensed stations came on air as part of a pilot project run by the Independent Radio and Television Commission. Early stations were represented by the National Association of Community-Radio Broadcasters, which in 1988 published a guide to setting up new stations. More recently licensed stations have formed CRAOL as a representative group.

Japan

Japan has a series of low power community radio stations across the country.

Jordan

The first community radio was established in Jordan using the internet. AmmanNet.net was established in November 2000 as a means of bypassing government restrictions on private non-governmental radio. In 2005 AmmanNet radio received license as an FM station and was able to broadcast to the people of Jordan's capital Amman. AmmanNet has also been involved in the training of other community radio stations in Jordan, one as part of the village in the twin villages of Lib and Mleih and another as part of King Hussein University in the southern city of Maan. Also AmmanNet is involved in training Arab media activists in Internet radio. A programme was launched to train and launch nine gulf-based radio stations as part of khaleejnet.net

Two new community radio stations were recently established in Jordan. Yarmouk FM is located at Yarmouk University in Irbed as part of the school's Journalism and Mass Communications programme. Farah FM is currently under construction but has a license to broadcast in Amman and Zarqa, Jordan's second largest city. This station will focus primarily on youth and women's issues.

Philippines

The very famous community radio in the Philippines is Radyo Natin. Radyo Natin is a set of radio stations in the Philippines. Its stations nationwide broadcast a live Manila feed through satellite. But sometimes some stations air local programming, cutting the Manila feed. It is considered a community network because local programmes are being aired in different RN stations. Radyo Natin is owned by Manila Broadcasting Company.

South Africa

From shortly after the end of the Second World War, the country's repressive State policies gave the SABC (South African Broadcasting Corporation) an effective monopoly. For almost half a century, it was the only broadcaster permitted to operate legally and faced no independent radio competition on South African territory until the early 1990s' transition to democracy. The first legally-permitted, non-SABC, broadcast was that of 1991's 'Festival Radio' from the campus radio studios at Rhodes University in Grahamstown. An Independent Broadcast Authority was created to oversee the freeing up of the country's airwaves with small, community radio stations being permitted to broadcast for the first time. Applications were discussed in open session to ensure transparency and accountability. Notable early community broadcasters included Bush Radio in Cape Town and Radio Unitra in Umtata. The Independent Communications Authority (ICASA) now regulates the telecoms and broadcasting sector.

South Korea

Korean government licensed a few small power community

radio stations in the year of 2005. Maximum power is 1 watt and it reaches 5 km.

Sweden

In Sweden, community radio (närradio) was introduced in 1978 with test transmissions. Regular transmissions started next year. Commercials were not allowed until 1993 but operations are mainly run as non-profit NGO's. There are 150 community radio stations in Sweden.

Thailand

Community radio in Thailand saw fast growth during the government of Thaksin Shinawatra, taking advantage of a delay in the establishment of a regulatory authority. Thailand's 2,000-3,000 community radio stations, often operating unlicensed, have been accused of causing interference with air traffic radio and other radio stations. However, selected community radio stations have been the target of police crackdowns, causing critics to accuse the government of political interference. Community radio in Thailand now is uncertain about their status.

United Kingdom

Community radio stations were in operation on cable systems from the early 1970s onwards and mostly situated in new town areas and staffed and operated by volunteers. In the late 1980s and early 1990s the then newly formed Radio Authority awarded licences (termed "Incremental" by the outgoing Independent Broadcasting Authority) to a number of new, ex-pirate and cable based community ventures. Notable stations included the championing Spectrum Radio and Radio Thamesmead (AKA—RTM Radio) one of the first cable radio stations which started on the Radiofusion cable system in South East London area in the mid-1970's. The old breed of community radio stations could raise funding by selling airspace and by receiving donations or grants.

United States

U.S. community radio stations are usually staffed by volunteers and air a wide variety of programming. They generally have smaller budgets than National Public Radio (NPR) network outlets, due to the small audience of potential contributors and/or business donors. Community radio stations are distinct from NPR stations in that most community radio programming is locally produced by non-professional disc jockeys and producers, where NPR tends to rely more on syndicated programming, both from its own sources and other outlets such as PRI; NPR stations almost always have paid staffs to handle most duties. Community stations often try, as a matter of principle, to reduce their dependence on financial contributions from corporations (and even governments) in comparison with other public broadcasters. Many community stations are licensed as full-power FM stations, while others—especially newer community stations—are licensed under low-power broadcasting rules. Many of the former were founded in the 1960s and 1970s, when cultural experimentation (*e.g.*, the New Left) in the U.S. had a significant following, particularly among the young.

The National Federation of Community Broadcasters was formed in 1970 as an umbrella organization for community-oriented, non-commercial radio stations. The NFCB publishes handbooks for stations and lobbies on behalf of community radio at the federal level. It has been criticized for encouraging the homogenization of community stations through its Healthy Station Project. The project encouraged stations to scale back volunteers' power over management and the content of their programmes, as well as embrace more predictable "strip" programming. The Grassroots Radio Coalition is a very loose coalition of stations that formed as a reaction against increasing commercialization of public radio and lack of support for volunteer-based stations (including in the NFCB). Some stations are part of both groups.

PIRATE RADIO

The term pirate radio usually refers to illegal or unregulated radio transmissions. Its etymology can be traced to the unlicensed nature of the transmission, but historically there has been occasional but notable use of sea vessels—fitting the most common perception of a pirate—as broadcasting bases. The term is most commonly used to describe illegal broadcasting for entertainment or political purposes, but is also sometimes used for illegal two-way radio operation. Rules and regulations vary widely from country to country. In countries such as the USA and many countries in Europe, many types of radio licenses exist, and often the term pirate radio generally describes the unlicensed broadcast of FM radio, AM radio, or shortwave signals over a wide range.

In some cases radio stations are deemed legal where the signal is transmitted, but illegal where the signals are received—especially when the signals cross a national boundary. In other cases, a broadcast may be considered "pirate" due to the nature of its content, its transmission format (especially a failure to transmit a station identification according to regulations), or the transmit power (wattage) of the station, even if the transmission is not technically illegal (such as a web cast or an amateur radio transmission). Therefore *pirate radio* means different things to different people, implying some licensing procedure has been violated somewhere within the reach of the signal. Pirate radio stations are sometimes called bootleg stations (a term especially associated with two-way radio), clandestine stations or *Free Radio* stations.

History and Examples

Radio "piracy" began with the advent of regulations of the public airwaves in the United States at the dawn of the Age of Radio. Initially, radio, or wireless as it was more commonly called, was an open field of hobbyists and early inventors and experimenters, including Thomas Edison, Lee De Forest, and Nikola Tesla. The United States Navy began using radio for time signals and weather reports on the east coast of the United States in the 1890s. Before the advent of valve technology, early radio enthusiasts used noisy spark-gap transmitters, such as the first the spark-gap modulation technology pioneered by the first real audio (rather than telegraph code) radio brodcaster, Charles D. Herrold, in San Jose, California, or the infamous Ruhmkorf coil used by almost all early experimenters. The Navy soon began complaining to a sympathetic press that amateurs were disrupting naval transmissions. The May 25, 1907, edition of *Electrical World* in an article called "Wireless and Lawless" reported authorities were unable to prevent an amateur from interferring with the operation of a government station at the Washington, D.C. Navy Yard using legal means.

In the run-up to the London Radiotelegraph Convention in 1912 (essentially an international gentlmen's agreement on use of the radio band, non-binding and, on the high seas, completely null), and amid concerns about the safety of marine radio following the sinking of the *Titanic* on April 15 of that year (although there were never allegations of radio interference in that event), the New York Herald of April 17, 1912, headlined President Taft's initiative to regulate the public airwaves in an article called "President Moves to Stop Mob Rule of Wireless." When the "Act to Regulate Radio Communication" was passed on August 13, 1912, amateurs and experimenters were not banned from broadcasting; rather, amateurs were assigned their own frequency spectrum and licensing and call-signs were introduced. By regulating the public airwaves, President Taft thus created the legal space for illicit broadcasts to take place. An entire federal agency, the Federal Communications Commission, was created eventually to enforce rules on call-signs, assigned frequencies, licensing and acceptable content for broadcast.

The 1912 Radio Act gave the president legal permission to shut down radio stations "in time of war," and during the first two and a half years of World War One, before US entry, President Wilson tasked the US Navy with monitoring US radio stations, nominally to ensure "neutrality." The Navy used this authority to shut down amateur radio in the western part of the US (the US was divided into two civilian radio "districts" with corresponding call-signs, beginning with K in the west and W in the east, in the regulatory measures; the Navy was assigned call-signs beginning with N). When Wilson declared war on Germany on April 6, 1917, he also issued an executive order closing most radio stations not needed by the US government. The Navy took it a step further and declared it was illegal to listen to radio or possess a receiver or transmitter in the US, but there were doubts they had the authority to issue such an order even in war time. The ban on radio was lifted in the US in late 1919.

In 1924, New York City station WHN was accused of being an "outlaw" station by AT&T (then American Telephone and Telegraph Company) for violating trade licenses which permitted only AT&T stations to sell airtime on their transmitters. As a result of the AT&T interpretation a landmark case was heard in court, which even prompted comments from Secretary of Commerce Herbert Hoover when he took a public stand in the station's defence. Although AT&T won its case, the furore created was such that those restrictive provisions of the transmitter license were never enforced.

In Europe, Denmark had the first known radio station in the world to broadcast commercial radio from a vessel in international waters without permission from the authorities in the country that it broadcast to (Denmark in this case). The station was named Radio Mercur and began transmission on August 2, 1958. In the Danish newspapers it was soon called a "pirate radio." In the 1960s in the UK, the term referred to not only a perceived unauthorized use of the state-run spectrum by the unlicensed broadcasters but also the risk-taking nature of offshore radio stations that actually operated on anchored ships or marine platforms.

A good example of this kind of activity was Radio Luxembourg located in the Grand Duchy of Luxembourg. The English language evening broadcasts from Radio Luxembourg were beamed by Luxembourg licensed transmitters. The audience in the United Kingdom originally listened to their radio sets by permission of a Wireless Licence issued by the British General Post Office (GPO). However, under terms of that Wireless Licence, it was an offence under the Wireless Telegraphy Act to listen to *unauthorized* broadcasts, which possibly included those transmitted by Radio Luxembourg. Therefore, as far as the British authorities were concerned, Radio Luxembourg was not a "pirate radio station" and British listeners to the station were not breaking the law (although as the term 'unauthorized' was never properly defined it was somewhat of a legal grey area). This did not stop British newspapers from printing programme schedules for the station, or a British weekly magazine aimed at teenage girls,

"Fab 208" from promoting the "DJs" and their lifestyle (Radio Luxembourg's wavelength was 208 metres (1440 kHz)).

Radio Luxembourg was later joined by three other well known pirate stations received in the UK in violation of UK licensing, Radio Caroline, North and South, plus Radio Atlanta which became Caroline South and Radio London, all of which broadcast from vessels anchored outside of territorial limits and were therefore legitimate. Indeed, all four stations had registered offices based in Britain which made them totally LEGAL, otherwise there would have been no office in the UK.

Where actual sea-faring vessels are not involved, the term *pirate radio* is a political term of convenience as the word "pirate" suggests an illegal venture, regardless of the broadcasts actual legal status. The radio station XERF located at Ciudad Acuña, Coahuila, Mexico, just across the Rio Grande from Del Rio, Texas, USA, is an example.

While Mexico issued radio station XERF with a license to broadcast, the power of its 250,000 watts transmitter was far greater than the maximum of 50,000 watts authorized for commercial use by the government of the United States of America. Consequently, XERF and many other radio stations in Mexico, which sold their broadcasting time to sponsors of English-language commercial and religious programmes, were labelled as "border blasters", but not "pirate radio stations", even though the content of many of their programmes were in violation of US law. Predecessors to XERF, for instance, had originally broadcast in Kansas, advocating "goat-gland surgery" for improved masculinity, but moved to Mexico to evade US laws about advertising medical treatments, particularly unproven ones.

Free Radio

Another variation on the term *pirate radio* came about during the "Summer of Love" in San Francisco during the hippie days when many things were named "free." Examples include "free store", "free love" and even *"free radio"*, which usually referred to clandestine and unlicensed land-based transmissions. These were also tagged as being pirate radio transmissions. Free Radio was only ever used to refer to Radio transmissions that were beyond Government control, as was offshore Radio in the UK and Europe.

The term *free radio* was adopted by the Free Radio Association of listeners who defended the rights of the offshore "radio stations" broadcasting from ships and marine structures off the coastline of the United Kingdom. Félix Guattari points out:

> "Technological development, and in particular the miniaturization of transmitters and the fact that they can be put together by amateurs, 'encounters' a collective aspiration for some new means of expression."
>
> —Félix Guattari

In Europe, in addition to adopting the term *free radio,* supportive listeners of what had been called pirate radio adopted the term offshore radio, which was usually the term used by the owners of the marine broadcasting stations.

While *pirate radio* became accepted as meaning to describe adventurous forms of unlicensed broadcasting that had roots in true offshore unlicensed broadcasting. To this end the British licensing authorities have allowed both independent stations and to date even one local BBC tribute station to use this name, while the government retained use of the term *pirate radio* to describe any stations on land or at sea, which are broadcasting without a licence and contrary to land-based law. No Pirate Radio station has ever actually been illegal as their activities are outside the jurisdiction of any country, therefore, all offshore stations are and always have been LEGAL operations.

Pirate Radio by Geographical Area

Since this subject covers both national territories, international waters and international airspace, the only effective way to treat this subject is on a country by country, international waters and international airspace basis. Because the laws vary, the interpretation of the term *pirate radio* also varies considerably.

Questions have been raised about various types of broadcasting conducted by national governments against the interests of other national governments, which have in turn created radio jamming stations transmitting noises on the same frequency so as to destroy the receivability of the incoming signal.

While the USA transmitted its programmes towards the USSR, which attempted to jam them, in 1970 the government of the United Kingdom decided to employ a jamming transmitter to drown out the incoming transmissions from the commercial station Radio North Sea International, which was based aboard the Motor Vessel (MV) *Mebo II* anchored off Southeast England in the North Sea.

Other examples of this type of unusual broadcasting include the Coast Guard Cutter *USCGC Courier*, which both originated and relayed broadcasts of the Voice of America from an anchorage at the island of Rhodes, Greece to Soviet bloc countries. Balloons have been flown above Key West, Florida to support the TV transmissions of TV Martí, which are directed at Cuba. Military broadcasting aircraft have been flown over Vietnam, Iraq and many other nations by the United States Air Force. The European Union financially supported a radio station broadcasting news and information into the former Yugoslavia from a ship anchored in international waters.

New Media Pirate Radio

Pirate radio has long been synonymous with AM (LW, MW and SW) and FM (VHF) unlicensed broadcasting and "border blasting" in most parts of the world. With the advent of the internet, many conventional AM/FM radio stations have also taken to simulcasting via the web. These range from public broadcasters, licensed commercial radio, and in some countries, the 3rd tier of low power license exempt radio stations.

Despite pirate radio being known for over the air transmission, a new type of so called "pirate radio" stations now operate online. The distinguishing feature is that these online pirates will usually not pay music copyright fees, like most of their AM/FM pirate cousins. These online stations will usually attract a small and loyal audience and may go unnoticed by the authorities, unlike the real AM/FM pirates who can easily be heard and traced on a conventional radio. The common term for this type of operation is better served by the term "Studio Pirates" rather than pirate radio, as no real radio transmitter is used.

A recent case of online studio pirate was seen in the UK. Hitz Radio (UK) and not to be confused with HitzRadio.com

(USA) managed to attract large amounts of mainstream media publicity in early 2007. This publicity resulted from Ryan Dunlop, the owner of the station, nominating Hitz Radio for various business awards. After this publicity, many people with radio industry knowledge began to probe the station, which had claimed "millions of fans" and tens of thousands of listeners online. These claims, along with others, were part of the portfolio put forward for the business awards. When industry insiders checked these claims, it resulted in the UK music copyright agencies PPL and MCPS-PRS Alliance chasing back fees owed by Ryan Dunlop and Hitz Radio. That in turn resulted in the audience claims to be false, based upon the amount of back dated fees owed for copyright.

Piracy in Amateur and Two-Way Radio

Illegal use of licensed radio spectrum (also known as bootlegging in CB circles) is fairly common and takes several forms:

- *Unlicensed operation*—Particularly associated with amateur radio and licensed personal communication services such as GMRS, this refers to use of radio equipment on a section of spectrum for which the equipment is designed but on which the user is not licensed to operate (most such operators are informally known as "bubble pack pirates" from the sealed plastic retail packaging common to such walkie-talkies). While piracy on the US GMRS band, for example, is widespread (some estimates have the number of total GMRS users outstripping the number of licensed users by several orders of magnitude), such use is generally disciplined only in cases where the pirate's activity interferes with a licensee. [A notable case is that of United States amateur operator and political activist Jack Gerritsen (operating under the revoked call sign KG6IRO), who was successfully prosecuted by the FCC for unlicensed operation and malicious interference.] A subcategory of this is free banding, the use of allocations nearby a legal allocation (most typically the 27 MHz Citizen's Band) on modified or purpose-built gear.

- *Inadvertent interference*—Common when personal communications gear is brought into countries where it is not certified to operate. Such interference results from clashing frequency allocations, and occasionally requires wholesale reallocation of an existing band due to an insurmountable interference problem; for example, the 2004 approval in Canada of the unlicensed use of the United States General Mobile Radio Service frequencies due to interference from users of FRS/GMRS radios from the United States, where Industry Canada had to transfer a number of licensed users on the GMRS frequencies to unoccupied channels to accommodate the expanded service.
- *Deliberate or malicious interference*—Refers to the use of two-way radio to harass or jam other users of a channel. Such behaviour is widely prosecuted, especially when it interferes with mission-critical services such as aviation radio or marine VHF radio.
- *Illegal equipment*—This refers to the use of illegally modified equipment or equipment not certified for a particular band. Such equipment includes illegal linear amplifiers for CB radio, antenna or circuit modifications on walkie-talkies, the use of "export" radios for free banding, or the use of amateur radios on unlicensed bands that amateur gear is not certified for. The use of marine VHF radio gear for inland mobile radio operations is common in some countries, with enforcement difficult since marine VHF is generally the province of maritime authorities.

List of Known Pirate Radio Stations

- Impact FM 87.5, United Kingdom and online at impact875.co.uk
- La Tremenda 106.5, Mexico
- Radio Caroline South, United Kingdom
- Radio Jackie, United Kingdom (Now licensed and legal)
- Radio Caroline North, United Kingdom
- Radio Scotland, United Kingdom
- Radio 270, United Kingdom
- Swinging Radio England, United Kingdom

- Britain Radio, United Kingdom
- Radio City, United Kingdom
- Radio 390, United Kingdom
- Radio Essex, United Kingdom
- Radio Mercur, Denmark
- Radio Milinda, Dublin
- Radio Kaleidoscope, United Kingdom
- Wonderful Radio London, United Kingdom
- Wicked Radio, 88.9 FM 25 watts Metal, Punk, Rock, Talk (English) Edgerton, Wisconsin United States.
- TSF (radio), from Portugal, originally a pirate radio, it was legalized during the 1989 forgiveness of private radios (since these were not allowed in Portugal).
- WTCR, Twentieth Century Radio, US-based shortwave pirate radio hosted by Dr. Morbius, from June 7-8, 2008 broadcast 0143-0314 UTC on 6925 kHz in USB mode. Uses call letters of the licensed WTCR and WTCR-FM stations in Virginia and West Virginia.

In Popular Culture

Movies

- In the motion picture *Born in Flames* (1983), two different radical feminist groups voice their concerns to the public with pirate radio stations. One group, led by an outspoken white lesbian, operates "Radio Ragazza." The other group, led by a soft-spoken African-American, operates "Phoenix Radio."
- Christian Slater's character in the movie *Pump Up the Volume* (1990) runs a pirate radio station from his basement.
- *Pirate Radio USA* (2006), a documentary of US pirate radio.
- The 2009 movie *The Boat That Rocked* is about UK pirate radio.

Novels

- In the best selling novel *Harry Potter and the Deathly Hallows*, rebels use a pirate radio station called "Potterwatch" to inspire the population to join them against the then Death Eater controlled Ministry of

Magic. They also use it to report whatever deaths the legitimate (meaning "Voldemort-controlled") media deem unworthy of mention.

TV

- In the *"Teenage Mutant Ninja Turtles"* Season 5 (1991) episode "Pirate Radio", Pirate Radio is something everyone listens to and Krang uses it to hypnotise people into walking through an inter-dimension portal into Krang's Chasm.
- In an episode of *"King of the Hill"* ("Father of the Bribe", Season 6, Episode 109), Dale runs a pirate radio station and is then forced to sell it to Octavio.
- In an episode of Sealab 2021, captain Murphy runs a pirate radio station using the emergency transmission equipment, until it is shut down by the FCC, whose draconian tactics are satirised.
- In an episode of *"Malcolm in the Middle"*, Hal finds a radio transmitter which he used to broadcast a pirate radio-station when he was in college (under the alias "Kid Charlemagne"). He decides to start his pirate radio broadcast again, without the knowledge of his family.

Video Games

- In the video game series, *Jet Set Radio* and *Jet Grind Radio,* the player receives instructions, objectives, and updates via pirate radio operated by a mysterious man known as "Professor K."
- In the video game *Grand Theft Auto: Vice City*, the Wildstyle radio station is purportedly a pirate radio station.
- In the video game *Fallout 3* the player can tune into "Galaxy News Radio" operated by Three Dog. This station plays 50s style music, satirical humor, and also news blurbs about the progress of your character. You can also complete a quest which adds to the station's broadcasting power, allowing all residents of the Wasteland to hear the transmissions. Galaxy News Radio used to be a TV News Station, as shown in *"Fallout."*

INTERNET RADIO

Internet radio (also known as *web radio, net radio, streaming radio* and *e-radio*) is an audio broadcasting service transmitted via the Internet. Broadcasting on the Internet is usually referred to as webcasting since it is not transmitted broadly through wireless means. Internet radio involves a streaming medium that presents listeners with a continuous "stream" of audio over which they have no control, much like traditional broadcast media; in this respect, it is distinct from "on-demand" file serving. Internet radio is also distinct from podcasting, which involves downloading rather than streaming. Many Internet radio "stations" are associated with a corresponding traditional (or "terrestrial") radio station or radio network. Only Internet radio stations are independent of such associations.

Internet radio services are usually accessible from anywhere in the world—for example, one could listen to an Australian station from Europe or America. Some major networks like Clear Channel in the US and Chrysalis in the UK restrict listening to in country because of music licensing and advertising concerns. Internet radio remains popular among expatriates and listeners with interests that are often not adequately served by local radio stations (such as progressive rock, ambient music, folk music, classical music, and stand-up comedy). Internet radio services offer news, sports, talk, and various genres of music—every format that is available on traditional radio stations.

Internet Radio Technology

Streaming

The most common way to distribute Internet radio is via streaming technology using a lossy audio codec. Popular streaming audio formats include MP3, Ogg Vorbis, Windows Media Audio, RealAudio and HE-AAC (sometimes called aacPlus). The bits are "streamed" (transported) over the network in TCP or UDP packets, then reassembled and played within seconds. (The delay is referred to as lag time.)

History

Internet radio was pioneered by Carl Malamud. In 1993, Malamud launched "Internet Talk Radio" which was the "first computer-radio talk show, each week interviewing a computer expert." However, as late as 1995, this service was not available via multicast streaming; it was distributed "as audio files that computer users fetch one by one."

A November 1994 Rolling Stones concert was the "first major cyberspace multicast concert." Mick Jagger opened the concert by saying, "I wanna say a special welcome to everyone that's, uh, climbed into the Internet tonight and, uh, has got into the M-bone. And I hope it doesn't all collapse."

On November 7, 1994, WXYC (89.3 FM Chapel Hill, NC USA) became the first traditional radio station to announce broadcasting on the Internet. WXYC used an FM radio connected to a system at SunSite, later known as Ibiblio, running Cornell's CU-See Me software. WXYC had begun test broadcasts and bandwidth testing as early as August, 1994. WREK (91.1 FM, Atlanta, GA USA) started streaming on the same day using their own custom software called CyberRadio1. However, unlike WXYC, this was WREK's beta launch and the stream was not advertised until a later date.

Some of the first Internet-only commercial radio stations emerged in 1995. NetRadio "was one of the Internet's original Webcasters," eventually "streaming more than 100 channels including both music and spoken material." Nonetheless, NetRadio Corporation ceased operations in 2001.

Another company to emerge in 1995 was Broadcast.com, founded by Todd R. Wagner and Mark Cuban. In 1998, the initial public stock offering for Broadcast.com set a record at the time for the largest jump in price in stock offerings in the United States. The offering price was $18 and the company's shares opened at $68 on the first day of trading. The company was losing money at the time and indicated in a prospectus filed with the Securities Exchange Commission that they expected the losses to continue indefinitely. Yahoo! purchased Broadcast.com on July 20, 1999.

In 2002, the Copyright Arbitration Royalty Panel (CARP) system was initiated by the United States Congress in order to oversee decisions regarding royalty rates and terms, particularly in regard to digital distribution of audio. Many webcasters believed the 2002 proposed royalty structure to be overly burdensome and intended to disadvantage independent Internet-only stations. CARP was later phased out in favour of the Distribution Reform Act of 2004.

On March 2, 2007, the United States Copyright Royalty Board approved a rate increase in the royalties payable to performers of recorded works broadcast on the internet. It was suggested that "while Internet giants like AOL may be able to afford the new rates, many smaller Internet radio stations will have to shut down." It was also suggested that some US based Internet broadcasts might be moved to foreign jurisdictions where US royalties do not apply. It was therefore predicted that "Internet radio services [were] likely to appeal the royalty ruling to the US Court of Appeals in Washington." Additionally, April 26, 2007, the Internet Radio Equality Act (HR 2060) was proposed to reverse the CRB's decision.

Day of Silence

US Internet broadcasters organized a nationwide coalition to oppose the rate hike and in support of the Internet Radio Equality Act. On June 26, 2007 many of them participated in a "Day of Silence"—either shutting off their audio streams entirely, or replacing their streams with static, ocean sounds or other ambience, interspersed with brief public service announcements—to focus attention on the consequences of the impending rate hike.

Rhapsody, Live365, MTV, Pandora, and SHOUTcast were among the participants in the Day of Silence. Last.FM and Slacker did not participate, saying that they did not want to punish their listeners for the station's problems. SoundExchange, representing supporters of the increase in royalty rates, pointed out the fact that the rates were flat from 1998 through 2005, without even being increased to reflect cost-of-living increases. They also point to the fact that CBS recently purchased Last. FM for 280 million dollars, and if internet radio is to build businesses from the product of recordings, the performers and owners of those recordings should receive fair compensation. Opponents argued that the purchase price paid for Last FM reflected that it was primarily a social network service that included a radio service.

Recent SoundExchange Developments

On May 1, 2007, SoundExchange came to an agreement with certain large webcasters regarding the minimum fees that were modified by the determination of the Copyright Royalty Board. While the CRB decision imposed a $500 per station or channel minimum fee for all webcasters, certain webcasters represented through DiMA negotiated a $50,000 "cap" on those fees with SoundExchange. However, DiMA and SoundExchange continue to negotiate over the per song, per listener fees.

SoundExchange has also offered alternative rates and terms to certain eligible small webcasters, that allows them to calculate their royalties as a percentage of their revenue or expenses, instead of at a per performance rate. To be eligible, a webcaster had to have revenues of less than $1.25 million dollars a year and stream less than 5 million "listener hours" a month (or an average of 6830 concurrent listeners). These restrictions would disqualify independent webcasters like AccuRadio, DI.FM, Club977 and others from participating in the offer, and therefore many small commercial webcasters continue to negotiate a settlement with SoundExchange.

An April 2008 survey showed that, in the US, more than one in seven persons aged 25-54 years old listen to online radio each week. In 2008, 13 per cent of the American population listened to the radio online, compared with 11 per cent in 2007.

An August 16, 2008, *Washington Post* article reported that although Pandora was "one of the nation's most popular Web radio services, with about 1 million listeners daily...the burgeoning company may be on the verge of collapse" due to the structuring of performance royalty payment for webcasters. "Traditional radio, by contrast, pays no such fee. Satellite radio pays a fee but at a less onerous rate, at least by some measures." The article indicated that "other Web radio outfits" may be "doom[ed]" for the same reasons.

On September 30, 2008, the United States Congress passed "a bill that would put into effect any changes to the royalty rate to which [record labels and web casters] agree while lawmakers are out of session." Although royalty rates are expected to decrease, many webcasters nevertheless predict difficulties generating sufficient revenue to cover their royalty payments.

PUBLIC BROADCASTING

Public broadcasting includes radio, television and other electronic media outlets that receive some or all of their funding from the public. Public broadcasters may receive their funding from individuals through voluntary donations, a specific tax such as a television licence fee, or as direct funding by the state.

The extent to which public broadcasters can be considered "non-commercial" varies from country to country. In the United States, most public radio and television stations are licensed as non-commercial broadcasters, yet many stations air underwriting spots (resembling advertisements on commercial broadcasting but with some content limitations) in exchange for corporate contributions. In some other countries, public broadcasters are permitted to air commercials.

Public broadcasting may be nationally and/or locally operated, depending on the country and the station. In some countries, public broadcasting is dominated by a single organization (such as the BBC in the UK and the ABC in Australia) and its radio and television services broadcast throughout the country. However, some countries have multiple public broadcasting organizations operating regionally (such as in Germany) or in different languages. In the United States, public broadcasting stations are always locally licensed, but range from stations that mostly broadcast programming from national networks [such as the Public Broadcasting Service (PBS) and National Public Radio (NPR)] to stations that broadcast only locally produced content.

Historically, in many countries (with the notable exception of the US), public broadcasting was once the only form or the dominant form of broadcasting. However, commercial broadcasting now also exists in most of these countries; the number of countries with only public broadcasting has declined substantially during the latter part of the 20th century. In some countries, commercial broadcasting and the emergence of a wider variety of broadcast media have created competition that makes it more difficult for public broadcasters to retain their audiences and survive.

Defining Public Broadcasting

There is no standard definition for public broadcasting, although a number of official bodies have attempted to identify key characteristics. Public-service broadcasters generally transmit programming that aims to improve society by informing viewers. In contrast, the aim of commercial outlets is to provide popular content that attracts a large audience, maximizing revenue from advertising and sponsorship. For this reason, the ideals of public broadcasting are often hard to reconcile with commercial goals.

The Broadcasting Research Unit lists the following as possible goals or characteristics of a public broadcaster.

1. *Geographic universality*—The stations' broadcasts are available nationwide, with no exception. This criterion is not met by Five in the UK, which a substantial minority of the population cannot receive. Generally, the "nationwide" criterion is satisfied by either having member stations across the country (as is the case with PBS) or, as is the case with most other public broadcasters around the world, the broadcaster's use of sufficient transmitters to broadcast nationwide.
2. *Catering for all interests and tastes*—As exemplified by the BBC's range of minority channels (BBC Two and BBC Radio 3).
3. *Catering for minorities*—Much as above, but with racial and linguistic minorities [for example S4C in Wales, BBC Asian Network, Radio-Canada, and Australia's multicultural Special Broadcasting Service (SBS)].
4. *Concern for national identity and community*—This essentially means that the stations mostly part commission programmes from within the country, which may be more expensive than importing shows from abroad.
5. *Detachment from vested interests and government* in which programming is impartial, and the broadcaster is not be subject to control by advertisers or government.

Even when a broadcast medium is removed from corporate and government interests, critics argue that it may nonetheless have a bias towards the values of certain groups, such as the middle class, the politics of the incumbent government, or in the case of partially or wholly commercially funded networks, the advertisers.

6. *One broadcasting system to be directly funded by the corpus of users*—For example, the licence fee in the case of the BBC, or member stations asking for donations in the case of PBS/NPR.
7. *Competition in good programming rather than numbers*—Quality is the prime concern with a true public service broadcaster. Of course, in practice, ratings wars are rarely concerned with quality, although that may depend on how "quality" is defined.
8. *Guidelines to liberate programme-makers and not restrict them*—In the UK, guidelines, and not laws, govern what a programme-maker can and cannot do, although these guidelines can be backed up by hefty penalties.

Some of these definition points may not be acceptable everywhere. For example, in the US, public broadcasting may see part of its mission to bring in foreign content, such as from the CBC/Radio-Canada and the BBC, since such content is not commonly aired by American commercial broadcasters.

An alternative model for implementing public-service media exists, known as Citizen Media. As it relates to broadcasting, this generally means a radio or television outlet which has some sort of public access, that is, most or much of the programming is created by members of the public which receives the programming. This can be in the form of community radio, campus radio, and public access television, although the latter is not a form of over-the-air broadcasting, as it is only available on cable television systems.

Advantages and Disadvantages

Public broadcasters may receive all or a substantial part of their funding from government sources, either from the general tax revenues or from licence fees. Public broadcasters do not rely on advertising as a source of revenue to the same degree as commercial broadcasters; this allows public broadcasters to air programmes that are less saleable to the mass market, such as public affairs shows, radio and television documentaries, and educational programmes. That public broadcasters do not chase ratings in the same way as commercial broadcasters can lead to the criticism that they are unresponsive to what their viewers want, but also to the positive claim that they can explore issues in greater depth and with more complexity than is possible in commercial media, and that they can present cultural fare that has social value but would not be supported by markets. It may also be pointed out commercial broadcasters programme not for audiences but for those audiences which will buy their products.

Additionally, public broadcasting facilitates the implementation of cultural policy (an industrial policy and investment policy for culture). Some examples include:

- The Canadian government is committed to official bilingualism (English and French). As a result, the public broadcaster, the CBC employs translators and journalists who speak both official languages and it encourages production of cross-cultural material. Quebec separatists argue that this is also a policy of cultural imperialism and assimilation.
- In the UK, the BBC supports multiculturalism and diversity, in part by using on-screen commentators and hosts of different ethnic origins.
- In New Zealand, the public broadcasting system provides support to Maori (native New Zealander) broadcasting, as a way to improve the opportunities, maintain the cultural heritage and promote the language of these New Zealanders.

Critics of public broadcasting systems argue that this implementation of cultural policy imposes the values of the public broadcaster on the populace. However, it can also be argued that commercial broadcasting has a bias for certain values or cultural forms, such as pop culture, militarism, culture bias, and consumerism.

Public broadcasting, and also some pirate broadcasting,

provides a counterweight to the commercial media. Advocates of deliberative democracy argue that public broadcasting helps to maintain modern democracies, since public broadcasters can engage in journalism for its own sake. In wealthier countries public broadcasters tend to not be beholden to political parties or the government of the day. This is especially true where the broadcaster is funded by licensing fees and so, theoretically, not dependent on the government for any of its funding.

Economics of Public Broadcasting

An economic rationale for public broadcasting is that it exists to provide coverage of interests for which there are missing markets. Public broadcasting can supply those topics which have social benefit that would otherwise not be broadcast due to believed unprofitability. Society is willing to pay for such programming, but markets fail to provide it. Typically, such underprovision exists when the benefits to viewers are relatively high in comparison to the benefits to advertisers from contacting viewers. This frequently is the case in undeveloped countries that normally have low benefits to advertising, which helps explain their tendency to have public broadcasting. However, concern exists that public broadcasting can crowd out potential private broadcasting. One study compared classical and jazz music programming provided by private radio to that provided by public radio. It found that in large markets, public broadcasting appears to displace private entry. Additionally, publicly funded broadcasting does not necessarily mean that the optimal level will be produced. A government failure can arise in which the cost of public funding exceeds its benefits.

One particular feature of public broadcasting in the United States, consumer funding, generates a unique economic dilemma. The free rider problem arises because individual certain consumers are who derive value from the programming do not donate and allow consumers to shoulder a larger portion of the funding. Consumers who value public broadcasting the most and those will the largest incomes tend to donate more than they would if all consumers donated their "fair" share. An expected result is that public broadcasting services which rely on consumer donations underprovide their services. Since consumer contributions are purely voluntary for National Public Radio, Public Broadcasting Service, and others these networks face the problem.

Economic Innovation

Public broadcasting has been a pioneer in introduced many new categories of programming. The market place was not willing to introduce new types of programming due to the cost of taking risks in these areas. Commercial media uses programmes that are typically well tested and proven by consumers. When looking at the programmes that came out of PBS, it is evident that categories such as cooking, science, home improvement, business, history and children shows all started at PBS many years and decades before the cable networks launched. PBS invested in these untested categories because the organization believed consumers could benefit from these programmes. PBS believed there were missing markets (show categories) that consumers would value and enrich their daily lives (giving higher utility). The commercial media industry was not willing to invest in unproven shows and without an organization such as PBS these categories might not exist in the market place. Public broadcasting has helped to introduce quality categories into the market place to benefit consumers. Without such an organization to test new quality programming, consumers would fail to receive the benefits. Consumers would have less choices and innovation would occur significantly slower.

Implementation of Public Broadcasting Around the World

The model, established in the 1920s, of the British Broadcasting Corporation (BBC)—an organization widely trusted, even by citizens of the Axis Powers during World War II—was widely emulated throughout Europe, the British Empire, and later the Commonwealth. The public broadcasters in a number of countries are basically an application of the model used in Britain.

Modern public broadcasting is often a mixed commercial model. For example, the CBC has always relied on a subsidy from general revenues of the government, in addition to advertising revenue, to support its television service. This means they must compete with commercial broadcasting. Some argue that this dilutes their mandate as truly public broadcasters, who have no commercial bias to distort their presentation. The rest of this section looks at some specific implementations of public broadcasting around the world.

Asia

Pakistan

In Pakistan, the public broadcaster is the state owned PBC which is short for "Pakistan Broadcasting Corporation." It consists of PTV (Pakistan Television) and Radio Pakistan. In the past PBC was funded publicly through money obtained from television, radio and VCR licensing. Pakistan entered into Television Broadcasting age with a small pilot TV Station established at Lahore from where transmission was first beamed in Black and White with effect from 26 November 1964. Television centres were established in Dhaka, Karachi and Rawalpindi/Islamabad in 1967 and in Peshawar and Quetta in 1974. PTV has various channels trasmitting throughout the world including PTV National, PTV World, PTV 2, PTV Global, PTV Bolan etc. Radio Pakistan has stations covering all the major cities, it covers 80 per cent; of the country serving 95.5 million listeners. It has world service in 07 languages daily.

Hong Kong

In Hong Kong, the Radio Television Hong Kong (RTHK) is the sole public service broadcaster. Although a government department under administrative hierarchy, it enjoys editorial independence, and its director is promoted from within the department. It operates seven radio channels, and produces television programmes and broadcast on commercial television channels, as these channels are required by law to provide time slot for RTHK television programmes.

Japan

In Japan, the main public broadcaster is the national NHK (Japan Broadcasting Corporation), sometimes informally referred to as Radio Tokyo by English speakers. The broadcaster was set up in 1926 and was modelled on the British Broadcasting Company, the precursor to the British Broadcasting Corporation created in 1927. Much like the BBC,

NHK is funded by a "receiving fee" by every Japanese household, with no commercial advertising and the maintenance of a position of strict political impartiality. NHK runs two national terrestrial TV stations (NHK General and NHK Educational) and three satellite only services (NHK BS-1, BS-2 and the hi-definition NHK Hi-Vision services). NHK also runs three national radio services and a number of international radio and television services, akin to the BBC World Service. NHK has also been an innovator in television, developing the world's first high definition television technology in 1964 and launched high definition services in Japan in 1981.

Malaysia

In Malaysia, the public broadcaster is the state owned RTM which is short for "Radio Televisyen Malaysia" (Malaysian Radio and Television). RTM was previously funded publicly through money obtained from television licensing, however, it is currently state subsidized as television licences have been abolished. At present, RTM operates 8 national, 16 state and 7 district radio stations as well as 2 national terrestrial television channels called RTM1 and RTM2. RTM is also currently doing tests on a new digital television channel called RTMi. Tests involving 2000 residential homes in the Klang Valley began in September 2006 and it was expected to be completed by March 2007.

Europe

In most countries in Europe, state broadcasters are funded through a mix of advertising and public money, either through a licence fee or directly from the government.

Germany

Following World War II, when regional broadcasters had been merged into one national network by the Nazis to create a powerful means of propaganda, the Allies insisted on a de-centralized, independent structure for German public broadcasting and created regional public broadcasting agencies that, by and large, still exist today. In addition to these nine regional radio and TV broadcasters, which cooperate within

ARD, a second national television service (ZDF) was later created in 1961 and a national radio service with two networks (Deutschland radio) emerged from the remains of Cold War propaganda stations in 1994. All services are mainly financed through license fees paid by everybody who keeps a radio or TV set "ready for use", and are governed by councils of representatives of the "societally relevant groups." Public TV and radio stations spend about 60 per cent; of the ~10 Bil. € spent altogether for broadcasting in Germany per year.

Ireland

In Ireland a system of TV licencing and advertising to fund public services operates. RTÉ the incumbent offers a range of free to air services on TV and Radio. Recently, there has also been a portion of revenue from the licence fee used to assist other broadcasters to produce home grown programming such as TV3 on television and Today FM on the radio. An off-shot of RTÉ, TG4 is an independent Irish language broadcaster that is funded by the government through subsidy, and through advertising revenue.

Italy

Italian national broadcasting company is the RAI—Radiotelevisione Italiana, born as URI in 1924. RAI transmits on analogical television on three channels, named Rai Uno, Rai Due and Rai Tre, but also works via satellite, in radiophonic sector, book and cinema. It is considered the biggest and one of the most authoritative television companies in Europe. With 54 per cent; of share, RAI also is the most viewed public television of the continent. Proceeds derive from a periodical standing charge and from advertising. The main competitors of RAI are Mediaset, the biggest national private television, divided in three channels, and La7, owned by Telecom Italia.

The Netherlands

In the Netherlands a different system is used to most other countries. Public broadcasting associations are allocated money and time to broadcast their programmes on the publicly owned television and radio channels. The time and money is allocated in proportion to their membership numbers. The system is intended to reflect the diversity of all the groups composing the nation.

United Kingdom

The United Kingdom has a strong tradition of public service broadcasting. In addition to the BBC, established in 1922, there is also Channel 4, a state-owned commercial public service broadcaster, and S4C, a Welsh language broadcaster in Wales. Furthermore, the two commercial analogue broadcasters ITV and Five also have significant public service obligations imposed as part of their licence to broadcast.

Scandinavia

National public broadcasters in the Scandinavian countries were modelled after the BBC and established only a few years later: Radioordningen (now DR) in Denmark, Kringkastingselskapet (now NRK) in Norway, and Radiotjänst (now Sveriges Radio) in Sweden (all in 1925), and YLE in Finland in 1926. All four are funded from television licence fees costing (in 2007) around 230 EUR (300 USD) per household per year.

North America

Canada

In Canada, the main public broadcaster is the national Canadian Broadcasting Corporation (the CBC), which operates two television networks (CBC Television and Télévision de Radio-Canada), four radio networks (CBC Radio One, CBC Radio Two, Première Chaîne and Espace musique) and two 24-hour news channels (CBC Newsworld and RDI) in both of Canada's official languages. CBC's television operations are funded in part by advertisements, in addition to tax dollars from the federal government (Newsworld and RDI are funded entirely by commercials). CBC's radio operations are commercial-free. In recent years, the CBC was frequently battered by budget cuts and labour disputes.

In addition, several provinces operate public broadcasters; these are not CBC subentities, but distinct networks in their own right. These include the English-language TVOntario and the French-language TFO in Ontario, Télé-Québec in Quebec, SCN in Saskatchewan, public radio station CKUA in Alberta, and Knowledge in British Columbia. Some of the provincial broadcasters operate through conventional transmitters, while others are cable-only channels.

Alberta also has a semi-public television network, Access, which is licensed to provide some public service programming but is owned and operated by a commercial broadcaster. The network, formerly a public broadcaster operated by the provincial government, was sold to CHUM Limited in 1995. CJRT-FM in Toronto also operated as a public government-owned radio station for many years; while no longer funded by the provincial government, it still solicits most of its budget from listener and corporate donations and is permitted to air only a very small amount of commercial advertising. One television station, CFTU in Montreal, operates as an educational station owned by the Université de Montréal. Some other universities have dedicated cable channels to broadcast educational programming, but no other university in Canada operates a conventional broadcast television station.

Some local community stations also operate non-commercially with funding from corporate and individual donors. In addition, cable companies are required to produce a local community channel in each licensed market. Such channels have traditionally aired community talk shows, city council meetings and other locally oriented programming, although it is becoming increasingly common for them to adopt the format and branding of a local news channel. Canada also has a large number of campus radio and community radio stations.

United States

Public broadcasting in the United States is as old as broadcasting itself. Most early public stations were operated by state colleges and universities, and were often run as part of the schools' cooperative extension services. Stations in this era were internally funded, and did not rely on listener contributions to operate; some accepted advertising. Networks such as Iowa, South Dakota, and Wisconsin Public Radio began in this way.

The concept of a "non-commercial, educational" station *per se* does not show up in US law until the 1940s, when the FM band was moved to its present location; the part of the band between 88.1 and 91.9 MHz is reserved for such stations, though they are not limited to those frequencies. For example, WBAA-West Lafayette, Ind. has its FM frequency at 101.3 MHz. Houston's KUHT was the nation's first public television station, and signed on the air in 25 May 1953 from the campus of the University of Houston. This phenomenon continued in other big cities in the 1950s; in rural areas, it was not uncommon for colleges to operate commercial stations instead (*e.g.*, the University of Missouri's KOMU-TV, an NBC affiliate).

In the United States, public broadcasting is decentralized and is not government operated, but does receive some government support. The majority of funding comes from community support to hundreds of public radio and public television stations, each of which is an individual entity licensed to one of several different non-profit organizations, municipal or state governments, or universities. Sources of funding also include on-air fund drives and—on public radio stations—the sale of underwriting "spots" (typically 15-30 seconds) to sponsors. Public radio and television organizations often produce their own programmes, but purchase or receive most of their programming from national producers and programme distributors such as National Public Radio (NPR), Public Broadcasting Service (PBS), Public Radio International (PRI), American Public Television (APT), and American Public Media. US Federal government support for public radio and television is filtered through a separate organization, the Corporation for Public Broadcasting (CPB).

Television

In the United States the Public Broadcasting Service (PBS) (formerly National Educational Television) television network operates on a largely viewer-supported basis (see telethon), with commercial sponsors of specific programmes. Over time, sponsorship announcements ("underwriting") have slowly transformed into something resembling regular TV advertisements, though they are usually shorter and have a more muted tone than what normally appears on commercial and cable TV, and many organizations still only receive a short thanks for their contributions. Underwriting may only issue declarative statements (including slogans) and may not include "calls to action." Most communities also have public access services on local cable television stations, which are sometimes supported in part through donations.

US public broadcasting for television has, from the late 1960s onward, dealt with severe criticism from conservative politicians and think-tanks, which allege that its programming has a leftist bias. In contrast to European public broadcasting systems, which tend to dominate their national marketplaces, US public broadcasting is, and has always been, a niche service that provides programming not found elsewhere on the system, such as cultural programmes, documentaries, and public affairs shows.

Radio

A public radio network, National Public Radio (NPR), was created in 1970, following the passage of the Public Broadcasting Act of 1967 which established the Corporation for Public Broadcasting. This network (generally exclusive of Pacifica) is colloquially though inaccurately referred to as *Public Radio*. Independent local public radio stations buy their programming from distributors such as NPR; Public Radio International (PRI); American Public Media (APM); The Public Radio Exchange (PRX); and Pacifica, most often distributed through the Public Radio Satellite System (PRSS). Around these distributed programmes, stations fill varying amounts of local programming.

Public radio stations in the US tend to broadcast a mixture of news and talk radio programming along with some music. Some of the larger operations split off these formats into separate stations or networks. Public music stations are probably best known for playing classical music, although other formats have been used, including the time-honoured "eclectic" music format that is rather free form in nature common among college radio stations; jazz is another public radio programming staple. Also, XM Satellite Radio provides a station of public radio programmes licensed from all three content providers.

Local stations derive most of the funding for their operations through regular pledge drives and corporate sponsorship (euphemistically termed "underwriting" on-air). The local stations then contract with programme distributors and also provide some programming themselves. NPR produces some of its own programming such as *Morning Edition; Weekend Edition;* and *All Things Considered.* PBS, by contrast, does not create its own content. NPR also receives some direct funding from private donors, foundations, and from the Corporation for Public Broadcasting. Some other public networks, such as Pacifica, are almost entirely member-funded and do not receive significant sponsorship from corporations or governmental sources.

Oceania

Australia

In Australia, the Australian Broadcasting Corporation (ABC) is funded entirely through an Australian Government grant-in-aid. The multicultural Special Broadcasting Service (SBS), another public broadcaster, now accepts limited sponsorship and advertising. Imparja is an Aboriginal community broadcaster in Australia that receives funding from the Federal Government. Most of its programmes are bought from Australia's commercial broadcasters, and it only airs a small amount of local content.

In addition, there is a large Australian community broadcasting sector, funded in part by Federal grants via the Community Broadcasting Foundation, but largely sustained via subscriptions, donations and business sponsorship. As of June 2005, there were 442 fully-licensed community radio stations (including remote Indigenous services) and a number of community television stations (most operating as Channel 31 despite being unrelated across different states). They are organized similarly to PBS and NPR stations in the US, and take on the role that public access stations have in the US.

New Zealand

In New Zealand, the former public broadcaster BCNZ (formerly NZBC) was broken up into separate state-owned corporations, Television New Zealand (TVNZ) and Radio New Zealand (RNZ). While RNZ remains commercial-free, about 90 per cent; of funding for TVNZ comes from selling advertising during programmes on their two stations. TVNZ continues to be a public broadcaster; however like CBC Television in Canada it is essentially a fully commercial network in continuous ratings battles with other stations.

Programmes offered on TVNZ include popular shows like *Desperate Housewives, ER, Lost, Cold Case,* and *Dancing with the Stars*. TVNZ operates five stations: *TV ONE, TV2, TVNZ 6, TVNZ 7* and *TVNZ Sport Extra* and hold majority ratings in the country. Because of its high ratings some of the most expensive advertising slots in the country are on TV ONE and TV2. TVNZ 6 and 7 are fully-funded and advertisement-free.

The Government owns a network of reserved channels for non-commercial regional access broadcasting, and some of them have been awarded to local community trusts to provide public service and access television. Examples are *Triangle TV* in Auckland and Wellington; and *Channel 7* in Taranaki.

Latin America

Despite a moderate state presence in television media since the 1970s, Latin America has never had a strong history of European style public service radio or television. The closest model to the British BBC is that of Chile's Televisión Nacional, an open channel which serves the entire country (including Easter Island and Antarctica bases). Televisión Nacional, popularly known as channel 7 because of its Santiago frequency, is governed by a seven-member board appointed by the Chilean Senate. It is meant to be independent of political pressures, although accusations of bias have been made, especially during election campaigns.

In most Latin American countries, the private sector has taken the leading role in the development of television networks. In opposition, state broadcasters tend to be either very weak and under-funded (as the Argentinian Canal 7, formerly known as ATC or the Brazilian TV Brasil), or to be clearly under the control of the party in power (like Cuban Cubavisión and Venezuelan VTV). Starting from these singularities, commercial broadcasting quickly and effectively conquered its audiences, leaving public and state broadcasting a token role. In some countries, such as Ecuador, where broadcasting was originally legally defined as a commercial venture, a public broadcaster was never born until 2008 (when Rafael Correa's government decided to set up Ecuador TV).

Recently, under the initiative of the Venezuelan government of Hugo Chávez, and with the support of the governments of Argentina, Uruguay and Cuba, the public news channel Telesur was created with the declared intent of giving Latin America a continent-wide news channel that can present world news with a Latin American vision and perspective. There is an ongoing debate on whether Telesur will be able become a neutral and fair news channel able to counter the huge influence of American networks like CNN, or whether it will end up as a propaganda tool of the Venezuelan government, which owns a 51 per cent share of said channel.

List of Public Broadcasters

North American

Canadian

- Canadian Broadcasting Corporation
- CBC Television
- Télévision de Radio-Canada
- CBC Radio One
- CBC Radio 2
- CBC Radio 3
- Première Chaîne
- Espace musique
- Bande à part
- CBC Newsworld
- RDI
- Radio Canada International
- Knowledge—British Columbia
- Saskatchewan Communications Network—Saskatchewan
- Télé-Québec—Quebec
- TFO—Ontario
- TVOntario—Ontario
- CKUA—Alberta

- CJRT-FM—Toronto, Ontario
- CFTU-TV—Montreal, Quebec

American

- National Public Radio
- Public Broadcasting Service
- Public Radio International
- Pacifica Radio Service
- Create
- American Public Media
- PRX
- Heartland Public Radio

Latin American

- Canal 7 Argentina—Argentina (nationwide)
- Canal 10—Tucumán—Tucumán, Argentina
- Televisión Nacional de Chile—Chile (nationwide)
- Señal Colombia—Colombia
- Telecaribe—Barranquilla, Colombia
- Telepacífico—Western Colombia
- Cubavision—Cuba
- Ecuador TV—Ecuador
- Venezolana de Televisión—Venezuela (nationwide)
- Televisión Educativa—Venezuela
- Visión Venezuela—Venezuela
- Telesur—Reaches the entire continent. Owned by Venezuela (a 51% share), Argentina (20%), Cuba (19%), and Uruguay (10%).
- TV Cultura—São Paulo, Brasil (some programming available nationwide)
- TV Brasil—Rio de Janeiro, Brasil (some programming available nationwide)

African and Middle Eastern

- SABC—South Africa
- Botswana Television—Botswana
- GBC—Ghana
- TPA—Angola
- SNRT—Morocco

- ENTV and TPA—Algeria
- ERTU—Egypt
- LJBC—Lybia
- Israel Broadcasting Authority—Israel
- IRIB—Iran
- Télé-Liban—Lebanon
- Al Jazeera—Qatar
- JRTV—Jordan
- Abu Dhabi TV—United Arab Emirates

Asian

- PTV—Pakistan
- MediaCorp—Singapore
- Korean Broadcasting System and Munhwa Broadcasting Corporation—South Korea
- CCTV—China
- NHK—Japan
- Prasar Bharati—India:
    - All India Radio
    - Doordarshan
- Taiwan Broadcasting System—Taiwan
- TDM—Macau
- Radio Television Hong Kong—Hong Kong
- Radio Televisyen Malaysia—Malaysia
- TVRI—Indonesia
- Vietnam Television—Vietnam
- Thai Public Broadcasting Service—Thailand
- National Broadcasting Network—Philippines

Oceanian

Australia

- Australian Broadcasting Corporation
- Special Broadcasting Service
- Imparja Television

New Zealand

- Radio New Zealand

European

- ARD—working partnership of German public-service broadcasters:
  - Mitteldeutscher Rundfunk—Leipzig
  - Westdeutscher Rundfunk—Cologne
  - Norddeutscher Rundfunk—Hamburg
  - Rundfunk Berlin-Brandenburg—Berlin
  - Bayerischer Rundfunk—Munich
  - Südwestrundfunk—Stuttgart
  - Saarländischer Rundfunk—Saarbrücken
  - Hessischer Rundfunk—Frankfurt
  - Radio Bremen—Bremen
- Arte—France/Germany
- BBC—United Kingdom
- BNT—Bulgaria
- BRF—German-speaking Community of Belgium
- BVN—Flanders and Netherlands Television
- Èeská televize—Czech Republic
- Channel 4—United Kingdom
- Danmarks Radio—Denmark
- Duna TV—Hungary
- ERT—Greece
- ETV—Estonia
- France Télévisions:
  - France 2
  - France 3
  - France 4
  - France 5
- GBC—Gibraltar
- HRT—Croatia
- LRT—Lithuania
- LTV—Latvia
- Magyar Televízió—Hungary
- MRT—FYR Macedonia
- NRK—Norway
- ORF—Austria

- Polish Radio—Poland
- PBS—Malta
- Publieke Omroep—Netherlands:
  - BNN
  - EO
  - KRO
  - LLiNK
  - MAX
  - NCRV
  - TROS
  - VARA
  - VPRO
- RTP—Portugal
- Radio France
  - France Inter
  - France Info
  - France Culture
  - France Musique
  - France Bleu
  - FIP
  - Le Mouv'
- Radio France Internationale
- RAI—Italy
- RAS—Italy
- RTBF—Wallonia, Belgium
- RTCG—Montenegro
- RTÉ—Ireland
- RTS—Serbia
- RTSH—Albania
- RTK—Kosovo
- RTV Slovenija—Slovenia
- RTVE—Spain
- RÚV—Iceland
- S4C—Wales, United Kingdom
- Sjónvarp Føroya—Faroe Islands
- SRG SSR idée suisse—Switzerland
- STV—Slovakia

- Sveriges Radio—Sweden
- Sveriges Television—Sweden
- UR—Sweden
- TG4—Ireland
- TVP—Poland
- Televisió de Catalunya—Catalonia
- TVR—Romania
- TRT—Turkey
- VRT—Flanders, Belgium
- Yleisradio—Finland
- ZDF—Germany

COMMERCIAL BROADCASTING

Commercial broadcasting is the practice of broadcasting for profit. This is normally achieved by interrupting normal programming to air advertisements, also commonly called "commercials" in this context. This is the dominant type of broadcasting in the United States and a large number of other countries such as most of Latin America. It is also common elsewhere, but usually exists alongside public broadcasting where programming is largely funded by broadcast receiver licences, public donations, or government grants.

In an hour of broadcast time on a commercial broadcast outlet, typically ten to twenty minutes are devoted to advertising. Advertisers pay a certain amount of money to air their commercials, usually based upon the popularity or ratings of a station or network. This effectively makes commercial broadcasters more answerable to advertisers than the public, which is a major criticism of commercial radio and television. Programming on commercial stations is often more sensationalistic—particularly during ratings periods such as sweeps in the US and also in some Latin American countries

Commercial broadcasting also has considerable overlap with pay services such as cable television, cable radio, satellite television and satellite radio; though such services are generally partially or wholly paid for by local subscribers, much of the programming, particularly on cable television, is produced by companies operating in much the same manner as commercial broadcasters, and both they and often the local cable provider will sell commercial time in the same manner. There does exist, however, completely advertisement-free commercial television and radio; premium cable services such as HBO and Showtime generally operate solely on subscriber fees with no need to sell ad space, as do the parts of the two major satellite radio systems that are produced in-house (mostly music material).

Commercial broadcasting (especially over-the-air) is often controversial for a great many reasons. Chief among them is a perceived lack of quality and risk in the programming (to which more conservative elements respond that it is too risque much of the time), an excessively high ratio of advertising to programme time (especially on children's television), and a perceived failure to serve the local interest due to media consolidation. Commercial radio in particular is often attacked for perceived homogeneity in programming, covert politicized censorship of content, and a desire to cut costs at the expense of giving the station an identifiable personality. Politics is a major force in media criticism, with an ongoing battle (especially in the United States) as to what moral standards, if any, are to be applied to the airwaves.

In much of the world, analogue broadcasting is giving way to digital, a process effectively complete some time ago for many satellite television providers and some cable systems. Standards such as DVB and ATSC promise to provide vastly enhanced picture quality and bandwidth usage, allowing the practical use of HDTV (which did not catch on anywhere until the arrival of digital technology) and multiple channels from the same broadcaster. The same transition is happening with radio transmissions but is unlikely to be complete for some time if ever; Digital Audio Broadcasting, HD Radio, and Digital Radio Mondiale are all rising formats for radio broadcasts.

Perhaps the best known commercial broadcasters are the venerable ABC, CBS, Fox and NBC television networks, as well as radio giant Clear Channel Communications, based in the United States. Major US commercial cable operators include Comcast, Adelphia, Time Warner Cable, and Cox Communications; satellite services include DirecTV, Dish Network, the UK's BSkyB, and the radio services Sirius, WorldSpace, and XM. In Asia the best known Commercial Service was with the oldest radio station in the region, Radio Ceylon.

RADIO COMEDY

Radio comedy, or comedic radio programming, is a radio broadcast that may involve sitcom elements, sketches, and many other forms of comedy found on other media. It may also include more surreal or fantastic elements, as these can be conveyed on a small budget with just a few sound effects or some simple dialogue. Because of this, it is often less restrictive and can allow for more imaginative and inventive comedy.

Background and History

Although traditional comedy was once a significant part of American broadcast radio programming, it is now mainly found in the archives of Old Time Radio enthusiasts and in Internet streaming of comedy recordings. The majority of mainstream radio comedy now consists of personality-driven shows hosted by talk-radio hosts such as Howard Stern or comedic duos such as Armstrong and Getty and Bob and Tom. Exceptions to this are WSRN's "Audience of Two", Garrison Keillor's work on Minnesota Public Radio: "A Prairie Home Companion" and "Comedy College", and NPR's Car Talk, a comedy show thinly disguised as car advice, and *Wait Wait...Don't Tell Me!*.

In Britain and Canada, however, the BBC and CBC respectively have continued making new radio comedy and drama. British radio comedy also has a home on Australia's Radio National and in Ireland there are always a few comedy shows in the week's programming on RTÉ.

Many of the BBC's most successful television comedies began life as radio shows. These include *Hancock's Half Hour*, *Goodness Gracious Me!*, *Knowing Me, Knowing You*, *The League Of Gentlemen*, *Whose Line Is It Anyway?*, *Room 101*, *Have I Got News For You*, (based on Radio 4's *The News Quiz*), *Dead Ringers* and most recently *Little Britain* and *Absolute Power*. The science fiction comedy *Red Dwarf* was developed from ideas in a radio show called *Son Of Cliché*. Another science fiction comedy *The Hitchhiker's Guide to the Galaxy* was created for radio, but also went on to great success in book, television and film formats. This has unfairly led to some people viewing radio as just a stepping stone to television, ignoring the many advantages of the medium.

Examples of American radio comedy can be heard on streaming internet radio stations. Garrison Keillor's "A Prairie Home Companion" can be heard on public radio stations in the United States and a different version of the shows can be heard on BBC7 and RTÉ under the name "Garrison Keillor's Radio Show." Old shows can be listened to online at the websites of "A Prairie Home Companion" or RTÉ. British radio comedy can be heard on BBC Radio 4, BBC Radio 2 and BBC 7. Minnesota Public Radio maintains a website where it is possible to listen to episodes of "Comedy College." A British commercial station "Oneword" broadcasted American vintage radio comedy as part of their 24 hour-a-day programming of books, comedy and drama and this was streamed on the internet until the station closed in 2008.

Interest in radio comedy and radio drama is currently enjoying a resurgence. Epguides.com (http://www.epguides.com) which provides encyclopedic information on television shows has recently begun to build a similar list of radio shows at: http://www.epguides.com/menu/radio.shtml

In America, new groups have formed to try to bring about a renewed interest in the art-form. At the fore-front of this new wave of audio—only comedic groups is Peeper Radio Theatre. Veteran NPR Producer Joe Bevilacqua is creating new radio comedy for The Comedy-O-Rama Hour, which airs on XM Satellite Radio's Sonic Theater Channel 163, five times per week. In the UK, recent standup and revue comedy performances are also now receiving airing on radio.

List of Radio Comedies

Produced Independently

- *Man of the People: The Only-Recently Discovered Secret Political Recordings of Acting Mayor Francis "Woody" Woodson*
- *The Sound of Young America*
- *The Comedy-O-Rama Hour*
- *The Wireless Theatre Company www.wirelesstheatrecompany.co.uk*

Produced by ABC (Australia)

- *The Idiot Weekly*
- *Yes, What?/The Fourth Form at St Percy's (Discontinued)*

Produced by or for the CBC

- *CBC Festival of Comedy*
- *CBC Festival of Funny*
- *Canadia 2056*
- *Chas Lawther's Stand Up Documentaries*
- *The Chumps Without a Net*
- *The Dead Dog Cafe Comedy Hour*
- *Double Exposure (comedy series)*
- *The Frantics Frantic Times, Fran of the Fundy, and The Frantics Look at History*
- *Gary and Ivan's Winnebago Tour*
- *Great Eastern*
- *Growing Up and Having Babies*
- *The Happy Gang*
- *Here Come the Seventies (radio show)*
- *How to Seem Smart*
- *The Irrelevant Show*
- *Laugh in a Half*
- *Madly Off in All Directions*
- *Mr. Interesting's Guide to the Continental United States*
- *The Muckraker*
- *The Norm*
- *Radio Free Vestibule*
- *Rick and Pete Grow Up and Have Babies*
- *The Royal Canadian Air Farce*
- *Running with Scissors with Mr. Interesting*
- *Steve, The First*
- *Steve, The Second*
- *Sunny Days and Nights*
- *This Hour Has 17 Programmes*
- *Those People Across the Street*
- *The Vinyl Cafe*
- *What a Week*

Produced by or for US Public Radio

- *A Prairie Home Companion* (Minnesota Public Radio)
- *Comedy College* (Minnesota PR)

- *Le Show* (KCRW)
- *NonProductive* (WRSU-FM)
- *Wait Wait... Don't Tell Me!* (Chicago Public Radio)
- *The Comedy-O-Rama Hour* (Joe Bevilacqua)

Produced by or for RTÉ

- *The Apocalypse of Bill Lizard*
- *The Comedy Improv Radio Show*
- *Beyond the Back of Beyond*
- *Scrap Saturday*

Produced by or for the BBC

- *15 Minute Musical*
- *15 Minutes of Misery*
- *15 Storeys High*
- *4 At The Store*
- *The 99p Challenge*
- *Absolute Power*
- *And Now in Colour*
- *The Arthur Smith Lectures*
- *Beat The Kids*
- Boothby Graffoe, *In No Particular Order* and *Big Booth Too*
- *The Christopher Marlowe Mysteries*
- *Creme de la Crime*
- *Concrete Cow*
- *The Consultants*
- *Dead Ringers*
- *Delve Special*
- *Dial M For Pizza*
- *Educating Archie*
- *Fist of Fun*
- *Flight of the Conchords*
- *The Franz Kafka Big Band*
- *Genius*
- *Giles Wemmbley Hogg Goes Off*
- *Geoffrey Boycott's Proper World History of Cricket*
- *Getting Nowhere Fast*
- *Goodness Gracious Me!*
- *The Goon Show*

- *Hancock's Half Hour*
- *The Harpoon*
- *The Hitch Hiker's Guide to the Galaxy*
- *The Hole In The Wall Gang*
- *The House of Milton Jones*
- *The Hudson and Pepperdine Show*
- *Hut 33*
- *I'm Sorry I Haven't a Clue*
- *I'm Sorry, I'll Read That Again*
- *In One Ear*
- *It's Been a Bad Week*
- *It's That Man Again*
- *Jackie Mason*
- *Jammin'*
- *Jeremy Hardy Speaks to the Nation*
- *Just a Minute*
- *King Street Junior*
- *Knowing Me, Knowing You*
- *The League of Gentlemen*
- *Lionel Nimrod's Inexplicable World*
- *Lines from My Grandfather's Forehead*
- *Linda Smith's A Brief History of Timewasting*
- *Little Britain*
- *Loose Ends*
- *The Mark Steel Lectures*
- *The Mark Steel Revolution*
- *The Mark Steel Solution*
- *The Mel and Sue Thing*
- *Men from the Ministry*
- *Mitch Benn's Crimes Against Music*
- *Much Binding in the Marsh*
- *The Museum of Everything*
- *The National Theatre of Brent*
- *The Navy Lark*
- *Nebulous*
- *The News Huddlines*
- *The News Quiz*
- *Nightcap*
- *The Now Show*
- *Old Harry's Game*

- *The Omar Khayyam Show*
- *On the Hour'*
- *The Party Line*
- *Paperback Hell*
- *People Like Us*
- *The Problem with Adam Bloom*
- *Quote... Unquote*
- *Radio Active*
- *Recorded for Training Purposes*
- *The Remains of Foley and McColl*
- *Robin and Wendy's Wet Weekends*
- *Room 101*
- *Ross Noble Goes Global*
- *Round the Horne*
- *Route One, USA*
- *Saturday Night Fry*
- *Son of Cliche*
- *Steptoe and Son*
- *The Sunday Format*
- *Take It From Here*
- *Think the Unthinkable*
- *The Very World of Milton Jones*
- *We've Been Here Before*
- *Whose Line Is It Anyway?*
- *World of Pub*
- *Yes Minister* (Adapted from television)
- *You'll Have Had Your Tea* (a spin-off from *I'm Sorry I Haven't a Clue*)

RADIO DOCUMENTARY

A radio documentary or feature is a radio documentary programme devoted to covering a particular topic in some depth, usually with a mixture of commentary and sound pictures. Some radio features, especially those including specially composed music or other pieces of audio art, resemble radio drama in many ways, though non-fictional in subject matter, while others consist principally of more straightforward, journalistic-type reporting—but at much greater length than found in an ordinary news report.

Quotes

"At its best, radio combines the power and immediacy of great documentary films with the intimacy and poetry of a *New Yorker*-style magazine piece."

—Columbia Graduate School of Journalism

"Staring red-eyed at the mirror in front of me, having spent another day and half of the night with my computer, I ask myself fundamental questions: Why radio? Why documentary? Answer: No other medium can provide me with more freedom of creation and investigation. It meets my urgent interest in reality and the desire for a 'musical' expression. The material (*der Werkstoff*) is sound. And sound always surrounds us. And: I'm not so much interested in the description of stable situations, but in processes. Our medium is not space, but time; our stories are not glued to the ground, but have motion, life... That's why!"

—Helmut Kopetzky, German author

Notable Radio Documentary and Feature Makers

- American RadioWorks
- Noah Adams
- Jay Allison
- Deb Amos
- John Biewen
- Melissa Bloch
- Alex Blumberg
- Kyla Brettle
- Scott Carrier
- Alex Chadwick
- Bill Drake
- Joe Frank
- John Gilliland
- Ira Glass (and This American Life)
- Berit Hedemann (Prix Europa Yleisradio 1997 and 1998)
- David Isay

- Kitchen Sisters
- Robert Krulwich
- Bill Lichtenstein
- Ewan MacColl
- Charles Parker
- Joe Richman
- Steve Rowland
- Keith Talbott
- Nancy Updike

TALK SHOW

A talk show (American) or chat show (Global) is a television or radio programme where one person or group of people come together to discuss various topics put forth by a talk show host. Sometimes, talk shows feature a panel of guests, usually consisting of a group of people who are learned or who have great experience in relation to whatever issue is being discussed on the show for that episode. Other times, a single guest discusses their work or area of expertize with a host or co-hosts. A call-in show takes live phonecalls from callers listening at home, in their cars, etc.

Genres

Television talk shows often feature celebrity guests who talk about their work and personal lives as well as the their latest films, TV shows, music recordings or other projects they would like to promote to the public. The hosts are often comedians who open the shows with comedy monologues.

Talk-radio host Howard Stern also hosted a talk show that was syndicated nationally, then moved to satellite radio's Sirius. The tabloid talk show genre, pioneered by Phil Donahue but popularized by Oprah Winfrey was extremely popular during the last two decades of the 20th century. Politics are hardly the only subject of American talk shows, however. Other radio talk show subjects include *Car Talk* hosted by NPR and *Coast to Coast AM* hosted by Art Bell and George Noory which discusses topics of the paranormal, conspiracy theories, fringe science and the just plain weird. Sports talk shows are also very popular ranging from high-budget shows like *The Best Damn Sports*

Show Period to Max Kellerman's original public access show *Max on Boxing*.

History

Talk shows have been broadcast on television since the earliest days of the medium. Joe Franklin, an American radio and television personality, hosted the first television talk show. The show began in 1951 on WJZ-TV (later WABC-TV) and moved to WOR-TV (later WWOR-TV) from 1962 to 1993. TV news pioneer Edward R. Murrow hosted a talk show entitled *Small World* in the late 1950s and since then, political TV talk shows have predominantly aired on Sunday mornings.

Syndicated daily talk shows began to gain more popularity during the mid-1970s and reached their height of with the rise of the tabloid talk show. Morning talk shows gradually replaced earlier forms of programming—there were a plethora of morning game shows during the 1960s and early to mid-1970s, and some stations formerly showed a morning movie in the time slot that many talk shows now occupy.

Current late night talk shows such as *The Tonight Show with Jay Leno* and *Late Show with David Letterman* have aired for years, featuring celebrity guests and comedy sketches. Syndicated daily talk shows range from tabloid talk shows, such as *The Jerry Springer Show* to celebrity interview shows like *Ellen* to industry leader *The Oprah Winfrey Show* which popularized the former genre and has been evolving towards the latter. Talk shows have more recently started to appear on Internet Radio. Also, several internet blogs are in talk show format including the Baugh Experience. The Guinness world record of 33 hours for longest talk show was broken in 28 August 2007 by Davor Dretar Drele and Kristijan Petroviæ—Kiky in Varaždin, Croatia during the Špancir festival. The show lasted for 35 hours.

List of Examples

Note: Some of the talk shows listed below are temporarily or permanently off the air or have not premiered yet.

Hungarian Language

- Nap-Kelte (Early Political Show—present)

- Reggeli (Early Show—present)
- Esti Showder Fábry Sándorral *(Late Show—present)*
- Mónika Show *(Afternoon Show—present)*
- Mokka *(Morning Show—present)*
- Szulák és Más *(Evening Talk Show—present)*
- Jam *(Morning Show—present)*
- Havas *(Evening Talk Show—present)*
- Joshi Bharat *(Afternoon Talk Show—present)*
- Esti Frizbi Hajdú Péterrel *(Evening Talk Show—present)*
- Barbara Show *(Afternoon Talk Show)*
- Szulák Andrea Show *(Late Talk Show)*
- Liptai Claudia Show *(Late Talk Show)*
- Claudia Show *(Afternoon Show)*
- Balázs Show *(temporarily not in the screen of RTL Klub)*

Portuguese Language

Portugal

- Sexta á Noite—*Friday at Night* (*January, 1 May 2008*)
- As Tardes da Júlia—*Júlia's Afternoons* (*April, 2007—present*)
- Contacto—*Contact* (*January 2006—present*)
- Dr. Preciso de Ajuda—*Dr I Need Help* (*2006 temporarily not in screen*)
- AB...Sexo—*AB...Sex* (*2006-07*)
- Clube Morangos—*Strawberries Club* (*2006*)
- Câmara Clara—*Clear Chamber* (*September 2005—present*)
- Fátima—*Fátima* (*December, 2005—present*)
- Bon Chic—*Bon Chic* (*2005*)
- Você na TV!—*You on TV* (*September, 2004—present*)
- Portugal no Coração—*Portugal in the Heart* (*February 2003—present*)
- Vidas Reais—*Real Lives* (*2003*)
- Domingo é Domingo—*Sunday is Sunday* (*2003*)
- A vida é bela—*Life is Wonderful* (*2002, 2004*)
- Olá Portugal—*Hi Portugal* (*September, 2002, 2004*)
- As Manhãs de Sofia—Sofia's Mornings (February, 2002—September 2002)
- Domingo Fantástico—*Fantastic Sunday* (*2002*)
- Noites Marcianas—*Martian Nights* (*February 2001-02*)

- Às duas por três—*Two by Three* (*2001-04*)
- Herman SIC—*Herman SIC* (*2000-06*)
- SIC 10 Horas—*SIC 10 Hours* (*1999-2005*)
- Fátima Lopes—*Fátima Lopes* (*1998*)
- Mundo VIP—*VIP World* (*1997-2001*)
- Praça da Alegria—*Joy Plaza* (*September 1995—present*)
- Big Show SIC—*Big Show SIC* (*1995-2001*)
- Perdoa-me—*Forgive Me* (*1995*)
- Ponto de Encontro—*Meeting Point* (*1994-96*)
- All You Need Is Love (*1994*)
- A Noite da Má Língua—*Gossip Night* (*1991-95—2004-05*)

Brazil

- *Programa do Jô*
- *Canal Livre*
- *Entrevista Record*

French Language

France

- On a tout essayé
- On n'a pas tout dit
- Le Grand Journal
- Tout le monde en parle
- On n'est pas couché
- On ne peut pas plaire à tout le monde
- T'empêches tout le monde de dormir
- La méthode Cauet
- Toute une histoire

English Language

- *After Dark*
- *American Morning*
- *Around the Horn*
- *The Arsenio Hall Show*
- *Attitudes*
- *The Bonnie Hunt Show*
- *Jerome T. Youngman's Bring it to Jerome*
- *The Charlie Rose Show*
- *The Charlotte Church Show*

- *Chelsea Lately*
- *The Colbert Report*
- *Crossfire*
- *Da Ali G Show*
- *The Daily Show*
- *The David Letterman Show*
- *Dennis Miller Live*
- *The Dick Cavett Show*
- *Dr. Phil*
- *The Early Show*
- *The Ellen DeGeneres Show*
- *For the People with Chuck Harder*
- *Friday Night with Jonathan Ross*
- *The Friday Night Project*
- *Gathering Texas*
- *The Gayle King Show*
- *The Gene Burns Programme*
- *Geraldo*
- *G'morning Didcot*
- *Good Morning America*
- *The Graham Norton Effect*
- *The Greg Behrendt Show*
- *The Hour*
- *The Howard Stern Show*
- *Insight with Javed Malik*
- *Jenny Jones*
- *The Jeremy Kyle Show*
- *The Jerry Springer Show*
- *Jimmy Kimmel Live!*
- *The John Kerwin Show*
- *The Joni Show*
- *Dr. Keith Ablow*
- *The Kumars at No. 42*
- *Larry King Live*
- *Last Call with Carson Daly*
- *The Late Late Show with Craig Ferguson*
- *The Late Late Show*
- *Late Night with Conan O'Brien*
- *Late Night with David Letterman*
- *Late Show with David Letterman*

- *Leeza*
- *Live with Regis and Kelly*
- *The Magic Hour*
- *The Mark Belling Late Afternoon Show*
- *The Mark Davis Show*
- *Martha*
- *The Martin Short Show*
- *The Maury Povich Show*
- *Meet the Press*
- *The Megan Mullally Show*
- *The Mike Malloy Show*
- *The Montel Williams Show*
- *MTV Live*
- *Night Stand with Dick Dietrick*
- *The Opie and Anthony Show*
- *The Oprah Winfrey Show*
- *The Paul O'Grady Show*
- *Pardon the Interruption*
- *Parkinson*
- *Person to Person*
- *The Phil Donahue Show*
- *Poolside Chats*
- *Pugs and Kelly*
- *Rachael Ray*
- *Real Time with Bill Maher*
- *Red Eye w/Greg Gutfeld*
- *Richard and Judy*
- *The Richard Bey Show*
- *Ricki Lake*
- *Kilroy*
- *The Robert Dodds Show*
- *Room 101*
- *The Roseanne Show*
- *The Rosie O'Donnell Show*
- *Rove Live*
- *The RuPaul Show*
- *The Rush Limbaugh Show*
- *Russel Harty Plus*
- *Sally*
- *Sex, Toys and Chocolate*

- *Shariah TV*
- *Sidewalks Entertainment*
- *The Sound of Young America*
- *Space Ghost: Coast to Coast*
- *Sports Kings Talk Show*
- *The Steve Wilkos Show*
- *Steven and Chris*
- *The Sunday Night Project*
- *Talk with Jordan Knight*
- *Talkshow with Spike Feresten*
- *Thicke of the Night*
- *This Spartan Life*
- *Topic A with Tina Brown*
- *The Today Show*
- *Tom Green's House Tonight*
- *The Tom Green Show*
- *The Tom Leykis Show*
- *The Tonight Show with Jay Leno*
- *The Tonight Show Starring Johnny Carson*
- *The Tony Danza Show*
- *TNC Talk with Rolfy Zhou and Nunymare Towowel*
- *Too Late with Adam Carolla*
- *Tough Crowd with Colin Quinn*
- *Trisha Goddard*
- *The Tyra Banks Show*
- *Unscrewed with Martin Sargent*
- *Vanessa's Real Lives*
- *The Vicki Gabereau Show*
- *The View*
- *The Wright Stuff*
- *Wogan*

German Language

- "3 nach 9" (NDR, since 1974)
- *Arabella* (ProSieben, 1994–2004)
- *Andreas Türck* (ProSieben, 1998–2002)
- *Nicole—Entscheidung am Nachmittag* (ProSieben, 1999-2001)
- *Hans Meiser* (RTL, 1992–2001)

- *Ilona Christen* (RTL, 1993–99)
- *Bärbel Schäfer* (RTL, 1995–2002)
- *Birte Karalus* (RTL, 1998–2000)
- *Sabrina* (RTL, 1999–2000)
- *Die Oliver Geissen Show* (RTL, since 1999)
- *Fliege—Die Talkshow* (ARD, 1994–2005)
- *Kerner* (Sat.1, 1996–1998)
- *Vera am Mittag* (Sat.1, 1996–2006)
- *Sonja* (Sat.1, 1997–2001)
- *NDR Talk Show (Jörg Pilawa)* (Sat.1, 1998–2000)
- *Ricky* (Sat. 1, 1999–2000)
- *Peter Imhof* (Sat. 1, 2000–01)
- *Franklin—Deine Chance um 11* (Sat.1, 2000–04)
- *Britt—Der Talk um eins* (Sat. 1, since 2001)

Bulgarian Language

- *Slavi's Show*

Croatian Language

- *Latinica*
- *Sanja*

Egyptian Language

- Al-Ashera Masaan
- Al-Kahira Al-Yom
- Teseen Dakika
- El-Beit Beitak

Finnish Language

- *A-talk*
- *Arto Nyberg*
- *Ben Furman*
- *Hyppönen Enbuske Experience*
- *Joonas Hytönen Show*
- *Krisse*
- *Lauantaivekkari*
- *Mirja Pyykkö*
- *Ruben & Joonas*

- *Sunnuntaivekkari*
- *Tuomas and Juuso*
- *Nevada*

Hebrew Language

- יאיר לפיד חי בעשר (Yair Lapid live at 10)
- יצפאן (Yatzpan)

Indonesian Language

- *Campur-Campur*
- *Ceriwis*
- *Dorce Show*
- *Empat Mata (Four Eyes)*
- *Kick Andy*
- *Ruming*
- *Rumpi*
- *Talk Life*

Italian Language

- *Al posto tuo* (1999-2006, show on Rai Uno)
- *AnnoZero* (2006-07, show on Rai Due and Raisat Extra)
- *Ballarò* (2001 present, show on Rai Tre and Raisat Extra)
- *Buon Pomeriggio* (2006-07, show on Canale 5)
- *Cronache marziane* (2004-05, show on Italia 1)
- *Festa Italiana* (2005 present, show on Rai Uno)
- *In famiglia* (1993 present, show on Rai Due)
- *Le inviasioni barbariche* (2005 present, show on La7)
- *L'Italia sul 2* (2002-08, show on Rai Due)
- *Liberitutti—Storie di italiani* (2005-06, show on Rete 4)
- *Loveline* (2005—present, show on MTV Italy)
- *Matrix* (2005—present, show on Canale 5)
- *Mattino Cinque* (2008—present, show on Canale 5)
- *Maurizio Costanzo Show* (1982-2008, show on Rete 4 and after on Canale 5)
- *Mezzanotte e dintorni* (1989-2003, show on Rai Uno)
- *Niente di personale* (show on La7)
- *Omnibus* (2002 present, show on La7)
- *Le inviasioni barbariche* (1997-1999, show on Rai Due)

- *Porta a Porta* (1996 present, show on Rai Uno)
- *Samarcanda* (1987-1992, show on Rai Tre)
- *Il senso della vita* (2005 present, show on Canale 5)
- *Sottovoce* (1994 present, show on Rai Uno)
- *Tappeto Volante* (1993 present, show on TeleMontecarlo and after on Canale Italia)
- *Tetris* (2006 present, show on Raisat Extra and after on La7)
- *Tutte le mattine* (2004 2006, show on Canale 5)
- *Tv Talk* (2005 present, show on Rai Tre and Rai Edu 2)
- *Unomattina* (1986 present, show on Rai Uno)
- *Uomini e donne* (1996 present, show on Canale 5)
- *Very Victoria* (2005 present, show on MTV Italy)
- *Voice* (2006, show on MTV Italy)

Japanese Language

- *Eigo de Shabera Night*

Norwegian Language

- *Først and sist*
- *Nytt på nytt*
- *Senkveld*
- *Grosvold*

Romanian Language

- *Realitatea Zilei with Andreea Crepulescu*
- *Chestiunea zilei* with Florin Cãlinescu
- *Marius Tucã Show* with Marius Tucã
- *De 3X femeie*
- *Dan Diaconescu in Direct*
- *Miezul Problemei*
- *Nasul*
- *Magic Nights* with Diana Singer and Eugen Huculici

Russian Language

- *Okna*
- *Bol'shaya stirka*
- *Pyat' vecherov*
- *Pust' govoryat*

Spanish Language

- *La Noche del 10*
- *Esta Noche Tunight*
- *El Show de Cristina*
- *Laura En America*
- *El Diario de Patricia*
- *La Señora León*
- *El Diario de Eva*
- *Entre Moria y Vos*
- *Geraldo*
- *Cállate con Carlos Sicilia*
- *El Show de Renny*
- *Stilos*
- *Maritere*
- *¿Quién Tiene La Razón?*
- *Caso Cerrado*
- *Cotorreando*
- *Escandalo TV*
- *El Gordo y la Flaca*
- *Despierta America*
- *Viva la Mañana*
- *Ya es 1/2 día en China*
- *Yo, José Gabriel*
- *Ya no hay respeto*
- *El diario de Eva*

Swedish Language

- *Carin 21:30*
- *Ett herrans liv*
- *Gäst hos Hagge*
- *Hylands Hörna*
- *Knesset*
- *Robins*
- *Sen kväll med Luuk*
- *Studio Virtanen*
- *Studio Belinda*
- *Wimans*

Thai Language

- *Muang Thai Rai Sapda*

Turkish Language

- *Beyaz Show*
- *Disko Kralý (King of Disco)*
- *Kime Diyorum Ben*
- *Anýnda Görüntü Show*
- *Mutfak*
- *Hiç Bunlari Kendine Dert Etmeye Değer mi?*
- *Hacý Yatmaz*
- *Sahan: Kime diyorum ben?*
- *Maksat Muhabbet*
- *Haydi Gel Bizimle Ol?*

Persian Talk Show

- *Shab-e-Shishei (Crystal Night)*

Chinese Language

Mandarin

- Kangxi Lai Le (ROC, Taiwan)

Cantonese

- Where Are They Now (Hong Kong)

Kazakhstan Talk Shows

- *Chto delat' (How to deal, KTK TV Channel)*
- *Na chistotu*
- *Dela zhiteyskie*

SOUND RECORDING

Beginnings: 1890-1900

The story of the sound recording industry is mostly a story of musical entertainment on phonograph discs for the whole period from the invention of the phonograph in 1877 to about the 1950s, when new technologies emerged. The major players in the industry were Victor, Columbia and HMV (which originally stood for His Master's Voice) until the end of World War II, and are still important today. These three companies all got their start in the 1890s, when the phonograph was still young. Thomas Edison's 1877 invention of the phonograph was followed by many imitators, most notably the "graphophone," which became the basis of the Columbia company. Both inventions used a cylinder record which captured sound in a groove. Just as the graphophone of 1887 borrowed many ideas from Edison, so too did Edison's "improved phonograph" of 1888 borrow back from the graphophone. Soon both machines were for sale or lease to the public. The primary market was intended to be businessman, lawyers, court reporters, and others who currently used stenography to capture important thoughts or compose letters. Although the sound recorder as a business machine has its own history, it is the entertainment uses of sound recording that made the biggest impact.

The First Peak, 1900-25

Business phonographs (and graphophones) were selling very poorly in the early years and the phonograph industry was near bankruptcy. But in 1899, someone had the bright idea to built a coin-operated phonograph, record some songs on cylinders, and put the machines into the arcades, which were quite popular at the time. The public loved it. The various companies making phonographs quickly went into the cylinder business, and some of them redesigned their players so that they were cheaper and simpler, hoping that people would buy them for their homes. The idea of a truly inexpensive machine that could play back (but not record) music was the inspiration for an even more successful technology—the disc record or "gramophone." Edison himself had considered a disc phonograph, but it was Emile Berliner who really got the ball rolling. Part of the reason for a disc instead of a cylinder was that Berliner thought it would be easy to stamp out large numbers of copies of disc recordings. In 1893 he began selling his cheap gramophone player and seven-inch disc records made of hard rubber. Emile Berliner in 1896 hooked up with Eldridge Johnson, a machinist from Camden, New Jersey who designed an improved gramophone player for the Berliner company. In a short time, the two joined forces to create what would become the Victor Talking Machine Company. Victor in the early 1900s became one of the largest manufacturers of "talking machines" and records. In 1889, Berliner had arranged for the establishment of a branch of his company in London. Although officially known as the Gramophone Company, it was better known by its brand of records, called His Master's Voice, or HMV, and by Nipper the dog, which later became the mascot for Victor. Meanwhile, the cylinder phonograph business had been in such a shambles that the original owners of the various companies lost control of their businesses to shrewd businessmen. The Columbia company had started life leasing business phonographs in Washington, D.C., but was soon making home cylinder graphophones from a factory in Bridgeport, Connecticut. The company's leader, Edward Easton, was not sure whether cylinders or discs would ultimately succeed, so soon Columbia was manufacturing both. Soon, three companies (Edison, Victor, and Columbia) were the Big Three in the record and record player businesses in the United States, while HMV and the various subsidiaries set up by Edison and Columbia dominated the market in Europe. They were selling about 3 million records a year by 1900 in the US alone. The success of the record industry during the next two decades was phenomenal. Soon, the record industry was one of the most important in the world.

Depression and Consolidation 1925-40

Unfortunately, the boom in talking machines was drawing to a close. Even before the general downturn in consumer spending in the 1930s, the recording industry was in decline. At first, the culprit seemed like excessive competition. Over 150 companies were making records or record players by about 1920, and they were all trying to undercut each other's prices. But the radio also acted as competition. Radio broadcasting began in some parts of the United States around 1922. During the 1920s, regular broadcasts began in many areas of the US and Europe. Radio networks appeared, which linked together stations and promised to bring in massive advertising revenue. The companies running these networks spent lavish amounts of money to create special programming that was more spectacular than what was available on records. Despite the poor sound quality of the early radios, people were attracted to the programmes and bought fewer records. The downturn was disastrous. The size of the industry in the US alone declined by about one half in the early 1920s, then stabilized for the rest of the decade. Manufacturers introduced an improved form of record in the late 1920s called the "electrical recording," hoping to lure customers back. This used microphones and electronic amplifiers in the studio to make the records, but could be played back on the old horn talking machines. Some manufacturers also introduced combination radio-phonographs. While these new technologies helped a little, when the Great Depression came the record companies were too weak to survive on their own. The phonograph division of the Thomas A. Edison company was the first to go, folding in 1929. Victor was bought by the Radio Corporation of America, and Columbia was purchased, appropriately enough, by the Columbia Broadcasting System. Most of the other names in the industry simply disappeared. In the 1930s, records continued to be sold in relatively small numbers. Classical music enthusiasts continued to buy records, but they were not a huge market. The radio broadcasters bought a fair number of records. There were new opportunities, too. When the talking motion pictures arrived, for a few years they actually used discs before switching to a system that put the "soundtrack" right on the edge of the film. In fact, the motion picture industry was where the real action was in the sound recording industry in the 1930s. Sales of recording equipment to motion picture producers sponsored research in improved technologies. The first stereophonic recordings released to the public were part of a motion picture, Walt Disney's Fantasia. It was only in the late 1930s that the number of record discs sold began to climb back toward the high of the 1920s. This was partly due to the gradually improving economy, particularly in the United States. It was also due to the growing number of jukeboxes in use. Jukeboxes consumed large numbers of records because they were usually changed every week or so. But the industry was still in trouble.

The War Years and Afterward, 1941-55

The coming of World War II was a worldwide tragedy but a boon for the record industry. Suddenly the governments and armed services of many nations had an interest in purchasing and using sound recording equipment. The entertainment industries of Hollywood and elsewhere were called into service to record music for the entertainment of troops. In the United States, the military sponsored the recording of both ordinary 10-inch discs (the standard consumer disc since about 1900) and "V-discs" for this purpose. V-discs were large, 16-inch diameter discs made of flexible vinyl plastic. They were similar to the discs then being used by radio broadcasters to record programmes. They held 15 minutes or so of recorded sound and could be shipped overseas without fear of breaking. The US army also experimented with other forms of recording, such as magnetic recording on wire, for the use of journalists. Although these devices did not have any real impact on the record industry at the time, they were a sign of things to come. While the troops were being fully entertained, consumers experienced a drought. Angered by the way radio used records without any payment to musicians, band leader Fred Waring filed suit in Pennsylvania to force the broadcasting industry to pay royalties. At the time, radio broadcasters paid a small royalty to the copyright owners every time a song was broadcast, but not to the musicians who had created the recording. Waring set off a battle that would take years to resolve. Even more dramatic was "Petrillo's War." James Petrillo (president of the American Federation of Musicians) in 1942 began demanding compensation to musicians for records being played on the radio or on jukeboxes. When the record companies refused, Petrillo called for a general strike—no records (except for those intended for the war effort) were made between the summer of 1942 and November 1944. With the end of the war, many in the record industry hoped for a renewed interest in music listening at home. Great technological changes were underway. During the 1930s and early 1940s, the German companies AEG and I.G. Farben had steadily improved the technology of magnetic recorders. These were "liberated" from Germany by the Allies in 1945 and became the basis of remarkable studio tape-recorders. The use of these recorders would soon revolutionize the making of records and movie soundtracks. What consumers saw in the stores was also changing. A few manufacturers in the late 1930s had offered what they called "high fidelity" electronic equipment. A relatively new English company, Decca, began selling high fidelity discs after World War II. Then, in 1948 and 1949, the Victor and Columbia companies introduced the new 45-rpm disc for singles and the Long Playing record for albums. These new high fidelity discs marked a new era in the home record player.

Show Tunes and Rock and Roll!

High fidelity was all the rage in the 1950s. The LP was a surprise hit—no one had expected that it would catch on as well as it did. It was much more expensive than the 45 rpm disc (or the older 10-inch disc, which survived until about 1955), and it was not intended for singles, which had been the main product of the music industry since its beginnings. LP sales were helped by the hi-fi movement, which emphasized listening to classical music (usually on LP), but also by the success of Broadway show tune and movie soundtrack albums. There was also some manipulation by the record companies, who discovered that when a song became a "hit" on the radio, if they simply refused to issue that song on a 45 rpm disc, the public would be forced to buy a whole album if they wanted to get that song. And while 45 rpm singles typically cost a dollar or less, albums were four dollars or more. Interestingly, technologies that were invented in order to attain "high fidelity" sound quality became the focus of music where "truth" to the original performance was irrelevant. Before the introduction of the tape recorder in the studio, musicians had to perform "live" in the studio to make a recording. High fidelity equipment was aimed at reproducing the exact sound of this studio performance in the home. With the introduction of the tape-recorder, suddenly it was practical to edit sound after the fact. If a soloist missed a note, a recording engineer could literally cut out that part of the tape and replace it with a better note. It was also possible with tape recorders to make recordings that could not possibly be captured "live." The musical team of Les Paul and Mary Ford often made recordings where they made recordings on top of existing recordings, resulting for example in a recording where Mary Ford apparently accompanied herself. When multitrack tape recorders were introduced, it was possible to do much more along these lines. Now it became more common for the various instruments, vocals, and solos to be recorded separately at different times, then "mixed" together later. Again, the trend was moving away from an artist or a group performing a whole piece that was recorded exactly as it actually sounded. Popular music (rather than classical) drove this forward. While classical musicians were constrained by tradition, popular music was free to experiment. In the studio, special effects and gimmicks were used freely. This was also true in the new rock and roll music, where studio effects like echo and reverb became the norm. When rock entered its "psychedelic" phase in the late 1960s, musicians pulled out all the stops and began using every technological trick available to them to create exotic new sounds. Two channel "stereophonic" recordings were developed as early as the 1930s as a way to create the illusion of reality—they were a "high fidelity" innovation. But by the 1960s the stereo effect was also being manipulated simply for the sake of producing a pleasing result, regardless of whether it was "true" to the original sound. On heavily "produced" records like the Beatles Sgt. Pepper album, the music was only remotely related to anything that could be performed live by the Beatles themselves.

Portable Music

A major trend of the postwar era was toward music portability. There were portable phonographs available from the very beginning, and small portable radios were common from the 1940s on. Of course, it depends on how you define "portable." The "portable" record players of the post-1945 era were usually just smallish models equipped with a handle. You still had to have a wall outlet to plug them into. True portability began with the commercialization of the transistor. This tiny electronic device replaced the vacuum tube, which sucked down electricity at such a prodigious rate that it demanded large batteries. Small, efficient transistor radios appeared around 1955 and became top sellers, especially after prices came down to the point where young people could own them. Transistor phonographs were available, but they were not as popular as transistor tape recorders. Although their sound quality was pretty lousy, transistor tape recorders became a big hit with teenagers in the US and Europe. People typically used them to re-record music from the radio or from records (their own or their friends'). When the Phillips Company in Europe introduced the Compact Cassette in 1962, it was initially rather expensive (about $75 for a battery-operated "Carry-Corder"). However, many other manufactures adopted the new tape format, and Asian firms soon introduced cut-rate models. By the end of the 1960s, battery operated portables were by far the best selling form of the tape recorder. The record industry paid little attention to the potential market for tape. Many record companies had introduced recorded reel-to-reel tapes beginning in the early 1950s. Some, like RCA-Victor, promoted both inexpensive home tape recorders and the tapes to play on them. But recorded reel-to-reel tapes were poor sellers compared to the LP, and cost at least a dollar more. The recorded reel-to-reel was an expensive failure for the record industry (although it did find a niche market among high fidelity aficionados). That is why the success of the 8-track tape was a bit of a surprise. The 8-track system was intended to be heard in the automobile—not surprisingly it was invented in the United States, where the car culture is strong. Home players could also be had, but manufacturers suspected that the tapes would be most appealing to commuters—and they were right. Introduced in 1965 by Ford, the 8-track sold in large numbers in the late 1960s and early 1970s until it took nearly a third of the market for recorded music. Ultimately the 8-track would fail, but it paved the way for music on cassettes. As cassette technology improved, it graduated from being a child's toy to being part of the home stereo system. Innovations such as Dolby B noise reduction and "metal" tape were created just for the cassette, and soon it took on the high-tech appeal that the LP had. At the same time, it retained the portability of music. The importance of this combination became clear in 1978 with the introduction of the Walkman tape player, which also combined high fidelity and portability. Along with the "boom box" type of radio/tape player combination, the Walkman (and its imitators) helped the cassette displace the LP as the dominant form of home music technology by about 1990. Record companies began cutting back on their LP releases to concentrate on the cassette, while only the most popular releases were available on LP. The combined effects of the introduction of high fidelity, the booming world economy, and the popularity of rock music stimulated huge growth for the record and electronics industry. The sale of records in the US alone grew from about $600 million in 1960 to $1.2 billion by 1970. While RCA-Victor, Columbia, and EMI thrived, so too did a number of new labels, such as Capitol, Atlantic, Motown, and Elektra. There was also a tendency, beginning in the 1960s, for conglomerates to form that included both motion picture and recording arms, since the two often complemented each other. Sales of music through the mail took off, with Columbia House emerging and the dominant firm in the US by the 1980s, Music Television (MTV) had emerged, linking TV and records through the exhibition of music videos. RCA by the 1980s was floundering, and after it was purchased by General Electric the RCA record division was sold to the German company Bertelsmann.

The Digital Era

The LP lives on, sort of, as the medium for disc jockeys, and a few rock groups insisted on releasing their music on LP records well into the 1990s. But both the LP and the cassette were pushed aside by the Compact Disc. The Phillips company, which had earlier introduced the cassette, had developed a laser disc for video recording in the late 1970s. Phillips teamed up with Sony, which had developed a digital tape recorder for making "master" recordings at about the same time. The new discs were created by re-recording ordinary studio tapes onto the digital tape, then using the digital tape to burn laser discs. A copy of the master laser disc was then used to press plastic duplicates, which were coated with shiny aluminum, encased in protective layers, and packaged for sale. Unlike the LP or the original Phillips video laser discs, which were quite large, the audio-only laser discs were "compact," and hence the name Compact Disc.

The CD was introduced to the public in 1982. Partly because of the high initial cost (a player cost over $2000, and the discs themselves cost $12-16), sales were limited. By about 1985, however, it was possible to buy a player for $350 or less, and prices were around $150 a few years later. Many consumers resented being pressured to abandon the collections of LP records they had accumulated over the years. However, the CD eventually won over the hearts of most consumers.

Sony also became a record company in the 1980s through the purchase of CBS Records (formerly Columbia). Sony followed this up in 1989 with the purchase of Columbia Pictures Entertainment.

In the studio, digital technology was making an important impact. Where the role of digital recorders was initially quite limited, soon it became easy and relatively inexpensive to use digital devices to compose, perform, record, edit, and mix songs. Previously, musical instruments had been separate from recording machines, and both had been separate from computers, but new technologies combined all three. Where tape-recorders had made it possible for individual musicians to play multiple instruments or record multiple vocal parts, or even become "one man bands," digital technology accelerated the tendency to do so. Many "bands" were really just one or two people manipulating drum machines and synthesizers, or re-recording bits and pieces of existing music.

If digital recording was a success in the studio, it was initially a failure as a consumer technology. The first consumer digital recorders were introduced in the late 1970s. They were essentially modified Betamax VCRs, and the cost was quite high. Digital recording re-appeared in 1990 with the introduction of Digital Audio Tape, and later with the Digital Compact Cassette, and again with the Sony Minidisc. Opposed by a recording industry fearful of music piracy, these formats failed to appeal to consumers.

Through the end of the 1990s, it appeared that the next home recording medium would undoubtedly be a recordable form of CD. It took many years for these to be introduced, and many more years for them to come down in price. Only in the early years of the 21st century did the price of a CD burner and the blank discs compete with a cassette deck.

By that time, however, the whole idea of storing sound on physical "records" was being called into question. Home computer users began sharing digitized music in a number of different formats in the late 1990s. The MP3 standard began to catch on, and Napster software appeared to make it possible for users to access each other's songs via the World Wide Web.

The recording industry freaked and shut down Napster, but the appeal of Internet-distributed music remained. It is not clear at this time whether the physical record—tape, disc, or what have you—will survive at all.

Overview History of the Technologies for Recording Music and Sound

The first recording devices were scientific instruments used to capture and study sound waves. These devices were capable of recording voices and other sounds long before the phonograph. The most famous of these was Leon Scott's 1857 Phonoautograph. This device used a horn to direct sound toward a flexible diaphragm placed at the small end. Attached to the diaphragm was a stylus and lever assembly that allowed the point to scratch out a line on a rotating cylinder beneath it. The cylinder (glass strips were later used) was coated with "lampblack," probably applied by holding it over a flame and allowing carbon to accumulate.

A 2001 search for original Phonautograph traces (many are published in facsimile form in books) turned up few from the period before the invention of the phonograph. The device probably lacked the sensitivity to record traces with enough detail to allow modern technology to reproduce intelligible sounds from them. The recordings are also very short—often less than one second. Alexander Graham Bell experimented with a Phonautograph in 1874, shortly before Edison's invention. Attempting to discover how the ear detected sound, he used a human ear (including the internal parts) from a cadaver, attaching a stylus to the eardrum and using it to make a recording.

Bell's ear Phonautograph was a very unusual variation on the basic technology. The recording mechanism was the human ear. By removing a chunk of skull including the inner ear from a human cadaver, and attaching a stylus to the moving parts of the ear, he was able to use this bio-mechanical device to make a recording of the sounds that entered a recording horn. It recorded on a moving glass strip, coated with a film of carbon, so there are probably no original recordings from it. When he learned of the invention of the phonograph, Bell wondered why he did not think of it himself.

Several researchers have investigated the possibility of using modern technology to reproduce these pre-Edison recordings, especially following the claim (probably false) that a recording of Lincoln's voice might exist. However, no one has yet been successful. A small collection of original Phonautograph recordings dating from the post-phonograph period is held by the Edison National Historic Site, but in part due to their poor quality, a signal processing engineer commissioned by the IEEE History Center was unable to extract any sounds from them.

Phonographs, Graphophones, Gramophones, and so on...

Thomas Edison had been working on telephone equipment at the time he conceived the phonograph. Alexander Graham Bell announced his telephone in 1876, and many inventors set out to duplicate and improve it. Edison, drawing on his vast experience in telegraph equipment, in July 1877 conceived of the idea of using a sensitive electromagnetic device to inscribe telephone messages on a strip of wax-coated paper. Probably unknown to Edison was a similar concept described in April 1877 by Frenchman Charles Cros. The latter would later claim precedence with some justification.

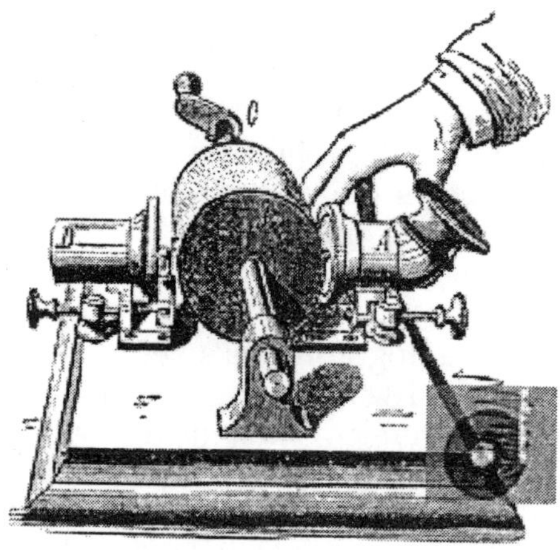

Fig. 4.1: Graphophone

A sketch of one of Edison's earliest phonographs. A sheet of thick tinfoil, wrapped around cylinder "C" is indented by a stylus attached to diaphragm "A." This hand-cranked machine was of the type used to demonstrate the principle. Production models had provisions for keeping the speed constant and other improvements.

After some experimentation, he turned instead to a device that could record straight from the air instead of relying on a telephone connection. This line of inquiry resulted in the construction of the first functional phonograph in early December, 1877. He demonstrated it almost immediately in the New York office of Scientific American magazine, and in subsequent months the publicity the invention generated resulted in a new nickname for Edison: "The Wizard of Menlo Park" (referring to his Menlo Park, New Jersey laboratories).

Fig. 4.2: Graphophone

Edison did little to commercialize the phonograph himself, and a limited number of licensees made unsuccessful attempts to sell the new device, including a German firm that introduced a talking doll. Within a decade, however, Edison had a new competitor in the form of the Graphophone. Essentially an improved phonograph, the new recorder stimulated Edison to return to his invention, and the result in 1886 was the improved phonograph. Phonograph and graphophone licensees attempted to lease or sell the devices to stenographers to replace handwriting. They made little money until someone had the bright idea to make a coin-operated phonograph for public amusement. By supplying ready made cylinders, they transformed the device into an entertainment technology. Following much legal wrangling over patents in the 1890s, Columbia Phonograph emerged as a major competitor to the Edison company, and survives today as part of CBS Records.

Electrical Recordings

The phonograph, graphophone and other players purely mechanical devices through the 1920s. However, in 1924, Columbia began experiments with a new technology developed by the Western Electric Company (the division of AT&T that made telephones and related equipment). Western Electric's recorder used electronic amplifiers to drive an electromagnetic cutting head, rather than relying on the acoustic horn. The result was a louder, clearer record. In the beginning, the record players still relied on acoustic playback with a horn, but as the home radio became popular, it became more common for people to purchase record players that had electric motors and electronic amplifiers. Some of them had a built-in loudspeaker, while others plugged into specially equipped radio sets and played through them. While some said the new "Orthophonic" records sounded harsh, they soon dominated the market.

Fig. 4.3: Library of Congress Photo

"Transcription" recorders like the one here were a later variation of the basic electrical recording technology. In this type of recorder, electrical signals are delivered to the electromagnetic cutting head, which is carried in a lathe-like mechanism (the operator has his right hand on the lathe).

Fig. 4.4: Edison National Historic Site

Edison, who had experimented with a form of electrical recording from the beginning, created his own version of the technology as well. Shown here is a close up of the machine from the side. Visible in the center is the large, heavy platter, the cutting head with its horseshoe-shaped electromagnet armature (left) and a microscope for observing the groove.

Hollywood's Influence

For the home consumer, the phonograph (or, as it was often called outside the US, the gramophone), was the only widely owned sound recording or reproducing technology through the end of World War II. But in recording studios, particularly in the radio and movie industries, times were changing.

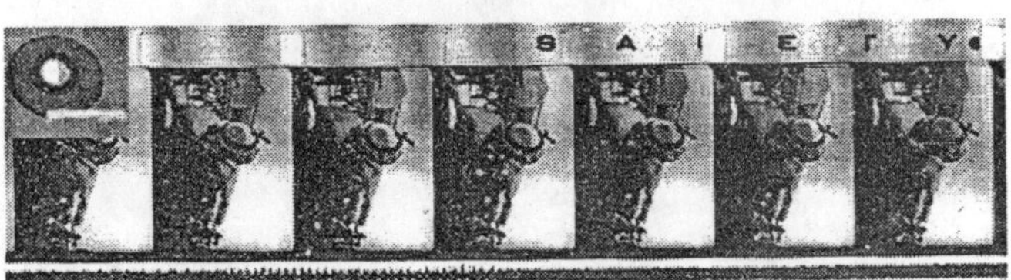

Fig. 4.5: Variable area Soundtrack

There were numerous attempts to record sound as a visible record rather than a groove, dating from the late 19th century. None was commercially successful until the early 1920s, when several firms introduced sound recording systems that recorded sound onto photographic film. They were all intended to be used with motion pictures, which had emerged as a major money maker in the 1910s. Thomas Edison, Western Electric system, and others had developed phonograph-based systems for adding sound to motion pictures, but none worked well due in part to the difficulty of synchronizing the sound to the picture. With the optical systems, the sound was recorded directly onto the same film that held the images, so it was always in synch. Between about 1906 and 1927, numerous "sound-on-film" optical systems emerged, but they still had technical problems. In fact, many of the early talkies, including the famous film The Jazz Singer of 1927, used the sound-on-disc technology introduced by Western Electric system. While perhaps the best of the disc systems, the Western Electric system began to be replaced by improved sound-on-film technologies as early as 1929. Sound-on-film became the standard way to record and reproduce sound in movies through the 1980s, and is still used some today.

Magnetic Recording

The era of the phonograph also saw the introduction of an alternative recording technology that was little seen by the public but increasingly used in studios. Magnetic recording, which is today used for video and audio tape, was first introduced around 1899-1900 by the Danish inventor Valdemar Poulsen.

Fig. 4.6: Graphophone

Poulsen envisioned that it would be useful for office dictation and telephone recording, but his "telegraphone," manufactured in the US and Europe by various firms, never took off. It was virtually forgotten in the US, but inventors in Germany and England persisted.

The earliest version of the telegraphone looked a bit like a cylinder phonograph. For simplicity's sake, the inventor wrapped the wire (onto which the recording was made) around a cylinder. The recording head tracked the wire along the surface.

Fig. 4.7: Gramophophone

The advent of electronic amplifiers for the telegraphone in the 1920s and the introduction of an oxide-coated tape in place of the solid steel wires and bands used before resulted in steady improvements in sound quality. The BBC, the CBC, and the RRG (the German broadcasting agency), among others, used steel-band magnetic recorders extensively all through the 1930s.

By the end of the decade, the German companies AEG and I.G. Farben had improved the tape-recorder and its coated-plastic recording medium to the point where it could approach the best disc recorders in sound quality. Its ability to make very long recordings and recordings under conditions of vibration and shock helped make the "magnetophon" popular for field and telephone surveillance recordings as well. For radio broadcasting, the best studio magnetophons rivaled or exceeded high quality American and British disc recorders by the time Berlin fell in the spring of 1945. This AEG magnetophon was one of several versions of the technology developed in Germany between the early 1930s and 1945. Like modern audio and video recorders, it employed a plastic tape coated with a layer of extremely fine iron powder (modern recorders use different mixtures of iron and other materials).

The Era of Tape-Recording

Despite its quiet start, it was tape recording that would eventually displace both the phonograph and optical recording methods. Eventually, Captured German recorders were widely copied, improved upon, and re-introduced by Ampex, EMI, and other firms in the late 1940s. Engineers used to editing optical film found it easy to learn to edit tape, and tape represented real improvements over optical recording in terms of convenience and low cost. In radio, record, and movie studios, tape was almost universally adopted by the early 1950s. The first consumer magnetic recorders also appeared in this period. Inexpensive wire recorders, developed more-or-less independently of the Europeans, were introduced around 1946 and proved to be a short lived hit. When the first cheap tape recorders appeared around 1948, they quickly stole the market. Millions of them were sold during the 1950s as part of a boom in "hi-fi," although many owners reported that they made little use of them. Record companies were willing to sell recorded tapes, but they could not compete in price with records, especially the LP record introduced in 1948 by CBS.

Studio Tricks and Stereo

The advent of tape recorders in recording studios led to innovations in recording that radically altered the making of music. Most radio and record studios in the US adopted Ampex recorders (although there were competitors from RCA, Presto and others) for making master recordings.

The less-expensive Magnecorders were popular in radio stations and studios where these workhorse machines were used for heavy production and editing work. The basic techniques of editing-cutting and splicing to remove, re-arrange, or compile pieces of recordings, mixing two or more sound sources into one recording, and fading sound in or out-were all innovations that were made easier with tape. Where in the past performers had to execute songs perfectly (or with minimal errors), or else face remaking the whole recording, now it was sometimes possible to splice together two or more flawed recordings to make a perfect one. Engineers and artists found that it was also easier to manipulate sounds on tape, leading to the use of all sorts of special effects, such as using a recorder to allow a single artist appear to accompany her/himself.

Even in the late 1940s, there were experiments with multitrack recording on tape. Multiple simultaneous soundtracks had been possible, though expensive, since the 1930s on motion picture film. As engineers reduced the size of tape recorder heads, it became possible to mount two or three heads on a single recorder, equip each with a recording/ reproducing amplifier, and record multiple simultaneous tracks on a single tape. This feature was used in two ways. In the studio, groups of musicians or singers could be separated into two or three groups, such as recording the rhythm section and the rest of the band separately. If there was a flub on one or the other tracks, it could be re-recorded without re-assembling the whole band. After years of perfecting this technique, it became the basis of increasingly complex recordings in the 1960s. More and more tracks were added to recorders to allow 24 or more tracks to be recorded on a single, very wide tape.

Stereo in the Home

The second outcome of the use of multitrack recordings was the most evident to the consumer; the advent of stereo sound. Engineers in the 1930s had discovered that a two-channel (or more) recording, utilizing two microphones, two amplifiers,

Fig. 4.8: Graphophone

and two loudspeakers, gave aurally pleasing results. The "stereo effect" as it was called was often described as "realistic," because human hearing has the capacity to identify the location of a sound source based on the slight time delay in the reception of sound in each ear. In the 1950s, engineers found that the stereo effect is false—the original location of the instruments in the studio is not perfectly simulated when a stereo recording is reproduced. However, most listeners prefer the three-dimensionality of the stereo effect, and it proved to be very popular. However, it required that consumers, like studio engineers, purchase equipment that could play stereo records, along with two-channel amplifiers and a second loudspeaker.

The first stereo recordings available to the public were in the form of reel-to-reel tape. Recorder manufacturers offered add-on stereo tape heads and off board amplifiers that could be added to existing recorders. Stereo recorders with a second head mounted next to the main head soon appeared. Almost simultaneously, tape-recorders with two miniaturized, stacked heads mounted in the same housing appeared; tapes for these recorders were incompatible with the earlier "staggered" head recorders. Then in 1957-58 RCA introduced a recorder with a super-compact tape head that stacked four heads in the place of just two, allowing a stereo tape to be flipped over and played on both sides like a mono tape. These large "four track" tape cartridges could not be played on either of the other two stereo systems. This lack of compatibility, combined with the high price of stereo tapes, discouraged sales. Meanwhile, another division of RCA introduced the stereo LP record, also in 1957-58, along with moderately priced stereo phonographs (stereo 45 rpm discs soon followed). Stereo LPs could not be played on monophonic players, so for many years mono and stereo versions of the same recordings were available. During the 1960s, most record companies discontinued mono LPs.

The Rise of the 8-Track

The 8-track was a distinctively American achievement in audio, reflecting the well-known fascination with automobiles in the US Automotive record players, some of questionable utility, were available as original equipment or aftermarket add-ons from about 1958 to the mid-1960s. They never sold in great numbers, and were eclipsed by the advent of automotive tape systems. Small cartridge tape systems appeared in the middle 1950s as a variation of the "cart" system that came to be widely used for spot announcements in radio stations. This was based on an endless loop tape cartridge that had a long playback time (over two hours was possible). In the early 1960s, an entrepreneur in California created a minor sensation with his "Stereo-Pak" auto tape system, and this was modified and reintroduced in a few years as the phonograph+history Stereo-8. Made by the same firm that made phonograph+history airplanes, it was first installed in Ford cars in 1965. Soon all the American auto makers offered this technology as optional equipment, and home and portable versions of the players appeared.

The 8-track took a large proportion of the music market in the late 1960s and peaked in the mid-1970s. Although it was a compromise in terms of sound quality, it required only one hand and minimal accuracy to insert into or remove from the players, which themselves were designed for extreme simplicity of operation. Once in the machine, the tape played automatically and required no rewinding. In terms of responsible engineering, the 8-track's design was a wise attempt at avoiding the introduction of an accessory that distracted the driver. At the end of its life in the early 1980s, it became the butt of jokes; a symbol of obsolescence and 1970s tackiness.

Cassette Culture

The cassette actually predated the 8-track by about a year, although it was cheap children's technology through the late 1960s. This small, two-reel cartridge was introduced by Phillips in Europe and Norelco in the US. It was based on, but intended for a different market than a similar small cartridge system that Phillips introduced for office dictation purposes. The "Carry-Corder" battery operated recorder/player made low quality recordings in mono only, but once prices for the recorders came down it proved to be a huge hit with teens. To overcome its sonic deficiencies, engineer Ray Dolby adapted his hiss reduction technology, versions of which appeared in pro and reel-to-reel recorders, for cassettes in 1968-69. The introduction of better quality home cassette decks by Ampex and others in the late 1960s and early 1970s elevated the reputation of the format and helped make it acceptable to the hi-fi crowd.

Meanwhile it had become the technology of choice for those interested in making copies of records for use in battery operated portables or in-car tape players. In terms of pre-recorded cassettes, sales overtook 8-tracks in the mid-1970s, then overtook LPs in the early 1980s. For a time in the 1980s, the cassette was the most popular home music format for both home recording and pre-recorded listening applications. Improved versions of Dolby appeared tailored for tape, and the venerable gamma-ferric oxide tape formulation, used since the 1940s for reel-to-reel tape, was superseded with mixtures that contained iron oxide mixed with or replaced by chromium dioxide or metal particles. The 90-minute tape became the best-selling blank tape, reflecting the fact that two full albums could usually be recorded on a single 90-minute cassette. The format spawned an ever-wider variety of portable and home recorders and players. In addition to the small battery operated portables available since the beginning, larger, more powerful "boomboxes" (also known by a number of other more offensive names, many reflecting the association of boomboxes with urban African-Americans, such as ghetto blasters, boomboxes, or even the Third World Briefcase). In reality, the boombox was a mass market, international phenomenon not associated with any particular race or nationality. These versatile devices were for most Americans at least the primary form of home audio technology, and some were even equipped with phonograph turntables. If the trend in boomboxes was toward bulkier and bulkier devices, the cassette spawned a second movement toward "personal audio." Following on the heels of its successful line of home VCRs, Sony Corporation in 1977-78 introduced its Walkman line of battery operated radios and tape players. Copycats jumped into the market the next year, and soon there was a bewildering variety of personal audio products. The CD-walkman was available by mid-decade, and the trend persists today with small MP3 players.

Digital Recordings and the CD

Digital audio began in the telephone industry, where it was used to digitize telephone conversations and, in effect, compress them so that more conversations could be handled on existing lines. Since the bandwidth of a telephone line is very narrow, the sound quality issues were focused on basic intelligibility of speech rather than realism and detail. However, the basic techniques could be applied to high quality recording. The earliest experiments with digital recording of high quality audio were probably those undertaken in Japan in the 1960s. Following the introduction of Betamax VCRs, which used a technology for video similar to what was needed to make digital audio recordings, Sony briefly offered an audio-only Betamax recorder, capable of recording audio digitally. This pioneering effort was largely forgotten by the time digital audio tape was reintroduced in the 1980s.

In the meantime, Phillips and Sony (among others) had been working on ways to record TV signals with a laser onto a reflective disc. As with the Betamax, some of the features of video recording are applicable to digital audio recording, so it was not a great leap from the early, analogue laser videodiscs introduced in 1978 and later to the compact audio disc, introduced in 1982-83. The CD was not an immediate hit, and it took nearly a decade for it to displace the audio cassette, but in the 1990s it became the most popular home format. Recordable CDs were not generally available until the mid-1990s, and few were sold before about 2000, when their sales took off. There were numerous variations of the CD and digital tape during the 1990s, few of which survived the decade. Today, the CD is being challenged by the DVD (which is also used for video), but it is unclear whether either of these formats will survive the challenge of media-free audio technologies such as MP3.

The Cultural Impact of Recorded Music

Sound recording has been a part of our culture since the late 19th century, gradually becoming more important. At the time of its invention, listening to the recording machine was a startling experience. Edison once recalled how taken aback he was when the prototype tinfoil phonograph actually worked. The ability of a machine to capture the human voice was an astonishing thing to people of the time. Shortly after first using the crude tinfoil recorder at his rural laboratory at Menlo Park, New Jersey, Edison took advantage of the proximity of New

York City (about 50 miles away) to demonstrate it to the public. After hearing it in the offices of the New York Times in December , 1877, a witness wrote that "it is impossible to listen to the mechanical speech without his experiencing the idea that his senses are deceiving him."

Yet the novelty soon wore off and the main commercial application of the phonograph-office dictation-fell flat. After achieving only limited acceptance as an office dictation machine in the late 1880s, the enterprising manager of the Pacific Phonograph Company set up the first coin-operated phonograph in a saloon in late 1889. While capable of playing only one song, this proto-jukebox helped launch the modern music industry. What Pacific Phonograph had innovated was the idea of using the phonograph to play back commercially made recordings, following the examples of the coin-operated player piano, music boxes, and other arcade-type entertainment technologies. Louis Glass of Pacific Phonograph reported to his business associates in 1890 that each of the two coin-operated phonographs he installed had generated about $1,000 in five months, all the more remarkable because the money was gathered five cents at a time.

5

News Writing, Feature Article and Column Writing: Basic Characteristics

NEWS STYLE AND NEWS WRITING

News style (also *journalistic style* or *news writing*) is the particular prose style used for news reporting (*i.e.* in newspapers) as well as in news items that air on radio and television. News style encompasses not only vocabulary and sentence structure, but also the way in which stories present the information in terms of relative importance, tone, and intended audience. News writing attempts to answer all the basic questions about any particular event in the first two or three paragraphs: *Who? What? When? Where? and Why? and occasionally How?* (*i.e.* 5 W's and 1H). This form of structure is sometimes called the "inverted pyramid," to refer to decreased importance of information as it progresses. News stories also contain at least one of the following important characteristics: proximity, prominence, timeliness, human interest, oddity, or consequence.

Overview

While newspapers, like encyclopaedias, generally adhere to an expository writing mode and style, this has changed over time as journalism ethics and standards have (debatably) increased to become more objective and less sensationalistic. There are debated degrees of professionalism among particular news agencies, and their reputability or public value, according to professional standards of idealism and depending on what the reader wants from a news story, may be tied to their ability to be objective. In its most ideal form, news writing strives to be intelligible to the vast majority of potential readers, as well as to be engaging and succinct. Within the limits created by these goals, news stories also aim for a kind of comprehensiveness. However, other factors are involved, some of which are practical and derived from the media form, and others stylistic.

Among the larger and more respected newspapers, fairness and balance is a major factor for the presentation of information. Commentary is usually confined to a separate section, though each paper may have a different overall slant. Editorial policy dictates the use of adjectives, euphemisms, and idioms. Papers with an international audience for example, usually use a more formal style of writing. The specific choices made by a news outlet's editor or editorial board are often collected in a style guide or stylebook; common commercial stylebooks are the "AP Style Manual" and the "US News Style Book." The main goals of news writing can be summarized by the ABCs of journalism: accuracy, brevity, and clarity.

Terms and Structure

Journalistic prose is explicit and precise, and tries not to rely on jargon. As a rule, journalists will not use a long word when a short one will do. They use subject-verb-object construction and vivid, active prose. They offer anecdotes, examples and metaphors, and they rarely depend on colourless generalizations or abstract ideas. News writers try to avoid using the same word more than once in a paragraph (sometimes called an "echo" or "word mirror").

Headline (or *hed*)

The head of a story, in newsman's jargon.

Subhead (or *dek*)

A phrase, sentence or several sentences near the title of an article or story.

Lede or Lead

The most important structural element of a story is the *lede* or *lead*—the story's first, or leading sentence. Charnley (1966) stated that an effective lead is a "brief, sharp statement of the story's essential facts." The lede/lead is usually the first sentence, or in some cases the first two sentences, and is ideally 20-25 words in length. The top-loading principle applies especially to ledes, but the unreadability of long sentences constrains its size. This makes writing a lede an optimization problem, in which the goal is to articulate the most encompassing and interesting statement that a writer can make in one sentence, given the material with which he or she has to work. While a rule of thumb says the lede should answer most or all of the 5 Ws, few ledes can fit all of these.

Article ledes are sometimes categorized into hard ledes and soft ledes. A *hard lede* aims to provide a comprehensive thesis which tells the reader what the article will cover. A *soft lede* introduces the topic in a more creative, attention-seeking fashion, and is usually followed by a *nut graf* (a brief summary of facts). Media critics often note that the lede can be the most polarizing subject in the article. Often critics find bias based on an editor's choice in headline and lede.

Example Lede-and-Summary Design

Humans will be going to the moon again. The NASA announcement came as the agency requested ten gazillion dollars of appropriations for the project...

Example Soft-Lede Design

NASA is proposing another space project. The agency's budget request, announced today, included a plan to send another person to the moon. This time the agency hopes to establish a long-term facility as a jumping-off point for other space adventures. The budget requests approximately ten gazillion dollars for the project...Two other terms common in editing are *hed* and *dek* or *deck*. *Hed* is used to denote an article's headline or heading. *Dek* refers to a quick blurb or article teaser.

Nut Graph

One or more paragraphs, particularly in a feature story, that explain the news value of the story.

Inverted Pyramid

Journalism instructors usually describe the organization or

structure of a news story as an inverted pyramid. The journalist top-loads the essential and most interesting elements of his or her story, with supporting information following in order of diminishing importance.

This structure enables readers to quit reading at any point and still come away with the essence of a story. It allows people to enter a topic to the depth that their curiosity takes them, and without the imposition of details or nuances that they would consider irrelevant. Newsroom practicalities represent another rationale. The inverted pyramid structure enables sub-editors and other news staff to quickly create space for ads and late-breaking news simply by cutting items (*"throw-aways"*) from the bottom ("cutting", literally, at the papers that still use traditional paste up techniques). The structure frees sub-editors to truncate stories at almost any length that suits their needs for space.

Poor structure typically begins with a faulty lede. Steeped in the raw material of their interviews and research, apprentice news writers often fail to anticipate what readers will find most interesting or to sum up the information quickly. These elements of their story they present only after their lede and in an article's later paragraphs. This is the reason for the popular newsroom admonition: *"Don't bury the lede!"* Some writers start their stories with the "1-2-3 lede." This format invariably starts with a 5 W opening paragraph (as described above), followed by an indirect quote that serves to support a major element of the first paragraph, and then a direct quote to support the indirect quote.

Feature Style

News stories are not the only type of material that appear in newspapers and magazines. Longer articles, such as magazine cover articles and the pieces that lead the inside sections of a newspaper, are known as *features*. Feature stories differ from *straight* news in several ways. Foremost is the absence of a straight-news lead, most of the time. Instead of offering the essence of a story up front, feature writers may attempt to lure readers in.

While straight news stories always stay in third person point of view, it is not uncommon for a feature magazine article to slip into first person. The journalist will often detail his or her interactions with interview subjects, making the piece more personal. A feature's first paragraphs often relate an intriguing moment or event, as in an "anecdotal lede." From the particulars of a person or episode, its view quickly broadens to generalities about the story's subject.

The section that signals what a feature is about is called the *nut graf* or *billboard*. Billboards appear as the third or fourth paragraph from the top, and may be up to two paragraphs long. Unlike a lede, a billboard rarely gives everything away. This reflects the fact that feature writers aim to hold their readers' attention to the end, which requires engendering curiosity and offering a "payoff." Feature paragraphs tend to be longer than those of news stories, with smoother transitions between them. Feature writers use the active-verb construction and concrete explanations of straight news, but often put more personality in their prose. Feature stories often close with a "kicker" rather than simply petering out.

FIVE WS

In journalism, the Five Ws [also known as the Five Ws (and one H) or simply the Six Ws] is a concept in news style, research, and in police investigations that most people consider to be fundamental. It is a formula for getting the "full" story on something. The maxim of the Five Ws and one H is that in order for a report to be considered complete it must answer a checklist of six questions, each of which comprises an interrogative word:

- Who?
- What?
- Where?
- When?
- Why?
- How?

The principle underlying the maxim is that each question should elicit a factual answer—facts that it is necessary to include for a report to be considered complete. Importantly, none of these questions can be answered with a simple "yes" or "no."

In the context of the "news style" for newspaper reporting, the Five Ws and one H are types of facts that should be contained in the "lead" (sometimes spelled lede to avoid confusion with the typographical term "leading" or similarly spelled words), or first two or three paragraphs of the story, after which more expository writing is allowed.

The "Five Ws" and one H were memorialized by Rudyard Kipling in his "Just So Stories" (1902), in which a poem accompanying the tale of "The Elephant's Child" opens with:

I keep six honest serving-men
(They taught me all I knew);
Their names are What and Why and When
And How and Where and Who.

History

Prof. William Cleaver Wilkinson popularized the "Three W's"—What? Why? What of it?—as a method of bible study in the 1880's, though he did not claim originality. This became the "Five W's", though the application was rather different from that in journalism:

> "What? Why? What of it?" is a plan of study of alliterative methods for the teacher emphasized by Professor W.C. Wilkinson not as original with himself but as of venerable authority. "It is, in fact," he says, "an almost immemorial orator's analysis. First the facts, next the proof of the facts, then the consequences of the facts. This analysis has often been expanded into one known as "The Five W's:" "When? Where? Whom? What? Why?" Hereby attention is called, in the study of any lesson: to the date of its incidents; to their place or locality; to the person speaking or spoken to, or to the persons introduced, in the narrative; to the incidents or statements of the text; and, finally, to the applications and uses of the lesson teachings.

By 1917, the "Five W's" were being taught in high school journalism classes, and by 1940, the "Five W's" were being characterized as old-fashioned and fallacious:

> The old-fashioned lead of the five W's and the H, crystallized largely by Pulitzer's 'new journalism' and sanctified by the schools, is widely giving way to the much more supple and interesting feature lead, even on straight news stories.
> All of you know about—and I hope all of you admit the fallacy of—the doctrine of the five W's in the first sentence of the newspaper story.

STYLE GUIDE

A style guide or *style manual* is a set of standards for design and writing of documents, either for general use or for a specific publication or organization. Style guides are prevalent for general and specialized use, for the general reading and writing audience, and for students and scholars of the various academic disciplines, medicine, journalism, the law, government, business, and industry. Some style guides focus on graphic design, covering such topics as typography and white space. Website style guides focus on a publication's visual and technical aspects, prose style, best usage, grammar, punctuation, spelling, and fairness. Many style guides are revised periodically to accommodate changes in conventions and usage. For example, the stylebook of the Associated Press is updated annually.

For Academia and Publishing

Publishers' style guides establish house rules for language use, such as spelling, italics and punctuation; their major purpose is consistency. They are rulebooks for writers, ensuring consistent language. Authors are asked or required to use a style guide in preparing their work for publication; copy editors are charged with enforcing the publishing house's style.

Academic organization and university style guides are rigorous about documentation formatting style for citations and bibliographies used for preparing term papers for course credit and manuscripts for publication. Professional scholars are advised to follow the style guides of organizations in their disciplines when they submit articles and books to academic journals and academic book publishers in those disciplines for consideration of publication. Once they have accepted work for publication, publishers provide authors with their own guidelines and specifications, which may differ from those required for submission, and editors may assist authors in preparing their work for press.

Indexing of the published work, which can be a tedious task, can be done by the author, by a professional editorial indexer, or by computer software. If done by the author or close collaborators of the author who are not professional indexers, the work is called "self-indexed."

For General Use

Some style guides are created for the general public, and may adopt the approaches of publishing houses and newspapers. Others, such as *Fowler's Modern English Usage,* 3rd ed., report how language is practiced in a given area and outline how phrases, punctuation and grammar are actually used.

About *Fowler's Modern English Usage,* Robert Burchfield states: "Linguistic correctness is perhaps the dominant theme of this book... I believe that 'stark preachments' belong to an earlier age of comment on English usage." John Updike comments in *The New Yorker*: "To Burchfield, the English language is a battlefield upon which he functions as a non-combatant observer."

Specialized Guides

A page from an "identity standards manual"—so named for the field of graphic design that focuses on corporate identity design and branding—that identifies colour standards to be used. Some organizations, other than the aforementioned ones, produce style guides for either internal or external use. For example, communications and public relations departments of business and nonprofit organizations have style guides for their publications (newsletters, news releases, Web sites). Organizations advocating for social minorities sometimes establish what they believe to be fair and correct language treatment of their audiences.

Graphic Design Guides

Many publications (notably newspapers) use graphic design

style guides to demonstrate the preferred layout and formatting of a published page. They often are extremely detailed in specifying, for example, which fonts and colours to use. Such guides allow a large design team to produce visually consistent work for the organization.

Examples

International

Several basic style guides for technical and scientific communication have been defined by international standards organizations. These are often used as elements of and refined in more specialized style guides that are specific to a subject, region or organization. Some examples are:

- ISO 8—Presentation of periodicals
- ISO 18—Contents lists of periodicals
- ISO 31—Quantities and units
- ISO 214—Abstracts for publication and documentation
- ISO 215—Presentation of contributions to periodicals and other serials
- ISO 690—Bibliographic references—Content, form and structure
- ISO 832—Bibliographic references—Abbreviations of typical words
- ISO 999—Index of a publication
- ISO 1086—Title leaves of a book
- ISO 2145—Numbering of divisions and subdivisions in written documents
- ISO 5966—Presentation of scientific and technical reports
- ISO 6357—Spine titles on books and other publications
- ISO 7144—Presentation of theses and similar documents
- ISO 9241—Ergonomics of Human System Interaction
- EN-15038:2006—Draft European Standard for Translation Services Annex D (informative)

Australia

- *Style Manual: For Authors, Editors and Printers* Snooks & Co for the Department of Finance and Administration. 6th ed. ISBN 0701636483.

Canada

- *The Canadian Style: A Guide to Writing and Editing* by Dundurn Press in co-operation with Public Works and the Government Services Canada Translation Bureau. ISBN 1550022768.

Newspapers

- *CP Stylebook*: Guide to newspaper style in Canada maintained by the Canadian Press. ISBN 0920009387.
- *The Globe and Mail Style Book*: Originally created to help writers and editors at the *Globe and Mail* present clear, accurate and concise stories. ISBN 0771056850.

United Kingdom

General

- *Copy-editing: The Cambridge Handbook for Editors, Authors and Publishers* Judith Butcher. 3rd ed. 1992 Cambridge: Cambridge University Press ISBN 0 521 40074 0.
- *Fowler's Modern English Usage*. Ed. R.W. Burchfield. Rev. 3rd ed. London: Clarendon Press, 2004. ISBN 0-19-861021-1 (hardcover). Based on *Fowler's Modern English Usage*, by Henry Watson Fowler.
- *The King's English*, by Henry Watson Fowler and Francis George Fowler.
- *The Oxford Style Manual* (2003 ed.). Combines *The Oxford Guide to Style* and *The Oxford Dictionary for Writers and Editors*, which concentrates on common problems.
- *Plain Words*, by Sir Ernest Gowers.
- *Usage and Abusage*, by Eric Partridge.

Journalism

- *The BBC News Style Guide* by the British Broadcasting Corporation.
- *The Economist Style Guide* by *The Economist* (UK).
- *The Guardian Style Guide* by *The Guardian* (United Kingdom)
- *The Times Style and Usage Guide* by *The Times*.

United States

In the United States, most books found in bookstores and libraries follow the *Chicago Manual of Style,* while most newspapers base their styles upon the *Associated Press Stylebook.* A classic style guide for the general public is *The Elements of Style,* by William Strunk, Jr. and E.B. White.

For General Writing

- *Bryson's Dictionary of Troublesome Words: A Writer's Guide to Getting It Right* by Bill Bryson.
- *The Classics of Style*—Presents writing guidance from William Strunk, Jr., Emerson, Whitman, Poe, and other writers.
- *The Elements of Style.* By William Strunk, Jr. and E.B. White. (Often referred to as "Strunk and White".)

For Legal Documents

- *The Bluebook: A Uniform System of Citation* by the Harvard Law Review.

For Academic Papers

- *MLA Handbook for Writers of Research Papers* by Joseph Gibaldi. (Often referred to as "MLA.")
- *Publication Manual of the American Psychological Association* by the American Psychological Association (APA).
- *A Manual for Writers of Research Papers, Theses, and Dissertations, Seventh Edition: Chicago Style for Students and Researchers* by Kate L. Turabian. Often referred to as "Turabian."

For Journalism

- *The Associated Press Stylebook* by the Associated Press (AP).
- *The New York Times Manual of Style and Usage* by Allan M. Siegal and William G. Connolly.
- *The Wall Street Journal Guide to Business Style and Usage,* by Ronald J. Alsop and the Staff of the *Wall Street Journal.*

For Technical Writing

Style guides are particularly important in technical writing projects. Where technical writing is undertaken in a large team or project, it is important that the finished documentation is devoid of any one individual's discernible personal style. A style guide is just one of the tools that can be used to help achieve this along with the use of specific standards, *e.g.*, ATA100 or AECMA S1000D in the aerospace and defense industries. Some disciplines use a style guide published by a professional society, such as the one offered by the American Physical Society or the one from the American Chemical Society referenced below.

For Electronic Publishing

- *The Columbia Guide to Online Style* by Janice Walker and Todd Taylor.
- *Web Style Guide: Basic Design Principles for Creating Web Sites* by Patrick J. Lynch and Sarah Horton.

For the Computer Industry (Software and Hardware)

- *Read Me First! A Style Guide for the Computer Industry* by Sun Technical Publications.
- *Microsoft Manual of Style for Technical Publications* by Microsoft Corporation. Provides a style standard for technical documentation including use of terminology, conventions, procedure, design treatments, and punctuation and grammar usage.

Editorial Style Guides on Preparing a Manuscript for Publication

- *The Chicago Manual of Style* by University of Chicago Press staff.
- *Words into Type* by Marjorie E. Skillin, Robert M. Gay, *et al.*

Academic

- *ACS Style Guide*—For scientific papers published in journals of the American Chemical Society.

- *American Medical Association Manual of Style*—For medical papers published in journals of the American Medical Association.
- *American Psychological Association Style Guide*—For the social sciences; published by the American Psychological Association.
- *American Sociological Association Style Guide*—For the social sciences; published by the American Sociological Association.
- *The Chicago Manual of Style*—Required by some academic publishers for books and journal publications.
- *Geoscience Reporting Guidelines*—For geoscience reports in industry, academia and other disciplines.
- *IEEE Style*—Used in many technical research papers, especially those relating to computer science.
- *MHRA Style Guide*—For the arts and humanities; published by the Modern Humanities Research Association. Available as a free download.
- *MLA Style Manual* and *MLA Handbook for Writers of Research Papers*, 6th ed.—For the arts and humanities; published by the Modern Language Association of America.
- *Scientific Style and Format: The CSE Manual for Authors, Editors, and Publishers*, 7th ed.—For scientific papers published by the Council of Science Editors (CSE), a group formerly known as the Council of Biology Editors (CBE).
- *The Style Manual for Political Science*—Used by many American political science journals; published by the American Political Science Association.
- *A Manual for Writers of Term Papers, Theses, and Dissertations* (frequently called "Turabian style")—Published by Kate L. Turabian, the graduate school dissertation secretary at the University of Chicago from 1930 to 1958. The school required her approval for every master's thesis and doctoral dissertation. Her stylistic rules closely follow those in *The Chicago Manual of Style*, although there are some differences.

CASE STUDY: NEWS WRITING AS PER ANNENBERG MEDIA

A video instructional series on writing and reporting for college and high school classrooms and adult learners; 15 half-hour video programmes and coordinated books.

Now on DVD

This series teaches the writing, reporting, editing, and communicating of information in the public interest. More than 100 journalists working in print, radio, and television reveal the secrets of their trade. Among those offering insights are Bob Woodward, Helen Thomas, Dave Barry, and Linda Ellerbee. Coverage of policy issues sheds light on journalism history, law, and ethics. A natural choice for students pursuing journalism or communications, *News Writing* is also an excellent resource for improving general writing skills, producing a school or university paper, continuing education for working journalists, or teacher professional development.

Individual Programme Descriptions

1. *What is News*?: Examines how journalists determine what the public needs and wants to know. Reporters and editors from diverse news organizations—including The Washington Post, The National Enquirer, and CNN—discuss editorial decision making and define news as it relates to journalism ethics and the news writing process.
2. *Hard News Leads*: Shows the power and process of the summary lead in newspaper, broadcast, and PR writing. A broad spectrum of writers—for example, White House correspondent Helen Thomas and Chicago Defender editor Michael Brown—discuss and demonstrate this basic journalism tool.
3. *News Writing Language and Style*: Explores the specifics of print journalism style—from the AP to Rolling Stone magazine focusing on accuracy and detail, enlivened by humor as Dave Barry and other writers confess their language sins and steer tomorrow's journalists toward production of professional and pristine prose.

4. *Development and Organization of a Story*: Deals with use of the inverted pyramid as well as hourglass and circle story shapes. Top journalists—such as Bob Woodward—along with Roy Peter Clark (The Poynter Institute) discuss and demonstrate focus sentences, transitions, and nut graphs as story development techniques.
5. *Dealing with Sources*: Illustrates how to interview sources and work quotes into a news story. Larry King (CNN), Deborah Wilgoren (The Washington Post), and others demonstrate the interviewing process, touching on the use of paraphrase vs. direct quotes, the mechanics of attribution, the ground rules for using "off the record" comments, and other issues.
6. *Good Writing vs. Good Reporting*: Considers the possibilities of conflict or compatibility between these two elements. Top reporters discuss essential issues such as accuracy, objectivity, fairness, and credibility along with the elements of writing that make a news story exciting, fun, and compelling to read.
7. *Beat Reporting*: Covers the wide variety of journalism career opportunities, with glimpses into the working conditions and daily experiences on crime, sports, business, government, and environmental beats as well as for general assignment and wire service reporters.
8. *Broadcast News Writing*: Compares the similarities and differences of broadcast and print journalism, with insightful comments from a host of radio and TV journalists—among them Sam Donaldson (ABC), Charles Kuralt (CBS), and Kurt Loder (MTV)—and follows a young reporter as he assembles a daily news package.
9. *Public Relations Writing*: Demonstrates the interaction of journalists and PR people. Professionals from Capital Records and the Golden State Warriors discuss the similarities of writing press releases and hard news stories, while sympathetic and unsympathetic journalists—including Andy Rooney (CBS) and Susan Antilla (*The New York Times*)—comment on the role of PR in the news.

10. *Beyond the Summary Lead*: Encourages novice writers to explore other creative introductory styles including anecdotal, quote, question, narrative, and direct address leads. Journalists—Gene Policinski (USA Today) and David Waldholz (*The Wall Street Journal*) among others—give tips on ways to avoid boring leads and grab readers in the first paragraph.
11. *Feature Writing Styles*: Explores the difference between feature news, soft features, and advocacy journalism, as Pulitzer Prize winner Tom Kundsen (Sacramento Bee), Joel Achenbach (The Washington Post), and others discuss their craft. Concepts such as trend stories, personality profiles, background stories, and human interest stories are also introduced and illustrated by working reporters.
12. *Column Writing and Editorial Writing*: Reveals the relationships among hard news writing, opinion writing, journalistic critique, and column writing, illustrating how "objective" front-page news can coexist with coverage in other sections. Dave Barry and Andy Rooney examine humor in column writing, Siskel and Ebert discuss criticism, and Pulitzer Prize-winning editorial writers dissect the elements of good opinion writing.
13. *Covering Disasters*: Demonstrates use of journalism's basic principles in crisis situations and under deadline pressure. Journalists who have covered earthquakes, chemical spills, severe weather, and plane crashes discuss the difference between theory and practice during community emergencies.
14. *The Ethics of Journalism*: Introduces a reporter's on-the-job ethical challenges. Journalists from a variety of beats discuss issues such as conflict of interest, honesty, thoroughness, objectivity, privacy, and balance, and one reporter demonstrates real-life ethical decision making as she covers a controversial local story.
15. *Media Law*: Focuses on reporters' rights and defenses for potential libel or invasion of privacy lawsuits as well as concepts like open meeting, shield, and freedom of information laws. In addition, Mark Goodman,

attorney for the Student Press Law Center, and author John Zelezny discuss legal issues that may confront students working for a school newspaper or other publication.

FEATURE STORY

A feature story (also known as a *feature article*) is an article in a newspaper, a magazine, or a news website that is not meant to report breaking news, but to take an in-depth look at a subject. While there are no precise guidelines on the differentiation between features and news stories, features are often significantly longer than news articles, are more likely to be written from a personal perspective, and unlike news stories do not always deal with the events of the immediate past.

Features are generally written in a different fashion from news stories, sometimes taking several paragraphs to arrive at the main story while trying to engage the reader and keep them reading by employing narrative hooks. Feature stories often delve deeper into their subjects, expanding on the details rather than trying to concentrate on a few important key points. The writing style of the articles can be more colourful and employ a more complex narrative structure, sometimes resembling the style of a nonfiction book more than a news report.

As the print media faces ever stiffer competition from other sources of news, feature stories are becoming more common as they can be more engaging to read. At many newspapers, news stories are sometimes written in "feature style," adopting some of the conventions of feature writing while still covering breaking events. Wire services such as the Associated Press, which previously made a point of distributing only news, now also include feature stories. The Pulitzer Prize for Feature Writing is awarded annually for a distinguished example of feature writing in an American newspaper or magazine, giving prime consideration to high literary quality and originality.

NARRATIVE HOOK

A narrative hook (or *hook*) is a literary technique in the opening of a story that "hooks" the reader's attention so that he or she will keep reading on. The "opening" may consist of several paragraphs for a short story, or several pages for a novel, but ideally is the opening sentence.

One of the most common forms is dramatic action, which engages the reader into wondering what the consequences of the action will be. This particular form has been recommended from the earliest days, stemming from Aristotle, and the widely used term *in medias res* stems from the Roman Empire. But action is not, in itself, a hook, without the reader's wondering what will happen next, or what caused the actions to occur. Overly dramatic openings may leave the reader indifferent because the characters acting or being acted on are non-entities; even murder of a faceless character may not engage interest.

The use of action as the hook, and the advice to so use it, is so wide spread as to sometimes lead to the use of the term to mean an action opening, but other things can be used for narrative hooks, such mysterious settings, or engaging characters, or even a thematic statement, as with Jane Austen's opening line, "It is a truth universally acknowledged, that a single man in possession of a good fortune, must be in want of a wife."

When a story does not lend itself to a good hook when it is laid out linearly, the writer may tell the story out of order to engage the reader's interest. The story may begin with a dramatic moment and, once the reader is curious, flashback to the history necessary to understand it. Or it may be told as a story-within-a-story, with the narrator in the frame story telling the story to answer the curiosity of his listeners, or by warning them that the story began in an ordinary seeming way, but they must follow it to understand latter actions.

NUT GRAF

In journalism, a *nut graf* (sometimes spelled *nut graph,* and also called a *billboard*) is one or more paragraphs, particularly in a feature story, that explain the news value of the story. In most news stories, the news style of writing is used, and the essential facts of a story are included in the lede (or lead), the first sentence or two of the story. For example, a story about crime statistics written in news style might start out with a lede like: "Violent crime is down in Anytown but shoplifting is soaring, according to statistics released by the Anytown Police Department Tuesday." Good ledes try to answer who, what, when, where, why and how as quickly as possible.

However, in feature stories, or in news written in a feature style, the story will often begin in a more narrative manner. For instance, if a story on crime statistics were written in feature style rather than news style, the first few paragraphs might start by introducing a local business owner who was affected by the boom in shoplifting. The nut graf, which often will start in the third or fourth paragraph, will explain what the story is about, including much but rarely all of the information that would have been contained in a lede, so as to keep the reader interested.

COLUMNIST

A columnist is a journalist who writes material on a regular basis for publication in a series. Columns appear in newspapers, magazines and other publications, including blogs on the Internet. Readers often open a publication with an expectation of reading a new essay by a specific writer who offers a personal point of view. Many columnists are strongly opinionated. In defining a column, Dictionary.com provides a breakdown of a few popular subjects covered by columnists:

> A regular feature or series of articles in a newspaper, magazine, or the like, usually having a readily identifiable heading and the byline of the writer or editor, that reports or comments upon a particular field of interest, as politics, theater, or etiquette, or which may contain letters from readers, answers to readers' queries, etc.

In at least one situation, a column expanded to become an entire successful magazine. When Cyrus Curtis founded the *Tribune and Farmer* in 1879, it was a four-page weekly with an annual subscription rate of 50 cents. He introduced a women's column by his wife, Louise Knapp Curtis, and it proved so popular that in 1883, he decided to publish it as a separate monthly supplement, *Ladies Journal and Practical Housekeeper*, edited by Louise Curtis. With 25,000 subscribers by the end of its first year, it was such a success that Curtis sold *Tribune and Farmer* to put his energy into the new publication, which became the *Ladies Home Journal.*

Radio and Television

Newspaper columnists of the 1930s and 1940s, such as Franklin Pierce Adams (aka FPA), Nick Kenny, Jimmie Fidler, Walter Winchell. Louella Parsons, Drew Pearson, Ed Sullivan and Walter Winchell, achieved a celebrity status and used their syndicated columns as a springboard to move into radio and television. In some cases, such as Winchell and Parsons, their radio programmes were quite similar in format to their newspaper columns. Rona Barrett began as a Hollywood gossip columnist in 1957, duplicating her print tactics on television by the mid-1960s. One of the more famous syndicated columnists of the 1920s and 1930s, O.O. McIntyre, declined offers to do a radio series because he felt it would interfere and diminish the quality of writing in his column, "New York Day by Day."

Books

However, FPA and McIntyre both collected their columns into a series of books, as did other columnists. McIntyre's book, *The Big Town: New York Day by Day* (1935) was a bestseller. FPA's *The Melancholy Lute* (1936), collected selections from three decades of his columns. H. Allen Smith's first humor book, *Low Man on a Totem Pole* (1941) and his two following books were so popular during World War II that they kept Smith on the *New York Herald Tribune*'s Best Seller List for 100 weeks and prompted a collection of all three in *3 Smiths in the Wind* (1946). While Smith's column, *The Totem Pole,* was syndicated by United Features, he told Time:

> Just between you and me it's tough. A typewriter can be a pretty formidable contraption when you sit down in front of it and say: 'All right, now I'm going to be funny.'

The Miami Herald promotes humor columnist Dave Barry with this description: "Dave Barry has been at *The Miami Herald* since 1983. A Pulitzer Prize winner for commentary, he writes about issues ranging from the international economy to exploding toilets." Barry has collected his columns into a series of successful books, and the newspaper offers a selection of memorable Barry columns on its website.

Types of Columnists

- Agony aunt, an advice columnist
- Critic reviewer
- Editorial opinion columnist
- Gossip columnist
- Humor columnist
- Food columnist

OBELISM

Obelism is the practice of annotating manuscripts with marks set in the margins. Modern obelisms are used by editors blue-penciling a manuscript or typescript. Examples are "stet" (which is Latin for "Let it stand," used in this context to mean "disregard the previous mark") and "dele" (for "delete"). The obelos symbol gets its name from the spit, or sharp end of a lance in ancient Greek. An obelos was placed by editors on the margins of manuscripts, especially in Homer, to indicate lines that were doubtfully Homer's. The system was developed by Aristarchus and notably used later by Origen in his Hexapla. Origen marked spurious words between obelos and metobelos.

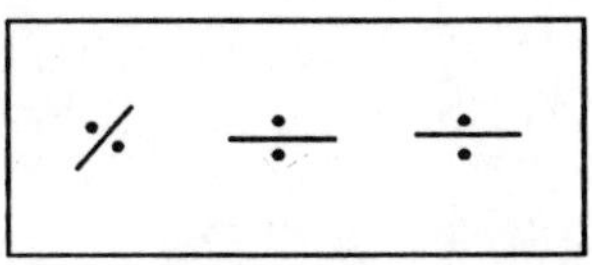

Fig. 5.1: Three Basic Variants of Dotted Obeles Glyphs

There were many other such shorthand symbols, to indicate corrections, emendations, deletions, additions, and so on. Most used are the editorial coronis, the paragraphs, the forked paragraphs, the reversed forked paragraphs, the hypodiastole, the downwards ancora, the upwards ancora, and the dotted right-pointing angle, which is also known as the diple periestigmene. Loosely, all these symbols, and the act of annotation by means of them, are *obelism*.

Following ancient Greek textual annotation symbols are also included in the supplemental punctuation list of ISO IEC standard 10646 for character sets.

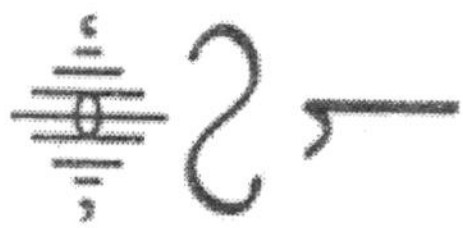

The coronis marked subsections.

The paragraphos was used for breaks.

The hypodiastole separated words before the use of spaces.

The dotted diple was also used for dubious lines.

Unicode encodes the following:

- U+2058—FOUR DOT PUNCTUATION
- U+2059—FIVE DOT PUNCTUATION = Greek pentonkion
- U+205A—TWO DOT PUNCTUATION
- U+205B—FOUR DOT MARK
- U+205C—DOTTED CROSS
- U+2E0E—EDITORIAL CORONIS
- U+2E0F—PARAGRAPHOS
- U+2E10—FORKED PARAGRAPHOS
- U+2E11—REVERSED FORKED PARAGRAPHOS
- U+2E12—HYPODIASTOLE
- U+2E13—DOTTED OBELOS
- U+2E14—DOWNWARDS ANCORA
- U+2E15—UPWARDS ANCORA
- U+2E16—DOTTED RIGHT-POINTING ANGLE = diple periestigmene

6

News Interview, News Conference and News Management: A Reflection

INTERVIEW

An interview is a conversation between two or more people (the interviewer and the interviewee) where questions are asked by the interviewer to obtain information from the interviewee. The word "Interview" is derived from french word "entirevior" it means "glimpse" to each other.

Fig. 6.1: An Interview

Famous Interviews

- *February 2003 Saddam Hussein interview*—Dan Rather interviewing Saddam Hussein days before the 2003 invasion of Iraq.
- *The Rolling Stone interview*—A number of influential pop-cultural interviews in the 1970s.
- *Microsoft interview*—The job interview method used by Microsoft.

- *Bashir interview*—An interview with Michael Jackson, later turned into a documentary.
- *Fellini*: I'm a Born Liar interview—Federico Fellini's last filmed interviews conducted in 1992 for a 2002 feature documentary.
- *The Paris Review*—Interviews with many of the finest novelists of the 20th century.

CASE STUDY: FEBRUARY 2003 SADDAM HUSSEIN INTERVIEW

The Saddam interview refers to a famous television interview that occurred between President of Iraq Saddam Hussein and American news anchor Dan Rather on February 24, 2003, very shortly before the 2003 Invasion of Iraq. The interview was aired both in the United States and on all three Iraqi television networks. British politician Tony Benn had also interviewed Hussein earlier that month.

Background

They drove for 45 minutes, in different directions, and switched cars on two separate occasions to keep Hussein's position secret. The interview was held at the Republican Palace. Neither Rather nor Murphy were allowed to bring their own tape-recorders. Hussein supplied his own translator, and CBS approved the translation of the recording. Rather and Murphy were treated well in the course of the interview, with Hussein offering Rather coffee at one point.

American Interview

In the 1980s, Rather had an on-air confrontation with the then president George H.W. Bush over the Iran-Contra Affair. His son, George W. Bush, has responded similarly, and has declined to give Rather an interview during his presidency. After the Hussein interview, the White House was interested in a rebuttal interview. CBS News would accept President Bush, Vice-President Dick Cheney or Secretary of State Colin Powell for the interview, but the White House only offered other officials for the interview, such as Ari Fleischer and Dan Bartlett. The

CBS network deemed these individuals inappropriate for the broadcast, and an American interview was never done.

Highlights

Memorable lines:

> *Hussein*:...Bear with me. My answers are long.
> *Rather*: Mr. President, I have all night.

Hussein invited President Bush to a live TV debate, to which Bush declined.

> *Rather*: Who would moderate this debate?
> *Hussein*: Yes, you Mr. Rather.
> *Rather*: With respect, Mr. President, I have other problems. I've got enough problems already.

On one occasion Hussein interrupted his translator and corrected his using the term "Bush" instead of "Mr. Bush", which Hussein explained was out of respect.

Summary

- Hussein declares his support of Allah, Islam and Palestine.
- Hussein denies possessing Weapons of Mass Destruction, or the possession of arms against U.N. Law.
- Hussein denies association with Osama bin Laden.
- Hussein declares he will not step down from presidency or ever surrender against a stronger opponent.
- Hussein also declares he will not go into asylum, or leave Iraq.
- Hussein claims that his armed forces lost only 10 per cent of their military equipment in 1991's Operation Desert Storm.

NEWS CONFERENCE

A news conference or press conference is a media event in which newsmakers invite journalists to hear them speak and, most often, ask questions.

Practice

There are two major reasons for holding a news conference. One is so that a newsmaker who gets many questions from reporters can answer them all at once rather than answering dozens of phone calls. Another is so someone can try to attract news coverage for something that was not of interest to journalists before.

Fig. 6.2: A Joint Press Conference by US President George W. Bush and British Prime Minister Tony Blair at the White House

In a news conference, one or more speakers may make a statement, which may be followed by questions from reporters. Sometimes only questioning occurs; sometimes there is a statement with no questions permitted. A media event at which no statements are made, and no questions allowed, is called a photo opportunity. A government may wish to open their proceedings for the media to witness events, such as the passing of a piece of legislation from the government in parliament to the senate, via a media availability.

Television stations and networks especially value news conferences: because today's TV news programmes air for hours at a time, or even continuously, assignment editors have a steady appetite for ever-larger quantities of footage. News conferences are often held by politicians (such as the President of the United States); by sports teams; by celebrities or film studios; by commercial organizations to promote products; by attorneys to promote lawsuits; and by almost anyone who finds benefit in the free publicity afforded by media coverage. Some people, including many police chiefs, hold news conferences reluctantly in order to avoid dealing with reporters individually.

A news conference is often announced by sending an advisory or news release to assignment editors, preferably well in advance. Sometimes they are held spontaneously when several reporters gather around a newsmaker. News conferences can be held just about anywhere, in settings as formal as the White House room set aside for the purpose to as informal as the street in front of a crime scene. Hotel conference rooms and courthouses are often used for news conferences.

U.S. Presidential Press Conference

When the President of the United States holds a press conference, he takes questions from the press pool in a specific order: wire services (for decades, Helen Thomas of UPI had the first question), broadcast networks, national newspapers, news magazines, radio and, lastly, regional newspapers.

NEWS MANAGEMENT

News Management is normally used to describe the way that individuals or organizations attempt to control the flow of news to the media and to 'set the agenda' for the media. This might involve issuing a press release which is embargoed, holding press conferences timed to make the lunch-time and early-evening news, or staging an event which is big enough or unusual enough to grab the media's attention. The government might, for example, choose to announce bad news on the same day that optimistic employment figures are announced. An extreme example of news management was the February 1996 'Scott report' on arms sales to Iraq. Expecting the report to be severely critical of the Government, ministers arranged for the report to be made available to them a week before it was scheduled for its first debate in parliament; a number of handpicked Opposition MPs were given a few closely supervised hours to 'read' the report which ran into several volumes; all other MPs had a matter of minutes only. The Government also made their own choice of quotes from the report avaibale to journalists.

MANAGING THE NEWS

Managing the news refers to acts which are intended to influence the presentation of information within the news media. The expression *managing the news* is often used in a negative sense. An example cited by the Communication, Cultural and Media Studies infobase concerns the February 1996 Scott Report on arms sales to Iraq. In the United Kingdom, the report was given early to certain officials. People or organizations who wish to lessen the publicity concerning bad news may choose to release the information late on a Friday, giving journalists less time to pursue the story. Staying "on message" is a technique intended to limit questions and attention to a narrow scope favourable to the subject.

7

Global News Agencies and Bureaus: Select Case Studies

NEWS BUREAU

A News bureau is an office for gathering or distributing news. Similar terms are used for specialized bureaus, often to indicate geographic location or scope of coverage: a *Tokyo bureau* refers to a given news operation's office in Tokyo, Japan; *foreign bureau* is a generic term for a news office set up in a country other than the primary operations centre; a *Washington bureau* is an office, typically located in Washington, D.C., that covers news related to national politics in the United States.

The term is related to but distinct from *News desk,* which refers to the editorial function of assigning reporters and other staff, and otherwise coordinating, news stories, and sometimes the physical desk where that occurs, but without regard to the geographic location or overall operation of the news organization. For example, a foreign bureau is located in a foreign country and refers to all creative and administrative operations that take place there, whereas a *foreign desk* describes only editorial functions and may be located anywhere, possibly as an organizational unit within the news organization's home office.

Operation of News Bureaus

A news bureau is traditionally operated out of an office by a single news outlet such as a radio, television, or newspaper news programme. A single news company such as CNN or NPR may use a single bureau and office staff for all of its programmes, and even those of subsidiary or other affiliated companies. For convenience, to save money and space, and to ensure the availability of necessary services (such as video feeds and studios), different companies may share an office space or co-locate at a single office building. News agencies may also operate news bureaus, and major public relations sources (such as governments, large companies, or advocacy groups) may operate news bureaus of their own to create, rather than simply report, news stories.

History of News Bureaus

Decline

Traditional news media, particularly television news and newspapers, have cut the number and size of news bureaus in recent decades for several reasons. They face declining profitability due to increasing competition from Internet news sources, and therefore have less money to spend on news-gathering.

Newspapers rely increasingly on cooperative arrangements with counterparts elsewhere, and often will accept stories from their sister organizations rather than investigating stories themselves. Similarly, smaller newspapers may formally affiliate to sponsor cooperative bureaus that operate as press pools to serve more than one news organization (and sometimes a large number of organizations) from a single office. When news sources combine operations following a merger or other business consolidation, the surviving company often combines or eliminates redundant bureaus. Growing multiculturalism has facilitated this process: rather than demanding a reporter from their own country or locale who has been sent on assignment, news audiences have come to tolerate or even expect to see stories in remote locations covered by people who live locally; this empowers the audience to make their own judgements about any apparent cultural difference between themselves and the news subjects, rather than leaving the function of cultural interpretation entirely up to the reporter.

The often-criticized practice of parachute journalism allows News media to cover stories remotely using journalists who are generalists rather than more specialized field experts. Rather than leaving journalists in place waiting for breaking news to occur, smaller staff can be assigned as needed to wherever there are breaking stories, either by commuting to the physical location or by synthesizing reports from remote sources. An even more controversial practice, sometimes described as a reaction to declining resources rather than a legitimate cost-saving measure, is to rely on and reprint information from press releases written by public relations professionals working for people or companies that are the subject of an article, or have an interest in an article, without spending the resources to verify or conduct independent research on the matter. Another practice that limits news bureaus is embedded reporting, whereby war correspondents travel under the care of military units rather than at their own direction. The ability to quickly and safely travel throughout a war zone, and to obtain interviews with soldiers and coverage of important conflicts, appeals to news media, but at the cost of journalistic independence and, according to some, objectivity.

Non-traditional Bureaus

The interaction between professional journalists, witnesses, and news subjects has evolved considerably. Whereas news subjects and bystanders were once treated simply as witnesses to be interviewed for a news story, media have now accepted them as part of the news process. There are many antecedents to Citizen journalism. For example, meteorologists would count on amateurs to gather weather data to report, or interview willing subjects unrelated to a news story for "man on the street" interviews. As early as the 1930s the Soviet Union encouraged millions of amateur People's correspondents to expose corruption and otherwise report on news. Beginning in the 1970s, media, unable to respond quickly enough to obtain compelling coverage of natural disasters and weather phenomena such as tornadoes would count on hobbyists for photographs and film footage. With improvements in technology and as video cameras and video-equipped cell phones became widely available, they set up formal programmes to gather material from nonprofessionals. For example, in August 2006, CNN launched "CNN Exchange", by which the public is encouraged to submit "I-Reports" comprising photographs, videos, or news accounts. More recently newspapers have incorporated blogs, once seen as a threat to conventional news practice, either by creating blogs of their own (and deputizing local or field-specific bloggers as a second, lower-paid tier among their recognized staff of independent contractors) or by covering blogs as news sources.

In 2006 Reuters opened its first virtual news Bureau, staffing real-life reporters in a virtual office in Second Life. CNN followed suit in October 2007, but took a citizen journalism approach, allowing residents of Second Life to submit their own reportage. Although the news audience of Second World is relatively small, and declining, media consider it a training ground for themselves and participants, applicable to future virtual news projects.

AGENCE FRANCE-PRESSE

Agence France-Presse (AFP) is the oldest news agency in the world, and one of the three largest with Associated Press and Reuters. It is also the largest French news agency.

AFP is based in Paris, with regional centres in Washington, Hong Kong, Nicosia, São Paulo, Montevideo and bureaux in 110 countries. It transmits news in French, English, Arabic, Spanish, German, and Portuguese.

AFP	
Type	News agency
Founded	1835
Headquarters	Paris, France
Website	www.afp.com

History

The agency was founded in 1835 by a Parisian translator and advertising agent, Charles-Louis Havas as *Agence Havas*. Two of his employees, Julius Reuter and Bernhard Wolff, later set up rival news agencies in London and Berlin respectively. In order to reduce overheads and develop the lucrative advertising side of the business, Havas's sons, who had succeeded him in 1852, signed agreements with Reuter and Wolff, giving each news agency an exclusive reporting zone in different parts of Europe. This arrangement lasted until the 1930s, when the invention of short-wave wireless improved and cut communications costs. To help Havas extend the scope of its reporting at a time of great international tension, the French government financed up to 47 per cent of its investments. When German forces occupied France in 1940, the news agency was taken over by the authorities and renamed the French Information Office (FIO); only the private advertising company retained the name Havas.

On August 20, 1944, as Allied forces moved on Paris, a group of journalists in the French Resistance seized the offices of the FIO and issued the first news dispatch from the liberated city under the name of Agence France-Presse. Established as a state enterprise, AFP devoted the post-war years to developing its network of international correspondents. One of them was the first Western journalist to report the death of Joseph Stalin, on March 6, 1953. AFP was keen to shake off its semi-official status, and on January 10, 1957 the French Parliament passed a law establishing its independence. Since that date, the proportion of the agency's revenues generated by subscriptions from government departments has steadily declined.

In 1982, the agency began to decentralize its editorial decision-making by setting up the first of its four autonomous regional centres, in Hong Kong. Each region has its own budget, administrative director and chief editor. In September 2007, the AFP Foundation was launched to promote higher standards of journalism worldwide.

Status

AFP is a government-chartered public corporation operating under a 1957 law, but is officially a commercial business independent of the French government. AFP is administered by a CEO and a board comprising 15 members:

- Eight representatives of the French press.
- Two representatives of the AFP personnel.

- Two representatives of the government-owned radio and television.
- Three representatives of the government. One is named by the prime minister, another by the minister of finance, and a third by the minister of foreign affairs.

The board elects the CEO for a renewable term of three years. The AFP also has a council charged with ensuring that the agency operates according to its statutes, which mandate absolute independence and neutrality.

Editorially, AFP is governed by a network of senior journalists. By statute, AFP 's mission is to report events, free of "all influences or considerations likely to impair the exactitude" of its news. And "under no circumstances to pass under the legal or actual control of an ideological, political or economic group." The primary client of AFP is the French government, which purchases subscriptions for its various services. In practice, those subscriptions are an indirect subsidy to AFP. The statutes of the agency prohibit direct government subsidies.

Investments

Notable investments include:

- *AFP GmbH*: AFP GmbH is the subsidiary of AFP in Germany, producing German-language services for local press, internet and corporate clients.
- *SID*: Sport-Informations-Dienst (SID) is producing a German-language sports service.
- *Citizenside*: In November 2007, AFP has announced its investment into Scooplive, a news photo and video agency online, created in France in 2006. Scooplive became Citizenside after this investment.

AGERPRES

AGERPRES is the national news agency of Romania.

History

The agency was founded with the name AGERPRES, standing for "Romanian Press Agency" (Romanian: *Agentia Română de Presă*)

AGERPRES National Press Agengy
(*Agentia Naþionalã de Presã AGERPRES*)

Type	Public
Founded	27 March 1889
Headquarters	Piaţa Presei Libere, Bucureşti, Romania
Key people	Ioan Roşca
Industry	News agency
Website	www.agerpres.ro

After 1989 the agency changed its name to ROMPRES (to underline the close relations of Romania with France, as an equivalent to Agence France-Presse). In 2008 the agency changed its name back to AGERPRES.

Fig. 7.1: The Logo Used Until the Name Rechange

ALGEMEEN NEDERLANDS PERSBUREAU

The Algemeen Nederlands Persbureau (ANP) is the leading news agency of the Netherlands. ANP was founded on December 11, 1934 by the association of Dutch newspapers NDP. The news agency's founders sought to produce a fast, fair and accurate alternative to the existing commercial news agencies.

Privatization

In 2000, the foundation was transformed into a private company, still owned by the newspaper publishers. In 2003 NPM Capital, the private equity firm of the Dutch family owned conglomerate SHV, bought 60 per cent of the shares from the publishers PCM Uitgevers, Telegraaf Media Groep en Wegener. Within a year NPM sold 15 per cent of the shares to the private equity firm Halder, a subsidiary of the Flemish governmental investment company Gewestelijke

Investeringsmaatschappij voor Vlaanderen. A minority stake remained in the hands of the Dutch newspapers (30%) and the management (10%).

Workings

With 140 reporters, correspondents, editors and photographers ANP produces over 160.000 news articles a year, accompanied by 600.000 photos. The ANP Multimedia staff airs radio bulletins and edits news for online media and mobile phones. ANP Video produces news footage for television and major news websites. Throughout a network of international correspondents and news agencies ANP delivers foreign news to its customers. The daily production (in Dutch) consists of general, political, financial, sports and entertainment news. A selection in English is available through NIS News Bulletin. The archives of ANP Photo consist of over 1 million digital images and 2, 5 million slides. ANP owns the archives of the former Dutch photoagencies Kippa and Benelux Press.

Offices

The staff of 220 people is headquartered in Rijswijk, just outside The Hague, with bureaus in Amsterdam (Economic, City and Entertainment), Rotterdam (City), The Hague (Government), Eindhoven (Regional) and Brussels (EU/NATO). In the Netherlands, ANP represents the news agencies Agence France Presse (AFP), Deutsche Presse Agentur (DPA), EFE (Spain) en Belga (Belgium).

ANSA NEWS AGENCY

Agenzia Nazionale Stampa Associata, best known with initials ANSA, is one of main press agencies in the world, and by far the most important one in Italy. It has been founded January 15, 1945, and it is based in Rome. ANSA holds 22 offices in Italy and 81 in 78 countries, all over the world.

ASSOCIATED PRESS

The Associated Press (AP) is an American news agency. The AP is a cooperative owned by its contributing newspapers, radio and television stations in the United States, which both contribute stories to the AP and use material written by its staffers. Many newspapers and broadcasters outside the United States are AP subscribers, paying a fee to use AP material without being contributive members of the cooperative.

AP Associated Press

Type	Not-for-profit cooperative
Founded	New York City, 1846
Headquarters	New York City
Key people	Tom Curley, President and CEO
Area served	Worldwide
Industry	News media
Products	Wire service
Revenue	$654,186,000 USD 2005
Operating income	$17,959,000 USD 2005
Net income	$18,528,000 USD 2005
Employees	4,100
Website	ap.org

As of 2005, the AP's news is published and republished by more than 1,700 newspapers, in addition to more than 5,000 television and radio broadcasters. The cooperative's photograph library consists of more than 10 million images. It operates 243 news bureaus and serves 121 countries, with a diverse international staff drawing from all over the world.

As part of their cooperative agreement with the Associated Press, most member news organizations grant automatic permission for the AP to distribute their local news reports. For example, on page two of every edition of *The Washington Post,* the newspaper's masthead includes the statement, "*The Associated Press is entitled exclusively to use for republication of all news dispatches credited to it or not otherwise credited in this paper and all local news of spontaneous origin published herein.*"

The *AP Stylebook* has become the de facto standard for news writing in the United States. The AP employs the "inverted pyramid formula" for writing that enables news outlets to edit a story to fit its available publication space without losing the story's essential meaning and news information.

The decline of AP's traditional rival, United Press International, as a major American competitor in 1993 left the AP as the only nationally oriented news service based in the United States. Other English-language news services, such as Reuters and the English language service of Agence France-Presse, are based outside the United States.

History

The AP was formed in May 1846 by a group of American newspapers that sought to pool resources in order to better collect and report news coming from Europe. Prior to this, the newspapers had competed by sending reporters out in rowboats to meet ships bringing news from Europe as they arrived in the harbor. The owners of these newspapers realized that they were all paying for essentially the same information and determined it would be more cost effective to have a service collect and pay for all the information once via telegraph. Their new organization originally was named the Harbor News Association; it later was renamed the Associated Press. A driving force in the organization's formation was Moses Yale Beach, publisher of the New York Sun, when he invited other New York publishers to join the Sun in a cooperative venture to cover the Mexican-American War. The four New York papers that joined in the agreement with the Sun were the Journal of Commerce, the Courier and Enquirer, the Herald, and the Express.

1849: The Harbor News Association opened the first news bureau outside the United States, in Halifax, Nova Scotia, to meet ships sailing from Europe before they reached dock in New York.

1861: Facing censorship in covering the American Civil War, reporters first filed under the anonymous byline "from the Associated Press agent."

1876: Mark Kellogg, a stringer, is the first AP news correspondent to be killed while reporting the news, at the Battle of the Little Bighorn. His final dispatch:

"I go with (Commander George Armstrong) Custer and will be at the death."

1893: Melville E. Stone becomes the general manager of the reorganized AP, a post he holds until 1921. Under his leadership, the AP grows to be one of the world's most prominent news agencies.

1899: AP uses Guglielmo Marconi's wireless telegraph to cover the America's Cup yacht race off Sandy Hook, New Jersey, the first news test of the new technology.

1914: AP introduces the Teletype, which transmitted directly to printers over telegraph wires. Eventually a worldwide network of 60-word-per-minute Teletype machines is built.

1919: Upton Sinclair includes a scathing criticism of the AP in his investigative book on contemporary journalism, *The Brass Check*.

1935: AP initiates WirePhoto, the world's first wire service for photographs. The first photograph to transfer over the network depicted an airplane crash in Morehouseville, New York, on New Year's Day, 1935.

1938: AP expands to new offices at 50 Rockefeller Plaza (known as "50 Rock") in the newly built Rockefeller Center in New York City, which would remain its headquarters for 68 years; in 2004 it relocated to larger facilities at 450 W. 33rd St. in Manhattan.

1941: AP expands from print to radio broadcast news.

1945: AP Paris bureau chief Edward Kennedy defies an Allied headquarters news blackout to report Nazi Germany's surrender, touching off a bitter episode that leads to his eventual dismissal by the AP. Kennedy maintains that he reported only what German radio already had broadcast.

1994: AP launches APTV, a global video newsgathering agency, headquartered in London.

2004: The AP moves its headquarters from 50 Rock to W. 33rd St.

2008: Associated Press President and CEO Tom Curley states that "shadow of the September 11 terror attacks is eclipsing press freedom and other constitutional safeguards in the United States."

AP Sports Polls

The AP is known for its Associated Press polls on numerous college sports in the United States. The AP polls ranking the top 25 NCAA Division I (Football Bowl Subdivision and Football Championship Subdivision) college football and NCAA Division I men's and women's college basketball teams are the most well known. The AP composes the polls by collecting and compiling the top-25 votes of numerous designated sports journalists. The AP poll of college football was particularly notable for many years because it helped determine the ranking of teams at the end of the regular season for the collegiate Bowl Championship Series until the AP, citing conflict of interest, asked for the poll to be removed from the bowl series. Beginning in the 2005 season, the Harris Interactive College Football Poll took the AP's place in the bowl series formula. The AP poll is the longest serving national poll in college football, having begun in 1936.

Each year on 31 March the AP announces the winner of the NCAA Men's basketball "player of the year" (POY) award.

Associated Press Television News

In 1994, London-based Associated Press Television (APTV) was founded to provide agency news material to television broadcasters. Other existing providers of such material at the time were Reuters Television and Worldwide Television News (WTN). In 1998, APTV left the Associated Press building in the Central London and merged with WTN to create Associated Press Television News (APTN) in the existing WTN building in North London.

Cancellations

2008 has seen an increase in the number of two-year notices of intent to cancel services. News organizations cited its cost, its commoditization in an era of free online news, and a renewed emphasis on original content to remain relevant in such an environment. Among the organizations cancelling are larger outlets like Dow Jones, New York Daily News, and Star Tribune of Minneapolis, as well as smaller-market publications such as The Spokesman-Review of Spokane, Wash and The

Bakersfield Californian. In addition, eight Ohio newspapers have created their own local network, the Ohio News Organization, including The Plain Dealer of Cleveland, The Columbus Dispatch and The Cincinnati Enquirer. While OHNO allows these newspapers to share local stories without submitting them to the AP, all remain Associated Press members.

Controversies

Jamil Hussein

Some questions were raised about the legitimacy of police captain Jamil Hussein as a source for AP reporting of sectarian violence in Iraq. On January 4, 2007 the Iraqi Interior Ministry recognized Jamil as an active member of the Baghdad police force, and said he faces arrest for talking to journalists. Ministry spokesman Abdul Karim Khalaf, who had previously denied the existence of Hussein, acknowledged that the officer was assigned to the Khadra police station.

Christopher Newton

The Associated Press fired Washington, D.C. bureau reporter Christopher Newton in September 2002, accusing him of fabricating at least 40 people and organizations since 2000. Some of the non-existent agencies quoted in his stories included "Education Alliance," the "Institute for Crime and Punishment in Chicago," "Voice for the Disabled," and "People for Civil Rights."

Tuvia Grossman

During the Second Intifada a caption of an Associated Press photograph of an Israeli police officer defending him from a violent Palestinian mob misidentified him as a Palestinian instead of as a Jewish-American. The photograph, publicized in *The New York Times, The Wall Street Journal,* and other newspaper publications worldwide, suggested Israeli brutality by the officer acting in Tuvia's defense.

Bloggers and Fair Use

In June 2008 Associated Press stated it would be defining

guidelines on how many words from its articles and broadcasts could be excerpted by internet bloggers and Web sites without infringing on its copyright. Its first initiative was a letter to Rogers Cadenhead's "Drudge Retort" news links site requesting the removal of items quoting from 39 to 79 words of AP articles. After an outcry from bloggers, AP admitted its letter to Drudge Retort was "heavy-handed." It later clarified that it would challenge blog postings "when we feel the use is more reproduction than reference, or when others are encouraged to cut and paste." It then retreated from that position, announcing it would be reviewing its standards.

Ron Fournier

In 2004, Ron Fournier, a reporter with the AP's Washington bureau, left the AP to take a Harvard Institute of Politics fellowship. During this period, he also cowrote the book *Applebee's America* with Matthew Dowd, a Republican strategist, and Doug Sosnik, a Democratic strategist. In 2006, he took a position as editor-in-chief of a new Internet website called Hotsoup.com, which aimed to foster discussion on a number of topics including politics. The site failed to catch on, however, and Fournier returned to the AP in March 2007 as its Online Political Editor, after considering "a senior advisory role" with John McCain's presidential campaign.

In May 2008, Fournier was named the acting Washington bureau chief, replacing his "mentor" Sandy Johnson. Since taking over the position, Fournier has led a dramatic shift in the AP's policy, moving it away from the neutral and objective tone it had become known for and toward a more opinionated style that would make judgements when conflicting opinions were presented in a story. On August 23, 2008, following US Senator and presumptive Democratic presidential nominee Barack Obama's announcement of his selection of Senator Joe Biden as a running mate, Fournier wrote a widely circulated piece entitled "Analysis: Biden pick shows lack of confidence." A *Washington Monthly* columnist described the piece as "mirror[ing] the Republican line with minimal variation." *Editor and Publisher* noted that Fournier's article "gained wide linkage at the Drudge Report, Hot Air and numerous other conservative sites...."

Coverage of the 2008 Democratic National Convention

Several media outlets, including *Editor and Publisher* magazine, MSNBC commentator Keith Olbermann, and the blog Gawker, raised issue with AP reporter Charles Babington's analysis "Obama spares details, keeps up attacks." According to *Editor and Publisher*, Babington's article, which was critical of the speech's supposed lack of substance, was transmitted alongside a second AP piece that "offered a detailed look at seven specific policy proposals in the speech (and expressed doubts about all of them)." Recently, Mr. Babbington has been more critical of the McCain campaign, writing an article on September 11th questioning the accuracy of his recent ads.

Governance

The Associated Press is governed by an elected board of directors:

- William Dean Singleton, Chairman and CEO, MediaNews Group, Denver, Colorado;
- Tom Curley, President and CEO;
- R. Jack Fishman, Publisher and Managing editor, Citizen Tribune, Morristown, Tennessee;
- Dennis J. FitzSimons, Chairman President and CEO, Tribune Company, Chicago, Illinois;
- Walter E. Hussman Jr., Publisher, Arkansas Democrat-Gazette, Little Rock, Arkansas;
- Julie Inskeep, Publisher, Fort Wayne Journal Gazette, Fort Wayne, Indiana;
- Boisfeuillet (Bo) Jones, Publisher and CEO, The Washington Post, Washington, D.C.;
- Mary Junck, President and CEO, Lee Enterprises, Davenport, Iowa;
- David Lord, President, Pioneer Newspapers, Seattle, Washington;
- Kenneth W. Lowe, President and CEO, E.W. Scripps Company, Cincinnati, Ohio;
- Douglas H. McCorkindale, Chairman, Gannett, McLean, Virginia;
- R. John Mitchell, Publisher, Rutland Herald, Rutland, Vermont;

- Steven O. Newhouse, Chairman, Advance.Net, New York, New York;
- Gary Pruitt, Chairman, President and CEO, The McClatchy Company, Sacramento, California;
- Michael E. Reed, CEO, Liberty Group Publishing, Inc., Downer's Grove, Illinois;
- Bruce T. Reese, President and CEO, Bonneville International, Salt Lake City, Utah;
- Jon Rust, Publisher, Southeast Missourian, Cape Girardeau, Missouri;
- Jay R. Smith, President, Cox Newspapers, Atlanta, Georgia;
- David Westin, President, ABC News, New York, New York; and
- H. Graham Woodlief, President, Publishing Division, Media General, Richmond, Virginia.

Web Resource

The AP's multi-topic structure has lent itself well to web portals, such as Yahoo, msn.com, etc. which all have news pages which constantly need to be updated. Often, such portals will rely on AP and other news services as their first source for news coverage of breaking news items. Yahoo's "Top News" page gives the AP top visibility out of any news outlet. This has been of major impact to the AP's public image and role, as it gives new credence to the AP's continual mission of having staff for covering every area of news fully and promptly. The AP is also the news service used on the Nintendo Wii's News Channel. In 2007 Google announced it was paying for Associated Press content displayed in Google News.

BLOOMBERG L.P.

Bloomberg L.P. is a financial software services, news and data company. It holds 33 per cent of international market share and is approximately the same size as Thomson Reuters, formed from the merger of its competitors Thomson Financial and Reuters into Thomson Reuters on 17 April 2008. Bloomberg L.P. was founded by Michael Bloomberg (current Mayor of New York City) with the help of Thomas Secunda and other partners (Bloomberg's former coworkers from Salomon Brothers) in 1981 with the help a 20 per cent ownership investment by Merrill Lynch. The company provides financial software tools such as analytics and equity trading platform, data services and news to financial companies and organizations around the world through the Bloomberg Terminal, its core money-generating product. Bloomberg L.P. has grown to include a global news service, including television, radio, the Internet and publications.

Bloomberg L.P.	
Type	Limited Partnership
Founded	1981
Headquarters	New York City, United States
Key people	Michael Bloomberg, Founder Peter Grauer, Chairman Dan Doctoroff, President Thomas Secunda, CTO Matthew Winkler, Editor-in-Chief, News
Industry	Financial Services
Revenue	US$4.7 billion (2006)
Employees	10,000 (February 2008, Bloomberg.com)
Website	http://www.bloomberg.com

Its current headquarters are located at the Bloomberg Tower, 731 Lexington Avenue in Midtown Manhattan, New York City. It was incorporated as a Delaware Limited Partnership (LP) in 1981 and has been in business since 1983. Michael Bloomberg owns 92 per cent of the group. Bloomberg's core business is leasing terminals to subscribers. It also runs Bloomberg Television, a financial TV station, and a business radio station WBBR in New York City. Forbes Magazine estimated, in 2000, Bloomberg's cash flow margins on its $2.3 billion in revenues exceed 35 per cent. Bloomberg reports more than 100,000 users in North America, and another 130,000 in the rest of the world. Its competitors include Thomson Reuters, Dow Jones Newswires, FACTSET and smaller companies such as New York Financial Press. In July 2008, Merrill Lynch agreed to sell its 20 per cent stake in the firm back to Bloomberg, for a reported $4.43 billion, valuing the firm at approximately $22.5 billion.

History, Services and Products

In 1981, Michael Bloomberg was fired from Salomon Brothers, where he was a general partner and given a $10 million severance package. Using this money, Bloomberg went on to set up a company named Innovative Market Systems. In 1982, Merrill Lynch became the new company's first customer, installing 20 Market Master terminals and investing $30 million in the company. In 1986, the company was renamed Bloomberg L.P. and by 1987, 5000 terminals had been installed. Within a few years, ancillary products including Bloomberg Tradebook (a trading platform), the Bloomberg Messaging Service, and the Bloomberg newswire were launched.

Bloomberg prospered during the boom of the 1980s and 1990s. It expanded internationally, opening offices in Europe, Asia, Latin America and Australia. In addition to its financial services offerings, Bloomberg launched its news services division in 1990. Bloomberg News (originally known as Bloomberg Business News) has some 2,000 staff in 125 bureaus around the world and is available on the web at www.bloomberg.com. It now provides information to approximately 350 newspapers and magazines worldwide, including *The Economist, The New York Times* and USA Today. In order to run for the position of Mayor of New York which he won against Democrat Mark Green in 2001, Mike Bloomberg gave up his position of CEO at Bloomberg and appointed Lex Fenwick as CEO in his stead.

Corporate Governance

As of March 2001, members of the board of directors of Bloomberg include: Peter Grauer, Arthur Levitt, Jane Bryant Quinn, Frank Savage, and Thomas Secunda.

Criticism

The Bloomberg Professional service is priced around $1800 per terminal per month (excluding exchange fees for live data) for the first terminal sold. Bloomberg has also pushed the introduction of Bloomberg Anywhere, a biometrically authenticated web-access system for Bloomberg Professional. This has forced firms to provide full Bloomberg subscriptions for users who would otherwise have been able to share terminals. The Bloomberg Messaging system has become the standard means of written communication in certain markets and the loss of the messaging service and the associated client contact is a significant switching barrier for anybody wishing to use a competing product, thus forcing many market participants to pay for a full Bloomberg subscription just to use the messaging service. The product is noticeably Americocentric. In particular, it is impossible to customize the date format.

DEUTSCHE PRESSE-AGENTUR

Deutsche Presse-Agentur GmbH (dpa) (German Press Agency) is a news agency founded in 1949 in Germany. Based in Hamburg, it has grown to be a major worldwide operation serving print media, radio, television, online, mobile phones, and national news agencies. News are available in German, English, Spanish, and Arabic. *Deutsche Presse-Agentur GmbH (dpa)* is the biggest Press Agency in Germany.

EUROPEAN PRESSPHOTO AGENCY

European Pressphoto Agency (epa) is one of the leading news photo agencies in the world. Established in 1985 by seven major Western European photo agencies the vision of the company was initially driven by a demand for an independent high quality world picture service to meet the needs of Europe's leading news agencies. In 2003, epa established a global network of bureaus to meet the needs of the growing world wide image market. Since establishing its global network the company has developed a reputation for its reliability, independence, flexibility and unconventional angle on news coverage.

For the first eighteen years epa built up a high reputation for its unique European photo coverage. Since 2003, when epa launched its global photo service, its strength has also been to cover global events from a perspective different from other picture agencies.

With global headquarters in Frankfurt, Germany the epa service today provides an average of 900 pictures per day to media clients around the world and a stock photo service of 1,500,000 images. The companies award winning picture service is provided by a broad network of epa staff photographers around the world and the daily production of its member agencies, which are all market leaders in their respective countries. The company is represented by Corbis in the United States, by Jiji Press in Japan and Yonhap in Korea.

Member Agencies

- ANA in Greece (http://www.ana.gr)
- ANP in the Netherlands (http://www.anp.nl)
- ANSA in Italy (http://www.ansa.it)
- APA in Austria (http://www.apa.at)
- BELGA in Belgium (http://www.belga.be)
- DPA in Germany (http://www.dpa.com)
- EFE in Spain (http://www.efe.es)
- KEYSTONE in Switzerland (http://www.keystone.ch)
- LUSA in Portugal (http://www.lusa.pt)
- MTI in Hungary (http://www.mti.hu)
- PAP in Poland (http://www.pap.pl)

INFORMATION TELEGRAPH AGENCY OF RUSSIA

The Information Telegraph Agency of Russia (Russian: *Informatsion-noye telegrafnoye agentstvo Rossii*), abbr. Итар-Тасс, *Itar-Tass* is the major news agency of Russia. It is headquartered in Moscow.

History

Its origin is in a letter sent by Finance Minister Vladimir Kokovtsov to foreign minister in March 1904 writing that "our trade and industrial circles, as well as the Finance Ministry, are ever more in need of an independent exchange of information with foreign countries by telegraph and of a way to make internal business developments widely-known."

In July 1904 a meeting was held about setting up an official telegraph agency, *St. Petersburg Telegraph Agency* (SPTA). Its purpose was "to distribute political, financial, economic, trade, and other information of public interest within the country and abroad..." SPTA began work as Russia's official news agency on September 1, 1904.

On August, 1914, one day after St. Petersburg was renamed Petrograd, SPTA was renamed the *Petrograd Telegraph Agency* (PTA). It was seized by Bolsheviks on November, 1917; on December, PTA is decreed to be the central information agency of the Soviet Russian Council of People's Commissars.'

On September, 1918, PTA and the Press Bureau of Council of People's Commissars' were merged into the Russian Telegraph Agency (Rosta). From it in July 1925 the Telegraph Agency of the Soviet Union (Russian: *Telegrafnoye Agentstvo Sovetskogo Soyuza*, abbr. Tass) was created by decree of the Soviet Union's Supreme Soviet.

Post-Soviet Period

In January 1992, following the dissolution of the Soviet Union, a Presidential Decree signed by President Boris Yeltsin re-defined status of Tass and changed its name to the *Information Telegraph Agency of Russia*. In May 1994 The Russian Government adopted a resolution *"On approval of the Charter of the Information Telegraph Agency of Russia"*, under which it operates as a central government news agency. It was wanted that the known Tass remains in the name abbreviation, so Tass became the specifier of the official name, Russian: *i.e.* the *Telegraph Agency of Communications and Report*.

It is state-owned and according to its website now produces about 700 newspaper pages per day. It has 74 bureaus and offices in Russia and other countries of the Commonwealth of Independent States and 65 bureaus in 62 other countries.

Legal Information

According to Russian law, Itar-Tass must be cited when its news reports are distributed by others.

INTERFAX

Interfax is a Russian non-governmental news agency based in Moscow. It was established in 1989. It employs around 1,500 journalists based in emerging markets. The organization concentrates on news concerning Europe and Asia and it has offices in London, New York, Frankfurt, Hong Kong, Shanghai, Beijing, Denver, Moscow, Warsaw, Budapest, Prague, Kiev, Minsk and Alma Ata.

Interfax Group at a Glance

Working for Decision-Makers

Interfax Information Services Group provides news and other information products that are essential for decision-makers in politics and business. Since early 1990s, Interfax has been the main provider of up-to-date news from Russia and countries of the former Soviet Union. This group has the most frequently quoted source of information on the region. Over the past few years, Interfax has also become a leading provider of political and business news from China and emerging markets of Central Europe. A network of about 30 companies operates all over Russia, the CIS, China and several Central European countries.

The Group publishes news in Russian, English, Ukrainian, Kazakh, and German and provides about 100 specialized services. Apart of news this group offers a number of unique information products based on the state-of-the-art technologies. Among them SPARK, the System for Professional Analysis of Markets and Companies, Russia's largest and most comprehensive database on companies.

Interfax Group produces company news, industry analysis and ratings, cooperating in this field with largest brands of the information industry. For example Moody's Investors Service is its partner in Moody's Interfax Rating Agency, which provides indispensable information for banks and investors reaching out to Russia's markets. At the end of 2004, the Group set up the Experian-Interfax credit bureau, which is a joint venture with the global leading information solutions company Experian. Interfax news is available through the information systems of Reuters and Bloomberg.

Interfax has thousands of clients throughout the world, including leading Russian and foreign media groups, state and government organizations, major banks, corporations, investment companies and funds.

KYODO NEWS

Kyodo News (*Kyōdō Tsūshinsha*) is a nonprofit cooperative news agency based in Minato, Tokyo. It was established in 1945 and it distributes news to almost all newspapers, and radio and television networks in Japan. The newspapers using its news have about 50 million subscribers. The subdivision Kyodo News International founded in 1982 is located in Rockefeller Center, New York. Their online news site is in Japanese, Chinese (Simplified and Traditional), and English. Satoshi Ishikawa is the news agency's president.

MAGYAR TÁVIRATI IRODA

MTI is a Hungarian news wire agency. MTI—Hungarian News Agency Corp. has now been in existence for over 125 years.

RIA NOVOSTI

RIA (Russian Information Agency) Novosti is a Russian press agency based in Moscow. The agency's clients include the presidential administration, Russian government, Federation Council, State Duma, leading ministries and government departments, administrations of Russian regions, representatives of Russian and foreign business communities, diplomatic missions, and public organizations.

History

RIA Novosti's history dates back to June 24, 1941, when by a resolution of the USSR Council of People's Commissars and the Communist Party Central Committee, "*On the Establishment and Tasks of the Soviet Information Bureau*", the Soviet Information Bureau (Sovinformburo) was set up under the USSR Council of People's Commissars and the Central Committee. Its main task was to oversee work to cover international, military events and the events of the country's domestic life in periodicals and on the radio (from October 14, 1941, to March 3, 1942, was based in Kuibyshev—modern-day Samara).

The bureau's main task was to compile reports on the situation on the frontline of the war, work on the home front, and the partisan movement for the radio, newspapers and magazines. Sovinformburo directed the activity of the All-Slavonic Committee, Anti-Nazi Committee of Soviet Women, Anti-Nazi Committee of the Soviet Youth, Anti-Nazi Committee of Soviet Scientists, and the Jewish Anti-Nazi Committee. In 1944, a special bureau on propaganda for foreign countries was set up as part of Sovinformburo.

Through 1,171 newspapers, 523 magazines and 18 radio stations in 23 countries, Soviet embassies abroad, friendship societies, trade unions, women's, youth and scientific organizations, Sovinformburo informed readers and listeners about the struggle of the Soviet people against Nazism and in the post-war years about the main areas of Soviet domestic and foreign policies. Sovinformburo heads: A.S. Shcherbakov (from 1941 to 1945), S.A. Lozovsky (from 1945 to 1948), Y.S. Khavinson, D.A. Polikarpov. In 1961, the Novosti Press Agency (APN) succeeded Sovinformburo. It became the leading information and press body of Soviet public organizations. The constituent conference was held on February 21, 1961. The conference of representatives of Soviet public organizations adopted a decision to create a press agency of public organizations named Novosti. The agency's guiding body was the Council of the Agency's Founders.

The APN founders were the USSR Journalists Union, USSR Writers Union, Union of Soviet Societies of Friendship and Cultural Relations with Foreign Countries, and the Znaniye Society. On April 3, 1961, the Agency charter was adopted. Under its charter, APN's aim was "to contribute to mutual understanding, trust and friendship among peoples in every possible way by broadly publishing accurate information about the USSR abroad and familiarizing the Soviet public with the life of the peoples of foreign countries." APN's motto was "Information for Peace, for the Friendship of Nations". APN had bureaus in over 120 countries. The Agency published 60 illustrated newspapers and magazines in 45 languages with a one-time circulation of 4.3 million copies. With the Union of Soviet Friendship Societies, APN published the newspaper, *Moscow News,* which in September 1990 became an independent publication. APN Publishing House put out over 200 books and booklets with a total annual circulation of 20 million copies. In 1989, a TV centre opened in APN. Later, it was transformed into the TV-Novosti TV company.

APN heads: Boris Burkov (1961-70), Ivan Udaltsov (1970-75), Lev Tolkunov (1975-83), Pavel Naumov (1983-86), Valentin Falin (1986-88), Albert Vlasov (1988-90).

By a decree of USSR President Mikhail Gorbachev, "On the Establishment of the Information Agency Novosti," the Information Agency Novosti (IAN) succeeded APN on July 27, 1990. "To provide information support for the USSR's state domestic and foreign policies and proceeding from the interests of the democratization of the mass media," the Novosti Press Agency was renamed the Information Agency Novosti (IAN). IAN's tasks remained the same—preparing and publishing printed, TV and radio materials in the USSR and abroad; studying public opinion on Soviet foreign and domestic policies in the USSR and abroad." A computer databank was created in the Agency. Initially, it contained over 250,000 documents. In 1991, the Infonews hotline started operating in the Agency. IAN had bureaus in 120 countries. It published 13 illustrated magazines and newspapers. The chairman of the IAN Board was Albert Ivanovich Vlasov.

Russian Federation

The Russian Information Agency Novosti was created in September 1991 on the basis of IAN and the Russian Information Agency. By a decree of the Russian president dated August 22, 1991, RIA Novosti was placed within the competence of the Press and Information Ministry. RIA Novosti had about 80 bureaus and news offices abroad, over 1,500 subscribers in CIS countries and about a hundred in non-CIS countries. In 1993, by a decree of the Russian president of September 15, 1993 *"On the Russian Information Agency Novosti"*, RIA Novosti became a state news-analytical agency. RIA Novosti's radio channel—RIA-Radio worked in 1996. In August 1997, the TV channel Kultura was set up on the basis of the RIA TV channel under the sponsorship of the VGTRK TV and radio broadcasting company. By a decree of the Russian president, "On Improving the Work of the State Electronic Media," the VGTRK information holding was created in May 1998, which RIA Novosti joined.

In May 1998, the Agency was renamed the Russian Information Agency Vesti. As a mass media body, it retained the name of RIA Novosti. The main criteria of RIA Novosti's information services were the combination of promptness, objectiveness, authenticity and its own opinion regardless of the political situation.

REUTERS

Reuters Group Limited is a British based news service and former financial market data provider that provides reports from around the world to newspapers and broadcasters. News reporting once accounted for less than 10 per cent of the company's income. Its main focus was on supplying the financial markets with information and trading products. These included market data, such as share prices and currency rates, research and analytics, as well as trading systems that allowed dealers to buy and sell such assets as currencies and shares on a computer screen instead of by telephone or on a trading floor like that of the New York Stock Exchange. Among other services, the most notable was analysis of 40,000 companies, debt instruments, and 3 million economic series. Competitors included Bloomberg L.P. and Dow Jones Newswires.

Reuters Group Limited

REUTERS

Type	Subsidiary
Founded	October 1851
Headquarters	London, England, UK
Industry	News Agency, Financial
Revenue	£2,605 m (2007)
Operating income	£292 m (2007)
Net income	£213 m (2007)
Parent	Thomson Reuters
Website	www.reuters.com

History

Paul Julius Reuter noticed that, with the electric telegraph, news no longer required days or weeks to travel long distances. In 1850, the 34-year-old Reuter was based in Aachen, Germany, close to the Netherlands' and Belgian borders, and he began using the newly opened Berlin–Aachen telegraph line to send news to Berlin. However, there was a 76-mile (122 km) gap in the line between Aachen and Brussels, the Belgian capital city and the financial centre of that country. Reuter saw there was an opportunity to speed up news service between Brussels and Berlin by using homing pigeons to bridge that gap in the telegraph lines.

In 1851, Reuter moved to London, England. After failures in 1847 and 1850, attempts by the Submarine Telegraph Company to lay an undersea telegraph cable from Dover to Calais appeared to promise success. Reuter set up his "Submarine Telegraph" office in October 1851 just before the opening of that undersea cable in November, and he negotiated a contract with the London Stock Exchange to provide stock prices from the continental exchanges in return for access to the London prices, which he then supplied to stockbrokers in Paris, France.

In 1865, Reuter's private firm was restructured, and it became a limited company (a corporation) called the Reuter's Telegram Company. Reuter had been naturalized as a British citizen in 1857. Reuter's agency built a reputation in Europe for being the first to report news scoops from abroad, like the news of Abraham Lincoln's assassination. After many decades of progress, almost every major news outlet in the world subscribes to the Reuters company's services. It operates in at least 200 cities in 94 countries, supplying news text in about 20 languages. Reuters was financed as a public company in 1984 on the London Stock Exchange and on the NASDAQ in the USA. However, there were concerns that the company's tradition for objective reporting might be jeopardized if control of the company later fell into the hands of a single shareholder. To counter that possibility, the constitution of the company at the time of the stock offering included a rule that no individual was allowed to own more than 15 per cent of the company. If this limit is exceeded, the directors can order the shareholder to reduce the holding to less than 15 per cent. That rule was applied in the late 1980s when Rupert Murdoch's News

Corporation, which already held around 15 per cent of Reuters, bought an Australian news company that also owned stock in Reuters. The acquisition meant that Murdoch then held more than 15 per cent, and then he was compelled to reduce the holding to less than 15 per cent to stay in line with the rules.

At the same time, as a further measure to protect the independence of Reuters news reporting, The Reuters Founders Share Company was set up. This is a company whose sole task is to protect the integrity of the company's news output. It holds one "Founders Share" which can outvote all other shares in the event that an attempt is made to alter any of the rules relating to the Reuters Trust Principles. These principles set out the company's aim to preserve its independence, integrity, and freedom from bias in its news reporting.

Reuters began to grow rapidly in the 1980s, widening the range of its business products and expanding its global reporting network for media, financial, and economic services. Recent key product launches include Equities 2000 (1987), Dealing 2000-02 (1992), Business Briefing (1994), Reuters Television for the financial markets (1994), 3000 Series (1996) and the Reuters 3000 Xtra service (1999).

In the mid-1990s, the Reuters company engaged in a brief foray in the radio sector—with London Radio's two radio stations, London News 97.3 FM and London News Talk 1152 AM. A Reuters Radio News service was also set up to compete with the Independent Radio News. In 1995, Reuters established its "Greenhouse Fund" to take minority investments in a range of start-up technology companies, initially in the USA, only.

On 15 May 2007, The Thomson Corporation reached an agreement with Reuters to combine the two companies, in a deal valued at US $17.2 billion. Thomsons now controls about 53 per cent of the new company, named *Thomson Reuters*. The new chief of Thomson Reuters is Tom Glocer, the former head of Reuters. The earlier rule of 15 per cent ownership (see above) was waived; the reason as given by Pehr Gyllenhammar, the chairman of the Reuters Founders Share Company, was "The future of Reuters takes precedence over the principles. If Reuters were not strong enough to continue on its own, the principles would have no meaning" citing the recent bad financial performance of the company. On 26 March 2008, shareholders of both organizations agreed the merger. The acquisition was closed on 17 April 2008.

In October 2007, Reuters Market Light, a division of Reuters, launched a mobile phone service for Indian farmers to provide local and customized commodity pricing information, news, and weather updates.

Journalists

Reuters has a team of several thousand journalists who over the years have covered major news events, sometimes at the cost of their lives. In May 2000, Kurt Schork, an American reporter, was killed in an ambush while on assignment in Sierra Leone. In April and August 2003, news cameramen Taras Protsyuk and Mazen Dana were both killed in two separate incidents by US troops in Iraq. During 2004, cameramen Adlan Khasanov in Chechnya and Dhia Najim in Iraq were also killed. In April 2008 Fadel Shana, a cameraman, was killed in the Gaza Strip after he was hit by an Israeli tank using controversial weapons known as flechettes.

The first Reuters journalist to be taken hostage in action was Anthony Grey. Detained while covering the Cultural Revolution in Peking in the late 1960s, said to be in response to the jailing of several Chinese terrorists by the colonial British Government in Hong Kong. He was considered to be the first political hostage of the modern age and was eventually released after almost two years solitary confinement. Awarded an OBE by the British Government in recognition of this, he went on to become a best selling author. In recent years Reuters news service was subject to severe budget cuts.

Fatalities

Name	*Nationality*	*Event Location*	*Event Date*
Kurt Schork	American	Sierra Leone	2000-05-24
Taras Protsyuk	Ukrainian	Iraq	2003-04-08
Mazen Dana	Palestinian	Iraq	2003-08-17
Adlan Khasanov	Chechen	Chechnya	2004-05-09
Dhia Najim	Iraqi	Iraq	2004-11-01
Waleed Khaled	Iraqi	Iraq	2005-08-28
Namir Noor-Eldeen	Iraqi	Iraq	2007-07-12
Saeed Chmagh	Iraqi	Iraq	2007-07-12
Fadel Shana	Palestinian	Gaza Strip	2008-04-16

Investments

Notable investments include:

- *Action Images*—On September 19, 2005, Reuters purchased North London-based Action Images, a deep collection of sports photography that includes more than 8 million images of which 1.7 million are online.
- *Application Networks*—In June 2006, Reuters acquired Application Networks, Inc., a provider of trade and risk management software based on JRisk, and agrees to acquire Feri Fund Market Information Ltd (FERI FMI) and its fund database subsidiary, FI Datenservice GmbH (FID).
- *AVT Technologies*—In December 2002, Reuters announced that it would acquire AVT Technologies, a specialist in foreign exchange transaction technology. Concurrent with the deal, Reuters established an Automated Dealing Technologies business unit, headed up by Mark Redwood, CEO of AVT Technologies.
- *Bridge Information Systems*—On September 28, 2001, it completed the largest acquisition in its history acquired certain businesses and assets of Bridge Information Systems Inc. Also during the year, the Group acquired 100 per cent of Diagram fip SA and 92 per cent of ProTrader Group LP. In October 2001, the Group disposed of its majority stake in VentureOne Corp.
- *Clearforest*—In June 2007, Reuters acquired Clearforest, a provider of Text Analytics solutions, whose tagging platform and analytical products allow clients to derive business information from textual content.
- *EcoWin*—In November 2005, Reuters acquired EcoWin, a Gothenburg (Sweden) based provider of global fianancial, equities, and economic data.
- *Factiva*—In May 1999, Reuters entered a joint venture with long-time rival, Dow Jones & Company, to form Factiva , a business news and information provider. In December 2006, Reuters sold its 50 per cent share in Factiva to Dow Jones, who is now the sole owner.

- *Instinet*—In May 2001, Instinet completed an IPO on NASDAQ; Reuters sold its majority stake in Instinet to The Nasdaq Stock Market in 2005.
- *Multex.com Inc.*—In March 2003, Reuters acquired Multex.com, Inc., a provider of global financial information.
- *TIBCO Software*—In July 1999, TIBCO Software completed an IPO on NASDAQ; Reuters retains a substantial proportion of the shares. Reuters announced in early 2000 a range of major initiatives designed to accelerate its use of internet technologies, open new markets and migrate its core business to an internet-based model.

Main Corporate Locations

From 1939, the Reuters corporate headquarters was in London's famous Fleet Street in a building designed for it by Sir Edwin Lutyens, but in 2005 Reuters moved to a larger building in the more modern Canary Wharf. The Reuters Building at 30 South Colonnade is near the One Canada Square tower, Jubilee Park and Canary Wharf tube station. The open space below the Reuters building has since been renamed Reuters Plaza. The company's North American headquarters is the Reuters Building at 3 Times Square, New York. It is on 7th Avenue between 42nd and 43rd Streets, and was constructed from 1998 to 2001.

Critique

Reuters has a strict policy towards upholding objectiveness and this policy has caused many to comment on the possible insensitivity of its reports covering major global events including: September 11, 2001, attacks. Reuters global news editor Stephen Jukes wrote, "We all know that one man's terrorist is another man's freedom fighter, and that Reuters upholds the principle that we do not use the word terrorist." *The Washington Post* media critic Howard Kurtz responded, "After the 1995 Oklahoma City bombing, and again after the attacks on the World Trade Center and Pentagon, Reuters allowed the events to be described as acts of terror. But as of last week, even that terminology is banned." Reuters later apologized for this characterization of their policy, although they maintained the policy itself.

The September 20, 2004, edition of the *The New York Times* reported that the Reuters Global Managing Editor, David A. Schlesinger, objected to Canadian newspapers' editing of Reuters articles through inclusion of the word "terrorist," stating that "my goal is to protect our reporters and protect our editorial integrity."

Due to this policy, Reuters was careful to only use the word "terrorist" in quotes, whether quotations or scare quotes. However, when reporting the 7 July 2005 London bombings, the service reported, "Police said they suspected terrorists were behind the bombings." The contrast between this and their aforementioned policy was criticized, although by that point Reuters policy was to use such words "when we are quoting someone directly or in indirect speech," and this headline is an example of the latter. The news organization has subsequently used the term "terrorist" without quotations when the article clarifies that it is someone else's words.

Photographs Controversies

Reuters was accused of bias against Israel in its coverage of the 2006 Israel-Lebanon conflict, in which the company used two doctored photos by a Lebanese freelance photographer Adnan Hajj. On August 7, 2006, Reuters announced it severed all ties with Hajj and said his photographs would be removed from its database.

UNITED PRESS INTERNATIONAL

United Press International (UPI) is a news agency headquartered in the United States with roots dating back to 1907. Once a mainstay in the newswire service along with Associated Press (AP) and Reuters, the popularity of the televised evening news and the resulting decline in the afternoon newspapers began a period of decline for UPI. This decline accelerated after the sale of UPI by the founding Scripps family culminating in two bankruptcies. In 2000 UPI was purchased by News World Communications, a media company to anyone, including his competitors. He later said: "I regard my life's greatest service to the people of this country to be the creation of the United Press."

Creating UPI

Frank Bartholomew, UPI's last reporter-president, took over in 1955, obsessed with bringing Hearst's International News Service (INS) into UP. He put the "I" in UPI on May 24, 1958, when UP and INS merged to become *United Press International*. Hearst, who owned King Features Syndicate, received a small share of the merged company. Lawyers on both sides worried about anti-trust problems if King competitor United Features Syndicate remained a part of the newly merged company, so it was made a separate Scripps company, which deprived UPI of a persuasive sales tool and the money generated by Charles M. Schulz' popular *Peanuts* and other comic strips.

The new UPI had 6,000 employees and 5,000 subscribers, 1,000 of them newspapers. Later that year, it launched the UPI Audio Network, the first wire service radio network. In 1960, subsidiaries included UFS, United Press Movietone, a television film service, was operated jointly with 20th Century Fox, the British United Press and Ocean Press.

Decline

The Associated Press—AP—was a publishers' cooperative and could assess its members to help pay for extraordinary coverage of such events as wars, the Olympic Games, or national political conventions. UPI clients, in contrast, paid a fixed annual rate; depending on individual contracts, UPI could not always ask them to help shoulder the extraordinary coverage costs. Newspapers typically paid UPI about half what they paid AP in the same cities for the same services: At one point, for example, the *Chicago Sun-Times* paid AP $12,500 a week, but UPI only $5,000; the *Wall Street Journal* paid AP $36,000 a week, but UPI only $19,300.

UPI was hurt by changes in the modern news business, including the closing of many of America's afternoon newspapers, resulting in its customer base shrinking. It went through seven owners between 1992 and 2000. UPI's end as a owned by Sun Myung Moon's Unification Church. Tl wire's daily coverage today includes domestic and inter top news, business, entertainment, sports, science, hea "Quirks in the News" through its NewsTrack service, as coverage and analysis of emerging threats, the s industry and energy resources. UPI's content is prese text, video and photo formats. Its news stories are f English, Spanish and Arabic.

History

United Press Associations

Newspaper publisher E.W. Scripps (1854–1926) created th chain of newspapers in the United States. After the Asso Press refused to sell its services to several of his papers, S together with partner Milton A. McRae combined regional news services (the Publisher's Press Associa Scripps McRae Press Association, and the Scripps N Association) into the *United Press Associations*, which b service on June 21, 1907. Scripps founded United Press o principle that there should be no restrictions on who c buy news from a news service.

United Press became the only privately-owned major r service in the world at a time when the world news scene dominated by the Associated Press in the United States an the news agencies abroad, which were controlled directl indirectly by their respective governments: Reuters in Brit Havas in France, and Wolff in Germany. William Rando Hearst entered the fray in 1909 when he founded Internatio News Service.

The AP was owned by its newspaper members, who co simply decline to serve the competition. Scripps had refu to become a member of AP, calling it a "monopoly, pure a simple" and declaring it was "impossible for any new paper be started in any of the cities where there were AP member (AP appeared in 1848, when six New York City newspap formed a cooperative to gather and share telegraph news, b the name *Associated Press* did not come into general use un the 1860s.)

Scripps believed that there should be no restrictions on wh could buy news from a news service and he made UP availab truly viable news service occurred in 1999 when its remaining contracts were sold to its one-time rival—AP.

UPI Purchased by the Unification Church

UPI was purchased in 2000 by Sun Myung Moon's global media conglomerate News World Communications, becoming an addition to the Unification Church media portfolio. At the time Moon said:

> "We even have to utilize the media for the sake of church development. The church is the mind and the media is the body, to reach the external world. We should begin that movement and activity in the United States, because the Washington Times and UPI are headquartered there. Once we establish our organization in the United States, it can be expanded to the world without much alteration."

After 57 years with UPI, its best-known reporter Helen Thomas resigned her position as UPI's chief White House correspondent in May 2000, the day after it was acquired by News World. Since the resignation of Thomas, UPI for the first time, does not have a reporter in the White House press corps. In 2004, UPI won the Clapper Award from the Senate Press Gallery and the Fourth Estate Award for its investigative reporting on the dilapidated hospitals awaiting wounded U.S. soldiers returning from Iraq.

By 2007, UPI, which once had 6000 employees in 223 news and picture bureaus around the world, thousands of nonstaff "stringers," and 7,500 customers in 100 countries, had fewer than 50 employees. In August 2007, the company reduced that number further, and currently has only five reporters in its Washington D.C. headquarters. Several dozen stringers still file regular reports from key regions of the world. More than a dozen editors are stationed in various cities in the United States and elsewhere.

People of UPI

United Press editor Lucien Carr, whose roommate Jack Kerouac wrote *On the Road* on a continuous roll of UP teletype paper, once said: "UP's great virtue was that we were the little guy

[that] could screw the AP." News people who worked for UPI are nicknamed "Unipressers." Famous Unipressers from UPI's past include journalists and reporters Oscar Fraley, Walter Cronkite, David Brinkley, Howard K. Smith, Eric Sevareid, Helen Thomas, Pye Chamberlayne, Frank Bartholomew, Hugh Baillie, Vernon Scott, Chauncey Bailey, Robert H. Tanji (Tokyo journalist/editor murdered on the job), William L. Shirer (who is best remembered today for writing *The Rise and Fall of the Third Reich, The New York Times's* Thomas Friedman, *The Times* of London's Marie Colvin, and Myram Borders, longtime reporter and chief of the Las Vegas bureau for nearly 25 years (and who broke numerous stories, including Elvis Presley's marriage to Priscilla as the wedding was in progress).

UPI photographers saw their work published in hundreds of publications worldwide, including *Life, Look,* and other magazines, as well as newspapers in the United States. Under their work, the only credit line was "UPI". Not until after the 1970s, when their names began appearing under their pictures, did a number of UPI's photographers achieve celebrity within the journalism community. UPI photographers who won Pulitzer Prizes include Andrew Lopez (1960), Kyoichi Sawada (1966), Toshio Sakai (1968) and David Hume Kennerly (1972). Tom Gralish won a Pulitzer Prize and the Robert F. Kennedy Journalism Award in 1986 after leaving UPI for *The Philadelphia Inquirer*. Dirck Halstead founded "The Digital Journalist."

Books about UPI include Joe Alex Morris's *Deadline Every Minute* (1957), Gregory Gordon and Ronald E. Cohen's *Down To The Wire* (1990); Richard M. Hartnett and Billy G. Ferguson's *Unipress* (2003), and Gary Haynes's *Picture This: The Inside Story of UPI Newspictures* (2006) with a foreword by former Unipresser Walter Cronkite. Well-known photographers from UPI include Joe Marquette, Darryl Heikes, Carlos Shiebeck, David Hume Kennerly, Ernie Schwork, James Atherton, James Smestad, Tom Gralish, and Bill Snead.

Richard Harnett, who spent more than 30 years at UPI, recalls what is often considered its greatest achievement: Merriman Smith's Pulitzer Prize-winning coverage of John F. Kennedy's assassination. "Smith was in the press car...When he heard shots, he called in to the Dallas office and sent a flash bulletin," Harnett says. "The AP reporter started pounding on his shoulder to get to the phone, but Merriman kept it from him." (Quoted—Brill's Content, April 2001)

Nine staffers have won eight Pulitzer Prizes while working for UPI: Russell Jones (International Reporting, 1957), Andrew Lopez (News Photography, 1960), Yasushi Nagao (News Photography, 1961), Merriman Smith (National Reporting, 1964), Kyoichi Sawada (News Photography, 1966), Toshio Sakai (Feature Photography, 1968), Lucinda Franks and Thomas Powers (National Reporting, 1971), and David Kennerly (Feature Photography, 1972). Arnaud de Borchgrave, *Newsweek*'s chief foreign correspondent for 25 years, covering more than 90 countries and 17 wars, is currently UPI Editor-at-Large. He began his journalistic career at United Press in 1946. Martin Walker, editor of UPI's English edition, was a winner of Britain's "Reporter of the Year" award when he was Deputy Editor-in-Chief at *The Guardian*. UPI also employs columnists, whose articles are sent to international papers and agencies. Current UPI columnists include, amongst others:

- Marc S. Ellenbogen with "Atlantic Eye"
- William S. Lind with "Military Matters"
- Loren B. Thompson with "Thompson Files"
- Martin Walker with "Walkers World"

US employees of UPI are represented by the News Media Guild.

Milestones

- In 1908, UP pioneered the transmission of feature stories and use of reporter bylines.
- In 1914, Edward Kleinschmidt invented the teletype, which replaced Morse code clickers in delivering news to newspapers. Press critic Oswald Garrison Villard credits United Press with the first use of the teletype.
- In the 1920s and 1930s, United Press pioneered its financial wire service and organized the United Feature Syndicate.
- Founded in the 1930's was "Ocean Press", a news service for oceanliners, consisting of copy from United Press and later United Press International. This ship-

board publication was published by a separate corporate subsidiary of Scripps, but essentially under one roof with UP/UPI at the Daily News Building in New York. The subheadline under the "Ocean Press" logo was: "WORLDWIDE NEWS of UNITED PRESS... TRANSMITTED by RADIOMARINE CORPORATION OF AMERICA"... which appears to have been a subsidiary of RCA. Some mastheads were labelled "UNITED PRESS—RCA NEWS SERVICE."

- In 1935, UP was the first major news service to offer news to broadcasters.
- 1945 saw it launch the first all-sports wire.
- In 1948, UP Movietone, a newsfilm syndication service, was started with 20th Century Fox.
- In 1951, United Press offered the first teletypesetter (TTS) service, enabling newspapers to automatically set and justify type from wire transmissions.
- In 1952, United Press launched the first international television news film service.
- The 'UPI March', as written and performed by the Cities Service Band of America under the direction of Paul Lavalle, debuted at the Belasco Theater in New York on December 9, 1952. The UPI March was also played at the coronation of Queen Elizabeth II.
- In 1953, UPI had the first, fully automatic photo receiver, UNIFAX.
- In 1958, it launched the UPI Audio Network, the first wire service radio network.
- In 1974, it launched the first "high-speed" data newswire—operating at 1,200 WPM.
- On April 19, 1979, UPI announced an agreement with Telecomputing Corporation of America to make the UPI world news report available to owners of home computers. Later, UPI was the first news service to provide news to dial-up services and web search pioneers Yahoo! and Excite.
- In 1981, UPI launched the first satellite data transmissions by a news agency.
- In 1982, UPI pioneered an eight-level Custom Coding system that allows clients to choose stories based on

topic, subtopic and location. It developed one of the first news taxonomies.

- In 1982, UPI is sold by Scripps to Douglas Ruhe and William Geissler for $1.
- In 1984, UPI descended into the first of two Chapter 11 bankruptcies.
- In 1985, Mario Vazquez Raña purchases UPI out of bankruptcy.
- In 1988, UPI broke the "all or nothing" news service tradition by introducing component products.
- In 1988, Vazquez Raña sells UPI to Infotechnology Inc.
- In 1993, UPI closed its bureaus and dismissed nearly all of its longtime employees, leaving them without pensions and medical benefits.
- In 1998, UPI sold its broadcast operations to AP Radio, which shut it down and converted clients to its own service.
- In 2000, UPI was acquired by the Unification Church.
- In 2005, UPI launched a direct-to-consumer website.
- In 2007, UPI launched "Ed" (Editorial Workshop System), a content management system to handle rich media content and distribution, and re-launched its Website, www.upi.com.
- In 2008, UPI launched UPIU, a multimedia journalistic forum for U.S. college and university students.

XINHUA NEWS AGENCY

The Xinhua News Agency is the official press agency of the government of the People's Republic of China (PRC) and the biggest centre for collecting information and press conferences in the PRC. It is one of the two news agencies in the PRC, the other being the China News Service. Xinhua is an institution of the State Council of China. Xinhua reports directly to the Communist Party of China's Public Information Department.

Xinhua employs more than 10,000 people—as compared to about 1,300 for Routes; has 107 bureaus worldwide both collecting information on other countries and dispensing information about China; and maintains 31 bureaus in China—one for each province plus a military bureau. As most of the newspapers in China cannot afford to station correspondents abroad, or even in every Chinese province, they rely on Xinhua feeds to fill their pages. *People's Daily,* for example, uses Xinhua material for approximately 25 per cent of its stories. Xinhua is a publisher as well as a news agency—it owns more than 20 newspapers and a dozen magazines, and it prints in Chinese, English, Spanish, French, Russian, and Arabic.

Beijing has been cutting funding to the news agency by an average of seven per cent per year over the past three years, and state funds currently cover only about 40 per cent of Xinhua's costs. As a result, the agency is raising revenues through involvement in public relations, construction, and information service businesses.

In the past, Xinhua was able to attract the top young journalists emerging from the universities or otherwise newly entering the field, but it can no longer do so as easily because of the appeal and resources of other newspapers and periodicals and the greater glamour of television and radio jobs. For example, mid-level reporters for the Xinmin Evening News in Shanghai often are given an apartment, whereas at Xinhua and People's Daily this benefit is reserved for the most senior journalists.

History

The Xinhua press agency was started in November 1931 as the *Red China News Agency* and changed to its current name in 1937. It began broadcasting to foreign countries in English from 1944. The Xinhua headquarters is located in Beijing. The Xinhua News Agency established its first overseas affiliate in 1947 in London, with Samuel Chinque as publisher. Now it distributes its news in Asia, Middle East, Latin America, Africa where run the superior offices; in Hong Kong, Macau and many foreign countries and districts. There are more than one hundred Xinhua affiliates.

Today, Xinhua News Agency delivers its news across the world in seven languages including Chinese, English, French, Russian, Spanish, Arabic, etc., as well as news pictures and other kinds of news. It has made contracts to exchange news and news pictures with more than eighty foreign news agencies or political news departments.

Unlike the *People's Daily*, which is an organization of the Communist Party of China rather than of the PRC government, Xinhua rarely offers editorials, but rather passes through speeches by government officials. Its position set as a platform of receiving and distributing the information all over the world and thus it covers the world news, live news and exclusive reports.

Like many other media organizations, Xinhua struggled to find the "right line" to use in covering the Tiananmen Square protests of 1989. Although more cautious than People's Daily in its treatment of sensitive topics during that period—such as how to commemorate reformist Communist Party leader Hu Yaobang's April 1989 death, the then ongoing demonstrations in Beijing and elsewhere, and basic questions of press freedom and individual rights—Xinhua gave some favourable coverage to demonstrators and intellectuals who were questioning top party leaders. Even so, many Xinhua reporters were angry with top editors for not going far enough and for suppressing stories about the Tiananmen Square crackdown. For several days after the violence on 4 June, almost no-one at Xinhua did any work, and journalists demonstrated inside the Agency's Beijing compound.

In 2001, Hong Kong-listed media company Sing Tao News Corporation Limited invested in joint ventures with Xinhua News Agency to set up a market information Website and offer audio and visual services planning and consulting.

Xinhua and the Internal Media

The Chinese media's internal publication system, in which certain journals are published exclusively for government and party officials, provides information and analysis not generally available to the public. The State values these internal reports because they contain much of China's most sensitive, controversial, and high-quality investigative journalism. Xinhua and many other Chinese media organizations produce reports for the "internal" journals. Informed observers note that journalists generally like to write for the internal publications—typically, only the most senior or most capable print and broadcast reporters are given such opportunities—because they can write less polemical and more comprehensive stories without having to omit unwelcome details as is commonly done in the print media directed to the general public.

The Chinese government's internal media publication system follows a strict hierarchical pattern designed to facilitate party control. A publication called Reference News—which includes translated articles from abroad as well as news and commentary by senior Xinhua reporters—is delivered by Xinhua personnel, rather than by the national mail system, to officials at the working level and above. A three-to-ten-page report called Internal Reference (*Neibu Cankao*) is distributed to officials at the ministerial level and higher. The most highly classified Xinhua internal reports, known as "redhead reference" (*Hong Tou Cankao*) reports, are issued occasionally to the top dozen or so party and government officials.

There are signs that the internal publication system is breaking down as more information becomes widely available in China. A Hong Kong-based political journal circulated on the Chinese mainland has questioned the need for such a system in light of China's modern telecommunications and expanding contacts with the outside world. Internal publications are becoming less exclusive; some are now being sold illegally on the street and are increasingly available to anyone with money.

Xinhua in Hong Kong

Xinhua's branch in Hong Kong was not just a press office. It was named a news agency under the special historic conditions before the territory's sovereignty was transferred from Britain to the PRC, because the PRC did not recognize British sovereignty over the colony, and an embassy cannot be set up within what it considered its soil. Until 1997, it served as the de facto diplomatic mission of the PRC in the territory. It was authorized by the special administrative region government to continue to represent the central government after 1997, and it was renamed *The Liaison Office of the Central People's Government in the Hong Kong SAR* on January 18, 2000. The State Council appointed Gao Siren as the director in August 2002. After renaming as liaison office, a Xinhua Agency which is a true press office was set up.

As suggested by the name change, Xinhua's present role is mainly about liaison with the broad spectrum of groups and associations in Hong Kong, or what is known as "united front" work in the terminology of the Communist Party of China.

According to some press reports in Hong Kong, the Liaison Office was under pressure from Beijing after the July 1 mass protest in 2003. Beijing officials reportedly criticized the Liaison Office for its inaccurate assessment of the public sentiment in Hong Kong during that period.

The former Hong Kong headquarters of Xinhua in Wan Chai was vacated in 2001, when the office relocated to Sai Wan, and sold in September 2002. The 23-storey building will be converted back into a four-star hotel with 480 rooms. Located at 387 Queen's Road East, the 1970s building had been Xinhua's home for more than 20 years.

Previous Directors of Hong Kong Xinhua

Xu Jiatun headed the Hong Kong branch of Xinhua until 1990, when he fled to the United States amid accusations that he sympathized with Beijing students during the Tiananmen Square protests of 1989.

Xu angered Beijing when he comforted Hong Kong students who staged a hunger strike outside the Xinhua office in support of the pro-democracy movement in Beijing in 1989. Years after, he joined to appeal for a reversal of the official verdict that the demonstrations were a "counter-revolutionary rebellion."

Zhou Nan succeeded exiled Xu Jiatun as the director of Xinhua in Hong Kong after the 1989 Tiananmen Square Crackdown. Zhou henceforth played a key role in the 13-year Sino-British argument on the handover in 1997.

During the hostile years, Zhou named Hong Kong's last governor Chris Patten as a 'sinner of a thousand years.' He said Patten had committed 'three violations', referring to Patten's political reforms, branded by Beijing as a breach of the Sino-British Joint Declaration, the Hong Kong Basic Law, and understandings between the two sovereign nations.

Zhang Junsheng, former Xinhua vice-director, was brought into the agency by its former Hong Kong director, Xu Jiatun, in 1985. He was one of the few pre-1989 staff to survive the post-Tiananmen purge. For 13 years, he was one of the few Xinhua officers who enjoy publicity by building up contacts in the film and arts world as the agency's cultural attaché.

His most famous manoeuvre was to repeat criticism of the Bill of Rights made in confidence by the then-chief justice Sir Ti Liang Yang. Zhang also openly called Hong Kong's last governor Chris Patten a liar. He accused Patten of trying to create chaos in the civil service by undermining its neutrality.

Xinhua in Macau

A Xinhua News Agency branch was set up in Macau in the late 1980s. The News Department of the Xinhua news Agency Macau Branch, a working organ sent by the central people's government of the PRC, is responsible for gathering news. The latter was renamed the *Liaison Office of the Central People's Government in the Macau SAR*.

Xinhua Online

The Xinhua News Agency runs the prominent news website Xinhuanet.com, which provides news in six different languages. The domain *xinhuanet.com* attracted almost 4 million visitors annually by 2008 according to a Compete.com survey.

Criticism

Propaganda

According to Reporters Without Borders, Xinhua's journalists are hand-picked and indoctrinated to produce media reports that give the official point of view of the Chinese Communist Party. The non-governmental organization accuses the Xinhua of being "the world's biggest propaganda agency", and claims that it distorts its international reports to express disdain toward China's opponents nations while supporting other nations accused of human rights violations. In 2006, Xinhua issued directives limiting foreign news agencies from directly selling news to other Chinese media outlets.

False News Report

A false news article appeared on *Xinhua News Agency*'s website on 25 September 2008, reporting the Shenzhou 7 mission events dated 27 September 2008; the article was reported in several mainstream news sources. The report described in detail the launch, which had not yet occurred, as well as the process of tracking and data transfer by a tracking ship, and dialogue between the crew members in space. The report was taken down the same day, and when contacted by the Associated Press, a xinhuanet.com staffer who refused to give his name allegedly stated that it had been a "technical error by a technician."

CHINA NEWS SERVICE

The China News Service is the second largest news agency in the People's Republic of China, trailing the Xinhua News Agency. It serves mainly overseas Chinese and residents of Hong Kong, Macau, and Taiwan. The CNS was established in 1952. It has established news offices and stations in every province in mainland China, as well as in Hong Kong and Macau. CNS also has news offices in foreign countries, including the United States, Japan, France and Australia.

NEWS WORLD COMMUNICATIONS

News World Communications, Inc. is a media corporation owned by the Unification Church. Two of News World's most well-known subsidiaries are *The Washington Times* and United Press International.

Relationship to the Unification Church

News World Communications, Inc. was founded by Unification Church founder and leader, Sun Myung Moon. Its board of directors are members of the Unification Church. In 1984, two years after founding the *Washington Times*, Moon said:

> *"The means of doing battle around the world have changed markedly. Instead of the conventional warfare of military forces, we have three major types of warfare today. First of all is ideological warfare; secondly is the warfare between intelligence forces; and thirdly, the warfare of propaganda. In today's warfare of ideology, intelligence and propaganda, nobody can compete with Reverend Moon."*

At a January 2, 1996 Unification Church leadership conference, Rev. Moon said:

> *"That is why Father has been combining and organizing scholars from all over the world, and also newspaper organizations, in order to make propaganda."*

Investigative journalist Robert Parry wrote about the rise of News World's publications:

> *"By the 1980s, the likes of South Korean theocrat Rev. Sun Myung Moon and Australian media mogul Rupert Murdoch were pouring billions of dollars into a rapidly expanding right-wing media. From these investments came a plethora of well-financed think tanks, year-round attack groups, and a vertically integrated conservative news media—from books, magazines and newspapers to radio, TV and eventually the Internet. Right-wing activists flocked to Washington and New York for good-paying jobs as journalists and pundits."*

News World also owns *Insight Magazine, The World and I* magazine, *Middle East Times, Tiempos del Mundo, Segye Ilbo, Sekai Nippo, GolfStyles, The World Peace Times,* and United Press International.

Publications

Washington Times

The *Washington Times* was founded in 1982 as a daily newspaper in Washington D.C., the capital of the United States. In 2002 Moon said:

> *"The Washington Times will become the instrument in spreading the truth about God to the world."*

In 2003, *The New Yorker* reported that a billion dollars had been spent on the *Washington Times* since the inception by News World. Moon noted in a 1991 speech that "Literally nine hundred million to one billion dollars has been spent to activate and run the *Washington Times*". By 2002, *Columbia Journalism Review* suggested Moon had spent nearly $2 billion on the *Times*. In 2008, Thomas F. Roeser of the Chicago Daily Observer said that Moon had "announced he will spend as many future billions as is needed to keep the paper competitive."

United Press International

In 2002, the news agency United Press International (founded in 1907) was purchased by News World. It now operates on a much reduced basis from its former importance.

Insight on the News

Insight on the News covered the United States political scene. It was often controversial for its conservative point of view.

The World and I

The World and I is an educational magazine published in the United States. It was formerly a print magazine but is now published online.

Middle East Times

The Middle East Times is a daily newspaper published in English in Cairo, Egypt. It covers news in the Middle East.

GolfStyles

GolfStyles covers the sport of golf. It publishes five regional editions in the Eastern and Midwestern United States.

Corporate Leaders

- Chairman and President, News World Communications and United Press International: Chung Hwan Kwak
- VP and CFO: Keith Cooperrider
- President and Publisher, *The Washington Times*: Tom McDevitt

YONHAP

Yonhap News Agency is a news agency in South Korea that supplies domestic and foreign news and information to newspaper and TV broadcast and other subscribers in South Korea. Yonhap (meaning "consolidated" in Korean) was established on December 19, 1980 through the merger of

Hapdong News Agency and Orient Press on the model of Japan's Kyodo News Agency. It maintains various agreements with 48 non-Korean news agencies, and also has a services-exchange agreement with North Korea's KCNA agency.

Yonhap was the host news agency of the 1988 Seoul Summer Olympics, and was elected twice to the board of OANA. Yonhap is South Korea's official news agency. It is the largest news agency in South Korea and receives an annual government subsidy of about US$20 million. Its largest shareholder is the Korean Broadcasting System (KBS), South Korea's largest public broadcaster. KBS is owned and operated by the government of South Korea.

AGÊNCIA BRASIL

Radiobras or *Agência Brasil* or ABr is the national broadcaster and a public agency of Brazil. The name is a portmanteau of *Radiodifusão Brasil* ("Brazil Broadcasting"). Radiobras operates several radio stations and TV stations throughout the country. It is also involved in international broadcasting, primarily on shortwave.

8

Major International News Channels and Networks: Select Case Studies

FOX NEWS CHANNEL

Fox News Channel (FNC) is a United States-based cable and satellite news channel. It is owned by the Fox Entertainment Group, and is a subsidiary of News Corporation. As of January 2005, it is available to 85 million households in the US and further to viewers internationally, broadcasting primarily out of its New York City studios. The channel was created by Australian media magnate Rupert Murdoch, who hired Republican political strategist Roger Ailes as its founding CEO. The network was launched on October 7, 1996 to 17 million cable subscribers. The network slowly rose to prominence in the late 1990s. In the United States, Fox News Channel has been rated as the cable news network with the largest number of regular viewers. Critics and some observers of the channel say that Fox News Channel promotes conservative political positions. Fox News Channel publicly disagrees with allegations of bias in the channel's reporting.

History

In May 1985, Australian publisher Rupert Murdoch announced that he and American industrialist and philanthropist Marvin Davis intend to develop "a network of independent stations as a fourth marketing force" to compete directly with CBS, NBC and ABC through the purchase of six television stations then owned by Metromedia. In July 1985, 20th Century Fox announced that publisher Rupert Murdoch had completed his purchase of 50 per cent of Fox Filmed Entertainment, the parent company of 20th Century Fox Film Corporation. A year later,

Twentieth Century Fox Film Corporation earned $5.6 million in its fiscal third period ended May 31, 1986, in contrast to a loss of $55.8 million in the year-earlier period.

Launched	October 7, 1996
Owned by	News Corporation
Picture format	480i/HDTV
Slogan	"We Report. You Decide"; "Fair and Balanced"; "The Most Powerful Name in News"
Country	United States
Language	English
Broadcast area	United States and International
Headquarters	New York, New York, United States
Sister channel(s)	Fox Business Network for Broadcasting Company, Sky News, Sky News Australia SKY TG 24
Website	foxnews.com
	Availability
	Satellite
DirecTV	360
Dish Network	205
SKY Italia	514
Sky Digital	509
	Satellite Radio
Sirius	131
XM	121
	IPTV over ADSL
Sky Angel	Channel 318

Prior to founding Fox News, Murdoch had gained significant experience in the 24-hour news business when News Corporation's BSkyB subsidiary started Europe's first 24-hour news channel, Sky News, in the United Kingdom in 1989. With the success of his fourth network efforts in the United States, experience gained from Sky News, and turnaround of 20th Century Fox, Murdoch announced on January 31, 1996 that News Corporation would be launching a 24-hour news channel to air on both cable and satellite systems as part of a News Corporation "worldwide platform" for Fox programming, reasoning that "The appetite for news—particularly news that explains to people how it affects them—is expanding enormously."

In February 1996, after well-known former Republican political strategist Roger Ailes left America's Talking (now MSNBC), Murdoch called him to start the *Fox News Channel.* A group of Ailes loyalists who followed him throughout the NBC empire joined him at Fox. From there, the CNBC expatriates, who joined a team already in place at Fox News, created the programming concept and proceeded to select space in New York. Ailes worked individuals through five months of 14-hour workdays and several weeks of rehearsal shows before launch, on October 7, 1996.

At launch, only 10 million households were able to watch Fox News, with none in the major media markets of New York City and Los Angeles. According to published reports, many media reviewers had to watch the first day's programming at Fox News studios because it was not readily available. The rolling news coverage during the day consisted of 20-minute single topic shows like *Fox on Crime* or *Fox on Politics* surrounded by news headlines. Interviews had various facts at the bottom of the screen about the topic or the guest. The flagship newscast at the time was called *The Schneider Report,* with Mike Schneider giving a fast paced delivery of the news. During the evening, Fox had opinion shows: *The O'Reilly Report* (now, *The O'Reilly Factor*), *The Crier Report* hosted by Catherine Crier, and *Hannity and Colmes*.

From the beginning, Fox News has placed heavy emphasis on visual presentation. Graphics were designed to be colourful and attention grabbing and to allow people to get the main points of what was being said even if they couldn't hear the host, through the use of on-screen text summarizing the position of the interviewer or speaker and "bullet points" when a host was giving commentary. Fox News also created the "Fox News Alert," which interrupted regular programming when a breaking news story occurred.

To accelerate its adoption by cable companies, Fox News paid systems up to $11 per subscriber to distribute the network. This contrasted with the normal practice, in which cable operators paid stations carriage fees for the programming of channels. When Time Warner bought out Ted Turner's Turner Broadcasting, a federal antitrust consent decree required Time Warner to carry a second all-news channel in addition to its own CNN. Time Warner selected MSNBC as the secondary news network, instead of Fox News. Fox News claimed that this violated an agreement to carry Fox News. Citing its agreement to keep its US headquarters and a large studio in New York City, News Corporation pressured Mayor Rudolph Giuliani's administration to pressure Time Warner, one of the city's two cable providers, to transmit Fox News on a city-owned channel. City officials threatened to take action affecting Time Warner's cable franchises in the city.

A lawsuit was filed by Time Warner against the City of New York claiming undue interference with, and inappropriate use of the city's educational channels for commercial programming. News Corporation countered with an antitrust lawsuit against Time Warner for unfairly protecting CNN. This led to an acrimonious battle between Murdoch and Turner, with Turner publicly comparing Murdoch to Adolf Hitler while Murdoch's *New York Post* ran an editorial questioning Turner's sanity. Giuliani's motives were also questioned, as his wife was a producer at Murdoch-owned WNYW-TV. In the end, Time Warner and News Corporation signed a settlement agreement to permit Fox News to be carried on New York City cable system beginning in October 1997, and on all of Time Warner's cable systems by 2001, though Time Warner still does not carry Fox News in all areas. In return, Time Warner was given some rights to News Corporation's satellites in Asia and Europe to distribute Time Warner programming, would receive the normal compensation per subscriber paid to cable operators, and News Corporation would not object to the continuation of Atlanta Braves baseball games being carried on TBS (which could have expired because of the Fox television network's contract with Major League Baseball).

On May 1, 2008, Fox News launched high definition channel simulcasts of its programming in selected regions of the United States. Time Warner Cable is carrying this channel in New York, NY, San Antonio, TX, and Kansas City, MO, while Cablevision is making it available in New York, NY and on Long Island. Recently, Comcast began adding the channel in Chicago, IL, Salt Lake City, UT, and few select markets.

Outlets

Fox News Channel maintains an archive of most of its programmes. This archive also handles the Fox Movietone newsreels. Licensing of the Fox News archive is handled by ITN Source, the archiving division of Independent Television News.

Television

Fox News Channel presents a variety of programming with up to 15 hours of live programming per day, in addition to programming and content for the Fox Broadcasting Company. Most of the programmes are broadcast from Fox News headquarters in New York City in their street-side studio on Sixth Avenue in the west extension of Rockefeller Centre. Audio simulcasts of the channel are aired on XM Satellite Radio and Sirius Satellite Radio.

Radio

With the growth of the Fox News Channel, the network introduced a radio division entitled *Fox News Radio* in 2003. Syndicated throughout the United States, the division provides short newscasts and talk radio programmes, featuring personalities from both the television and radio divisions. In addition, the network has also introduced Fox News Talk in 2006, a satellite radio station which features programmes syndicated by and featuring Fox News personalities.

Online

Like other news networks, Fox News Channel produces a news website featuring the latest coverage, including video clips from the network's television division, audio clips from Fox News Radio, in addition to columns from the network's assorted television, radio, and online personalities. Introduced in December 1995, the network's website ranks below many other news websites, ranking in the lower teens in the list of top news websites "net top 20" Retrieved on 2008-03-17.

Fox News Mobile is a part of the Fox News website that is dedicated to streaming news clips that are formatted for video enabled mobile phones.

Personalities

Producing a variety of different programming, Fox News Channel has a number of different programme hosts, news anchors, correspondents, and contributors which appear throughout daily programming on the network. The network has a number of different signature hosts, including Bill O'Reilly, Sean Hannity, Alan Colmes, Greta Van Susteren, and Shepard Smith, all of whom host programmes which are on the list of the top ten most watched programmes on cable news.

Fig. 8.1: FNC's Studio A for *The O'Reilly Factor* and *America's Newsroom*

Ratings

Fox News leads the cable news market in the United States in regular viewership. Fox News saw huge growth in its ratings during the early stages of the Iraq conflict. By some reports, at the height of the conflict they enjoyed as much as a 300 per cent increase in viewership, averaging 3.3 million viewers daily.

In 2004, Fox News Channel's ratings for its broadcast of the Republican National Convention beat those of all three broadcast networks. During President George W. Bush's address, Fox News notched 7.3 million viewers nationally, while NBC, CBS, and ABC scored ratings of 5.9, 5.0 and 5.1, respectively.

Fig. 8.2: FNC's *Hannity and Colmes* Production Area

In late 2005 and early 2006, Fox saw a brief decline in ratings. One of the most notable decline in ratings came in the second quarter of 2006, when compared to the previous quarter, Fox News had a loss in viewership for every single prime time programme. One of the most noteworthy losses of viewership was that of *Special Report with Brit Hume*. The show's total viewership was down 19 per cent compared to the previous quarter. However, several weeks later, in the wake of the North Korean Missile Crisis and the 2006 Lebanon War, Fox saw a surge in viewership and remained the #1 rated cable news channel. Fox still held eight of the ten most-watched nightly cable news shows, with *The O'Reilly Factor* and *Hannity and Colmes* coming in first and second places, respectively.

For the year 2007, Fox News was the number-one rated cable news network in the United States. It was down one per cent in total daily viewers and down three per cent in the 25-54 year old demographic, but it still boasted most of the top-rated shows on cable new led by The O'Reilly Factor. For primetime TV Fox News ranked #6 of all cable networks.

Slogan

"Fair and Balanced" is a trademarked slogan used by the

broadcaster. The slogan was originally used in conjunction with the phrase *"Real Journalism."*

Author and comedian Al Franken used the slogan in the subtitle for his 2003 book *Lies and the Lying Liars Who Tell Them: A Fair and Balanced Look at the Right*. In the book, he cites examples of Fox News' bias. On August 22, 2003, Fox sued based upon its trademark on the phrase. Fox News dropped the lawsuit three days later after Judge Denny Chin refused their request for an injunction.

In December 2003, Fox News found itself on the other end of a legal battle concerning the slogan, when AlterNet filed a cancellation petition with the United States Patent and Trademark Office to have Fox's trademark rescinded as misdescriptive. AlterNet included the documentary film *Outfoxed* as supporting evidence in its case. After losing early motions, AlterNet withdrew its petition and the USPTO dismissed the case.

In April 2008 FNC's sister network, Fox Business Network (which launched on 2007-10-15) adopted a new slogan: *Start here. Start now* (as of May 12, 2008). This is the network's current advertising slogan. These ads currently air on all Fox Cable Networks programmes and as newspaper ads in New York Post, Dow Jones newspapers, and others.

Controversies

Political Bias

Some critics, politicians, and observers have accused Fox News of having a bias towards the political right or Republican point of view at the expense of neutrality. Murdoch and Ailes have reacted against allegations of bias, with Murdoch claiming that Fox has "given room to both sides, whereas only one side had it before."

Internal Memos

A series of internal memos issued by Fox News V.P. John Moody to news personnel in 2003 and 2004 were leaked to the media in July 2004. These editorial directives contained comments such as "[the then Democratic presidential candidate] John Kerry may wish he'd taken off his microphone before trashing the GOP." Journalists and media watchdog groups such as Media Matters for America, cite the leaked memos as evidence that top-down pressure is the source of Fox News channel's pro-Republican bias.

Talking Points from Bush White House

While promoting his memoir, *What Happened,* Scott McClellan, former White House Press Secretary (2003–06) for President George W. Bush stated on the July 25, 2008 edition of Hardball with Chris Matthews that the Bush White House routinely gave talking points to Fox News commentators—but not journalists—in order to influence discourse and content. McClellan stated that these talking points were not issued to provide the public with news; instead, they were to provide Fox News commentators with issues and perspectives favourable to the White House and Republican Party. McClellan later apologized to Fox News commentator, Bill O'Reilly for not responding to Matthews' suggestion that "Bill" or "Sean" received the talking points; McClellan said he had no personal knowledge that O'Reilly ever received the talking points. Furthermore he pointed out "the way a couple of questions were phrased in that interview, along with my response left things open to interpretation and I should not have let that happen."

Outfoxed

In 2004, director Robert Greenwald produced the documentary film *Outfoxed: Rupert Murdoch's War on Journalism.* The film argues that Fox News has a conservative bias, including as evidence internal memos from editorial Vice-President John Moody which, the film claims, exposes attempts to distort the content of Fox News. This was later distributed on DVD by MoveOn.org.

International Transmission

The Fox News Channel feed is available internationally, while the Fox News Extra segments provide alternate programming.

Fox News Extra

Initially, US advertisements were replaced on Fox News with

viewer e-mail and profiles of Fox News anchors set to music. In 2002 these were replaced with international weather forecasts. In 2006, the weather segments were replaced with 'Fox News Extra' segments, various narrated reports from FOX reports on a variety of topics. These reports are generally on lighter issues not related to current news events, and the segments are repeated. Fox News Channel also shows international weather forecasts when the Fox News Extra segments run short.

The Fox News feed in the United Kingdom does not feature Fox News Extra, and instead features break fillers from sister channel Sky News's International Variant. For a short period in 2001, a still of the Fox News logo replaced this other content.

Australia

In Australia, Fox News Channel is broadcast on the three major Pay-TV providers, Foxtel, Austar and Optus Television. Foxtel is 25 per cent owned by News Corporation. The Australian version previously featured some local programming, including a John Laws current affairs programme in place of part of *Fox and Friends*. Local advertisements and promotions are aired in place of every second 'Fox News Extra' segment. Sky News Australia is Fox's sister channel.

Brazil

Since 2002 Fox News has been broadcast to Brazil, but the commercials are replaced with Fox News Extra. It is broadcast by Sky (satellite operator, a joint-venture between News Corporation and Globosat) and in the digital packages of NET.

Canada

On December 14, 2000, the Canadian Radio-television and Telecommunications Commission (CRTC) approved Fox News Canada on behalf of the Global Television Network, for broadcast in Canada. Fox News Canada was to be a domestic Canadian version of Fox News. The channel, or "speciality television service", was never implemented by Fox, and the deadline for commencement of the service expired on November 24, 2004. That same day, a similar license was granted to Rogers Communications for "MSNBC Canada", which went to air in September 2001. During this period, it was speculated by some, and repeated by Fox News personalities, that the station was being "banned in Canada." The CRTC's previous refusal to grant Fox News an outright license had been contested by some Canadians, as well as American fans of the channel, who believed the decision to be politically motivated. However, it is rare for any American cable network to be licensed in Canada outright.

On November 18, 2004 the CRTC announced that a digital license would be granted to Fox News. In its proposal, Fox News stated, with reference to Fox News Canada, that "Fox News does not intend to implement this service and therefore will not meet the extended deadline to commence operations." On December 16, 2004, Rogers Communications became the first Canadian cable or satellite provider to broadcast Fox News, with other companies following suit within the next several weeks.

New Zealand

In New Zealand, Fox News is broadcast on Channel 92 of pay satellite operator Sky TV's digital platform. It is also broadcast overnight on New Zealand TV channel Prime, owned by Sky. Fox News parent corporation News Corp has a stake in both Sky and Prime.

Scandinavia

Between 2003 and 2006, in Sweden and the other Scandinavian countries, Fox News was broadcast 16 hours a day on TV8, with Fox News Extra segments replacing U.S. advertising. Fox News was dropped by TV8 and replaced by German news channel Deutsche Welle in September 2006.

United Kingdom

Fox News is also carried in the United Kingdom by the British Sky Broadcasting (BSkyB) satellite television network (Sky Digital) which is 40 per cent owned by Fox's parent News Corporation. It is run as a sister channel to BSkyB's popular Sky News. Fox News is usually broadcast as a VideoGuard encrypted channel but during major news stories it may be simulcast on Sky Active, which is free to air. As of September 2006 the channel has carried UK specific advertising, along with headlines and weather provided by Sky News during its breaks. These run under the brand of Fox News International. Due to the shared ownership of Fox and Sky, Fox News and Sky News routinely share bureaus and reporters for breaking news stories from around the world.

Other Countries

Fox News Channel is also carried in more than 40 countries. Although service to Japan stopped in the summer of 2003, it can still be seen on Americable (distributor for American bases), Mediatti (Kadena Air Base), and Pan Global TV Japan.

- Argentina
- Australia
- Bahamas
- Bahrain
- Barbados
- Belize
- Bermuda
- Cambodia
- Cayman Islands
- Chile
- Colombia
- Costa Rica
- Dominican Republic
- Finland
- Greece
- Grenada
- Guam
- Guatemala
- Hong Kong
- Iceland
- Indonesia
- Ireland
- Israel
- Italy
- Jamaica
- Kazakhstan
- Kyrgyzstan
- Lebanon
- Macau
- Malaysia
- Maldives
- Mexico
- Netherlands
- New Zealand
- Nigeria
- Norway
- Pakistan
- Palau
- Panama
- Peru
- Papua New Guinea
- Philippines
- Portugal
- Russia
- Saudi Arabia
- Singapore
- Saint Kitts
- Saint Lucia

- Saint Vincent and the Grenadines
- Slovenia
- Sweden
- Thailand
- Trinidad and Tobago
- Tonga
- United Arab Emirates
- United Kingdom
- Venezuela

BBC SERVICES ON TV, RADIO AND ONLINE

BBC World Service

BBC World Service is the world's most respected voice in international broadcasting. It provides authoritative and impartial news and information in 33 languages worldwide. In the UK, its English service is available via DAB digital radio, digital television (terrestrial, satellite, cable and broadband) and online. BBC World Service is trusted for its accuracy, editorial independence and expertize and provides a forum for the exchange of ideas across cultural, linguistic and national boundaries. It projects British values of trustworthiness, openness, fair dealing, creativity, enterprise and community. BBC World Service is a public service funded by the UK Foreign and Commonwealth Office. It is permitted to generate additional income subject to the BBC's Fair Trading Commitment and Commercial Policy Guidelines. It is financed separately from the UK licence fee and cross-subsidies are forbidden.

Mission

To enrich people's lives with programmes and services that inform, educate and entertain.

Vision

To be the most creative organization in the world.

Values

- Trust is the foundation of the BBC: we are independent, impartial and honest.
- Audiences are at the heart of everything we do.
- We take pride in delivering quality and value for money.

- Creativity is the lifeblood of our organization.
- We respect each other and celebrate our diversity so that everyone can give their best.
- We are one BBC: great things happen when we work together.

The Royal Charter and Agreement also sets out six public purposes for the BBC.

Television

Public services funded by the licence fee:

1. BBC One
2. BBC Two
3. BBC Three
4. BBC Four
5. CBBC
6. CBeebies
7. BBC News
8. BBC Parliament
9. BBC Red Button
10. BBC iPlayer
11. BBC HD

Radio

Public services funded by the licence fee:

1. Radio 1
2. 1Xtra
3. Radio 2
4. Radio 3
5. Radio 4
6. Radio 5 Live
7. 5 Live Sports Extra
8. 6 Music
9. Radio 7
10. Asian Network

Around the UK

Public services funded by the licence fee:

1. English regions
2. Scotland
3. Wales
4. Northern Ireland
5. BBC Online
6. BBC on YouTube

Around the World

Public service funded by the UK government:

- BBC World Service

Separate commercial ventures whose profits help fund BBC public services:

1. BBC America
2. BBC Canada
3. BBC Food
4. BBC Kids (Canada)
5. BBC Prime
6. BBC World News
7. Animal Planet
8. People+Arts
9. UKTV
10. UK.TV (Australia)
11. BBC Worldwide on YouTube

Royal Charter

The BBC is established under a Royal Charter. The current Charter came into force in 2007 and runs until the end of 2016. It explicitly recognizes the BBC's editorial independence and sets out its public purposes.

BBC Trust

Under the new Charter, the BBC is governed by the BBC Trust, which sets the strategic direction of the BBC and has a clear duty to represent the interests of licence fee payers. The Trust sets purpose remits, issues service licences and holds the Executive Board to account for its performance in delivering BBC services.

The Trust works closely with National Audience Councils in order to understand the needs and concerns of audiences.

Executive Board

Operational responsibility rests with the Executive Board. It is responsible for delivering the BBC's services and running the organization in accordance with the overall strategy set by the Trust. For more details and an explanation of purpose remits and service licences, see the most recent Annual Report.

Media Regulators

Government responsibility for broadcasting and creative industries in the UK lies with the Department for Culture, Media and Sport (DCMS). Ofcom is the independent regulator and competition authority for the UK communications industries, with responsibilities across television, radio, telecommunications and wireless communications services.

BBC NEWS

BBC News, formerly BBC News and Current Affairs, is the department led by Helen Boaden within the BBC responsible for the corporation's news-gathering and production of news programmes on BBC television, radio and online. Producing 120 hours of output daily, the organization is the largest broadcasting news gatherer in the world while carrying out the key objective of the BBC's Royal Charter to *"collect news and information in any part of the world and in any manner that may be thought fit."*

Fig. 8.3: The Current BBC News Logo

The department is based at the News Centre within BBC Television Centre in West London, W12, and is represented by regional centres across the United Kingdom together with 44 news-gathering bureaux based around the world; only three are based within the UK. Political coverage is based at the Millbank Studios in 4 Millbank in Westminster. With an annual budget of £350 million, BBC News consists of 3,500 staff—2,000 of whom are journalists. Competition within the UK comes mainly from rolling news channel Sky News, but also from ITN, a major independent provider of news services to commercial networks. Around the world the BBC complements other news providers' services. Conversely, some countries have restricted BBC broadcasts and BBC journalists' movements for internal political reasons.

History

The Early Years

The British Broadcasting Company broadcast its first radio bulletin from 2LO on 14 November 1922. Televised bulletins came later on 5 July 1954, broadcast from leased studios within Alexandra Palace in London. However, newsreels had been in use for some time—shown at cinemas and other places of public gathering—and these had been adapted as *Television Newsreel* programmes, which before the advent of news coverage proper had run on the BBC since 1948. A weekly *Children's Newsreel* was inaugurated on 23 April 1950.

The public's interest in television and live events was stimulated by Elizabeth II's coronation in 1953. It is estimated that up to 27 million people viewed the programme in the UK—overtaking radio's audience of 12 million for the first time—and those live pictures were fed from 21 cameras in central London to Alexandra Palace for transmission, and then on to other UK transmitters opened in time for the event.

1950s

Television news, although physically separate from its radio counterpart, was still firmly under its control—with correspondents providing reports for both outlets—and that first bulletin, shown in 1954 on the then BBC television service and presented by Richard Baker, involved him providing narration off-screen while stills were shown—and this was then followed by the customary *Television Newsreel* with a recorded commentary by John Snagge (and on other occasions by Andrew Timothy).

It was revealed that this had been due to producers fearing a newsreader with their facial movements could distract the viewer from the story in question. On-screen newsreaders were finally introduced a year later, in 1955—Kenneth Kendall (the first to appear in vision), Robert Dougall and Richard Baker—just three weeks before ITN's launch date of 22 September.

Mainstream television production had started to move out of Alexandra Palace in 1950 to larger premises—mainly at Lime Grove Studios in west London—taking Current Affairs department with it, and it was here that the topical early-evening programme *Tonight,* hosted by Cliff Michelmore and designed to fill the airtime provided by the abolition of the Toddlers' Truce, started on 18 February 1957. Prior to this, in the same Shepherd's Bush studios, the first *Panorama* had been transmitted on 11 November 1953, with Richard Dimbleby taking over as anchor in 1955.

Later in 1957, on 28 October in central London, radio launched its morning programme *Today* on the Home Service. In 1958 Hugh Carleton Greene became head of News and Current Affairs, and set up a BBC study group whose findings, published in 1959, were critical of what the television news operation had become under Greene's predecessor Tahu Hole. The solution proposed was that the head of television news should take control (away from radio), and that the television service should have a proper newsroom of its own, with an editor-of-the-day...

1960s

On 1 January 1960, Greene became Director General and under him big changes were afoot not only for BBC Television, but also for BBC Television News—a separate news department, formed in 1955 as a response to the founding of ITN—the aim was to make BBC reporting a little more like ITN, which had been praised by Greene's study group.

A newsroom was created at AP, television reporters recruited, and given the opportunity to write and voice their own scripts—without the "impossible burden" of having to cover stories for radio too.

In 1987, almost thirty years later, John Birt resurrected the practice of correspondents working for both TV and radio with the introduction of bi-media journalism, and 2008 saw tri-media introduced across TV, radio and online. Also in 1960, Nan Winton the first female BBC network newsreader appeared in vision on 20 June, and 19 September saw the start of the radio news and current affairs programme *The Ten O'clock News*. Greene was a great innovator and (on a lighter note) asked Ned Sherrin, the then producer of *Tonight* to "prick the pomposity of public figures" with a weekly television show. So on 24 November 1962 *That Was The Week That Was*, hosted by David Frost, was born at Lime Grove Studios and is mentioned here because (of Greene's actions) it was a product of Current Affairs department rather than Light Entertainment. BBC 2 started transmission on 20 April 1964, and with it came a new news programme for that channel—*Newsroom*.

Fig. 8.4: Newsroom Launched in 1964—in 1968 it Became the UK's First Colour Television News Programme

The World at One (WATO) began on 4 October 1965 on the then, Home Service, and the year before *News Review* had started on television.

News Review was a roundup of the weeks news, first broadcast on Sunday 26 April, 1964 on BBC 2 and harking back to the weekly *Newsreel Review of the Week* (produced from 1951)

to open programming on Sunday evenings—the difference being that this incarnation had subtitles for the deaf and hard-of-hearing. As this was the decade before electronic caption generation, each "super" (superimposition) had to be produced on paper or card, synchronized manually to studio and news footage, committed to tape during the afternoon and broadcast early evening—thus Sundays were no longer a quiet day for news at AP. The programme ran until the 1980s—by then using electronic captions, known as Anchor—to be superseded by Ceefax subtitling (a similar format), and the signing of such programmes as *See Hear* (from 1981).

On Sunday 17 September 1967 *The World This Weekend* launched on the then, Home Service, but soon-to-be Radio 4.

Preparations for colour began in the autumn of 1967 and on Thursday 7 March 1968 *Newsroom* on BBC 2, moved to an early evening slot, became the first UK news programme to be transmitted in colour—from Studio A at Alexandra Palace—*News Review* and *Westminster* (the latter a weekly review of Parliamentary happenings) were "colourized" shortly after.

Much of the insert material was still in black and white however, as initially only a part of the film coverage shot in and around London was on colour reversal film stock—and all regional and many international contributions were still in black and white too. Colour facilities were also technically very limited for the next eighteen months at AP, as it had only one RCA colour videotape machine and, eventually two, Pye colour telecines—although the news colour service started with just one.

Black and white national bulletins on BBC 1 continued to originate from Studio B on weekdays, along with *Town and Around*—the London regional "opt out" programme broadcast throughout the 1960s (and the BBC's first regional news programme for the South East)—until it started to be replaced by *Nationwide* on Tuesday to Thursday from Lime Grove Studios early in September 1969. *Town and Around* was never to make the move to Television Centre—instead it became *London This Week* which transmitted on Mondays and Fridays only from the new TVC studios.

Television News Moves to Television Centre

The final news programme to come from Alexandra Palace was

a late night news on BBC 2 on Friday 19 September, 1969 in colour. BBC Television News resumed operations the next day with a lunchtime bulletin on BBC 1 (in black and white) from Television Centre, where it has remained ever since.

This move to better technical facilities, but much smaller studios, allowed *Newsroom* and *News Review* to replace back projection with CSO. And it also allowed *all* news output to be produced in PAL colour, in preparation for the "colourization" of BBC 1 from 15 November, 1969—the studios were capable of operating in NTSC too for the US, Canada and Japan as the BBC sometimes provided facilities for overseas broadcasters. During the 1960s satellite communication had become not only possible, but popular, however colour field-store standards converters were still in their infancy in 1968 and we would have to wait until the 1970s for line-store conversion to do the job seamlessly.

1970s

On 14 September 1970 the first *Nine O'Clock News* was broadcast on television with Robert Dougall presenting the first week from studio N1—described by *The Guardian* as "a sort of polystyrene padded cell"—the bulletin having been moved from the earlier time of 8:45 pm as a response to the ratings achieved by ITNs *News at Ten* introduced three years earlier. Richard Baker and Kenneth Kendall presented subsequent weeks, thus echoing those first television bulletins of the mid 1950s. The *Nine* made history again in 1975 with the appointment of Angela Rippon as the first female presenter. Her work outside the news was controversial for the time, appearing on the Morecambe and Wise show singing and dancing. The early evening news on BBC 1 remained at its regular time of 5:50 pm—there would be another fourteen years before it got a similar makeover to become the *Six O'Clock News*.

The first edition of *John Craven's Newsround*—initially intended only as a short series and later renamed just *Newsround*—came from studio N3 on 4 April, 1972. Afternoon television news bulletins during the mid to late 1970s were broadcast from the BBC newsroom itself, rather than one of the three news studios. The newsreader would present to camera while sitting on the edge of a desk; behind him staff would be seen working busily at their desks. This period corresponded with when the *Nine O'Clock News* got its next makeover, and would use a CSO background of the newsroom from that very same camera each weekday evening.

Also in the mid seventies, the late night news on BBC 2 was briefly renamed *Newsnight,* but this was not to last, or be the same programme as we know today—that would be launched in 1980—and it soon reverted to being just a news summary with the early evening BBC 2 news expanded to become *Newsday*.

News on radio was to change in the 1970s, and on Radio 4 in particular, brought about by the arrival of new editor Peter Woon from television news and the implementation of the *Broadcasting in the Seventies* report. These included the introduction of correspondents into news bulletins where previously only a newsreader would present, as well as the inclusion of content gathered in the preparation process. New programmes were also added to the daily schedule, PM and The World Tonight as part of the plan for the station to become a "wholly speech network." *Newsbeat* launched as the news service on Radio 1 on 10 September 1973.

The 23 September 1974 saw the launch of the Ceefax teletext system, developed to bring news content on television screens using text only. Engineers originally began developing such a system as a form of communicating news for deaf viewers but the system was expanded. The service is now much more diverse, listing details such as weather, flight times and film reviews. The decline in shooting film for news broadcasts became more prevalent, as ENG equipment became less cumbersome—the BBC's first attempts had been using a Philips colour camera with backpack base station and separate portable Sony U-matic recorder in the latter half of the decade.

1980s

By 1982 ENG technology had become so stable that an Ikegami Tsushinki camera was used by Bernard Hesketh to cover the Falklands War-winning him the RTS TV Cameraman of the Year award and a BAFTA nomination for his "footage"—the first time that the electronic camera had been relied upon in a conflict zone by BBC News, rather than film. BBC News won the BAFTA for its actuality coverage, however the event has become remembered in television terms for Brian Hanrahan's reporting where he coined the phrase "I counted them all out and I counted them all back" to circumvent restrictions, and which has become cited as an example of good reporting under pressure. Two years prior to this the Iranian Embassy Siege had been shot electronically by the BBC Television News OB team with Kate Adie reporting, again nominated for BAFTA actuality coverage, but this time beaten by ITN for the 1980 award.

Newsnight, the news and current affairs programme still running to this day, was due to go on air on 23 January 1980, although trade union disagreements meant that its launch from Lime Grove was postponed by a week." On 27 August, 1981 Moira Stuart became the first Afro-Caribbean female newsreader to appear on British television. The first BBC breakfast television programme, *Breakfast Time* also launched during the 1980s, on 17 January 1983 from Lime Grove Studio E and two weeks before its ITV rival TV-am. Presenters including Frank Bough, Selina Scott and Nick Ross helped to wake viewers with a relaxed style of presenting.

Fig. 8.5: 1980s Computer Generated Titles

The *Six O'Clock News* first aired on 3 September 1984, eventually becoming the most watched news programme in the UK (however, since 2006 it has been overtaken by the *Ten O'Clock News* on TV). Starting in 1981, the BBC gave a common theme to the main news bulletins, with a set of animated computerized "stripes" forming a circle on a red background with a "BBC News" typescript appearing below the circle graphics, and a theme tune comprised of brass and keyboards. The red background was replaced by a blue from 1985 until 1987. The *Nine* used a similar (stripey) number 9.

By 1987, the BBC had decided to re-brand its bulletins and established individual styles again for each one with differing titles and music, the weekend and holiday bulletins branded in a similar style to the *Nine,* although the "stripes" introduction continued to be used until 1989 on occasions where a news bulletin was screened out of the running order of the schedule.

1990s

During the 1990s, a wider range of services began to be offered by BBC News, with the split of BBC World Service Television to become BBC World (news and current affairs), and BBC Prime (light entertainment). Content for a 24-hour news channel was thus required, followed in 1997 with the launch of domestic equivalent BBC News 24. Rather than set bulletins, ongoing reports and coverage was needed to keep both channels functioning and meant a greater emphasis in budgeting for both was necessary.

Fig. 8.6: The *Nine O'clock News* Moved to 10 pm in 2000

In 1998 after 66 years at Broadcasting House, the BBC Radio News operation moved to Television Centre. New 'Silicon Graphics' technology came into use in 1993 for a relaunch of the main BBC One bulletins, creating a virtual set which appeared to be much larger than it was physically. The relaunch also brought all bulletins into the same style of set with only small changes in colouring, titles and music to differentiate each. A computer generated glass scultpure of the BBC coat of arms was the centrepiece of the programme titles until the largescale corporation rebranding of news services in 1999.

In 1999, the biggest relaunch occurred, with BBC One bulletins, BBC World, BBC News 24 and BBC News Online all adopting a common style. One of the most significant changes was the gradual adoption of the corporate image by the BBC regional news programmes, giving a common style across local, national and international BBC television news. This also included *Newyddion*, the main news programme of Welsh language channel S4C, produced by BBC News Wales. The introduction of regional headlines at the start of bulletins followed in 2000 though the English regions lost five minutes at the end of bulletins, due to a new headline round-up at 18:55.

It was also in 2000 that the *Nine O'Clock News* moved to the later time of 10 pm. This was in response to ITN who had just moved their popular *News at Ten* programme to 11 pm. ITN briefly returned *News at Ten* but following poor ratings when head to head against the BBC's *Ten O'Clock News*, the ITN bulletin was moved to 10.30 pm, where it remained until January 14, 2008.

2000s

The retirement of Michael Burke and departure of Peter Sissons from the *Ten O'Clock News* led to a change in the BBC One bulletin presenting team on 20 January 2003. The changes saw a relaunch with the *Six O'Clock News* becoming double headed, and Huw Edwards and Fiona Bruce moving to present the *Ten*. A new set design with a projected background image of a fictional newsroom was introduced, and new programme titles were launched on 16 February 2004 to match those of BBC News 24. BBC News 24 and BBC World introduced a brand new style of presentation in December 2003, that was slightly altered on 5 July 2004 to mark 50 years of BBC Television News.

Editorial changes were announced for the main news bulletins on 8 November 2005 when it was announced that a new single daytime editor position would replace the role of two editors for the *One* and *Six O'Clock News*. The position of Controller of BBC News 24 was created as a replacement for the role of editor, and was awarded to Kevin Bakhurst, then editor of the *Ten O'Clock News* on 16 December. Amanda Farnsworth became daytime editor and Craig Oliver was later named editor of the *Ten O'Clock News*. A further step taken by Head of Television News, Peter Horrocks, was to begin simulcasting the main BBC One news bulletins with News 24, a move he explained would allow for the pooling of operations and "beef up" news operations.

The outgoing set design for BBC One bulletins was introduced on in May 2006, with programme titles slightly updated. This change was to allow for *Breakfast* to move into the same studio as the main bulletins for the first time since 1997. Barco videowall screens provide a backdrop for the set; a view of the London skyline for main news bulletins progressively darkening during the day, while *Breakfast* began with images of cirrus clouds against a blue sky but changed this following criticisms from viewers that it appeared 'too cold' for the time of day. The studio bears similarities to changes made at ITV News in 2004, though ITN uses a CSO Virtual studio rather than the actual screens at BBC News.

A new graphics and playout system was introduced for production of television bulletins in January 2007. This coincided with a new structure to BBC World News bulletins, editors favouring a section devoted to analysing the news stories reported on. The first new BBC News bulletin to be introduced since the *Six O'Clock News* was announced in July 2007 after a successful trial in the Midlands. The summary lasting 90 seconds has broadcast at 8 pm on weekdays since December 2007 and follows a similar style to *60 Seconds* on BBC Three, but also includes headlines from the various BBC regions. BBC News television bulletins underwent their largest change since 1999 on 21 April 2008, as part of a long-term cost cutting plan at the BBC. BBC News 24 was renamed the *BBC News Channel* and moved into the same studio, N6, as the BBC One bulletins at BBC Television Centre. BBC World was renamed *BBC World News* and the BBC One bulletins renamed *BBC News at One, Six* and *Ten* respectively. All the changes followed the redesign of the BBC News website earlier in the year. Regional news programmes were also relaunched following the new style. The studio moves also meant that Studio N9, previously used for BBC World, was closed, and operations moved to the previous studio of BBC News 24.

Organizational Changes

BBC News became part of the new BBC Journalism group in November 2006 as part of a major restructuring of the BBC. Helen Boaden remains Director of BBC News, reporting to Mark Byford, head of the new group and Deputy Director-General.

It was announced on 18 October 2007 as part of Mark Thompson's new six year plan, *Delivering Creative Future,* that there would no longer be a television Current Affairs department in its own right—it would become a unit within the new News Programmes department. The Director General's announcement, in response to a £2 billion shortfall in funding, would deliver *"a smaller, but fitter, BBC"* in the digital age—along with imminent job cuts and the sale of Television Centre in 2013.

The various newsrooms of the BBC: television, radio and online, were merged together to create a multimedia newsroom—programme making within the newsrooms was brought together to form the multimedia programme making departments. Peter Horrocks, referring to the changes, stated that the move would bring about a greater efficiency—particularly at a time of cost-cutting at the BBC. He highlighted the dilemma faced with such a change in his blog: that by using the same resources across the various broadcasting mediums means fewer stories can be covered—or by following more stories, there would be fewer ways to broadcast them.

The entire News Operation is due to move from Television Centre to new facilities at Broadcasting House at Portland Place, Central London. Refurbishment and extension work was scheduled for completion in 2008 though delays have seen the deadline extended until 2010, with news expecting to move in in 2012. The new building will also become home to the BBC World Service once the lease on Bush House expires.

Broadcasting Media

Television

BBC News is responsible for the main news bulletins on BBC One as well as other programmes on BBC Two, BBC Three, BBC Four, the BBC News Channel, and the provision of 22 hours of programming for BBC World News. Production of BBC Parliament is carried out on behalf of the BBC by Millbank Studios though BBC News provides editorial and journalistic content.

BBC News content is also output onto the BBC's digital interactive television services under the BBCi brand, and the legacy analogue CEEFAX teletext system.

The distinctive music on all BBC television news programmes was introduced in 1999 and composed by David Lowe. It was part of the extensive rebranding which commenced in 1999 and features the classic 'BBC Pips'. The general theme was used not only on bulletins on BBC One but News 24, BBC World and local news programmes in the BBC's Nations and Regions. Lowe was also responsible for the music on Radio One's *Newsbeat*. The theme has had several changes since 1999. The new BBC Arabic Television news channel launched in early 2008, with a Persian language channel set to follow; both will include news, analysis, interviews, sports and highly cultural programmes.

Radio

BBC Radio News produces bulletins for the BBC's national radio stations and provides content for local BBC radio stations via the General News Service (GNS). BBC News does not produce the BBC's regional news bulletins, which are produced individually by the BBC nations and regions themselves. The BBC World Service broadcasts to some 150 million people in English as well as 32 languages across the globe.

Online

BBC News Online is the BBC's news website. Launched in November 1997, it is one of the most popular news websites in the UK reaching over a quarter of the UK's internet users, and worldwide, with around 4 million global readers every month. The website contains exhaustive international news coverage as well as entertainment, sport, science, and political news. Many reports are accompanied by audio and video from the BBC's television and radio news services within the BBC News player.

Television and radio bulletins are also available to view on the site, together with current affairs programmes including *Newsnight* and *Question Time* are available to view on the site after they have been broadcast, while BBC News 24 is available to view 24 hours a day. Certain radio and television broadcasts are available for download as podcasts as part of the BBC's download trial.

Opinions

Political and Commercial Independence

The BBC is required by its charter to be free from both political and commercial influence and answers only to its viewers and listeners. Nevertheless, the BBC's political objectivity is sometimes questioned. For instance, *The Daily Telegraph* (3 August 2005) carried a letter from the KGB defector Oleg Gordievsky, referring to it as "The Red Service." Books have been written on the subject, although rarely from people writing neutrally themselves, including anti-BBC works like *Truth Betrayed* by W J West and *The Truth Twisters* by Richard Deacon.

The BBC is regularly accused by the government of the day of bias in favour of the opposition and, by the opposition, of bias in favour of the government. Similarly, during times of war, the BBC is often accused by the UK government, or by strong supporters of British military campaigns, of being overly sympathetic to the view of the enemy. This gave rise, in 1991 during the first Gulf War, to the satirical name "Baghdad Broadcasting Corporation." During the Kosovo War, the BBC were labeled the "Belgrade Broadcasting Corporation" by British ministers, although Slobodan Milosevic later complained that the BBC's coverage had been biased *against* the Serbs. Conversely, some of those who style themselves anti-establishment in the United Kingdom or who oppose foreign wars have accused the BBC of pro-establishment bias or of refusing to give an outlet to "anti-war" voices. Following the 2003 invasion of Iraq a study, by the Cardiff University School of Journalism, of the reporting of the war, found that nine out of 10 references to weapons of mass destruction during the war assumed that Iraq possessed them, and only one in 10 questioned this assumption. It also found that out of the main British broadcasters covering the war the BBC was the most likely to use the British government and military as its source. It was also the least likely to use independent sources, like the Red Cross, who were more critical of the war. When it came to reporting Iraqi casualties the study found fewer reports on the BBC than on the other three main channels. The report's author, Justin Lewis, wrote of his findings: "Far from revealing an anti-war BBC, our findings tend to give credence to those who criticized the BBC for being too sympathetic to the government in its war coverage. Either way, it is clear that the accusation of BBC anti-war bias fails to stand up to any serious or sustained analysis."

Some have argued that a current of anti-BBC thinking exists in many parts of the political spectrum and that, since the BBC's theoretical impartiality means they will broadcast many views and opinions, people will see the bias they wish to see. This argument is buttressed by the fact that the BBC is frequently accused of bias from all directions.

Prominent BBC appointments are constantly assessed by the British media and political establishment for signs of political bias. The appointment of Greg Dyke as Director-General was highlighted by press sources because Dyke was a Labour Party member and former activist, as well as a friend of Tony Blair. The BBC's current Political Editor, Nick Robinson, was some years ago a chairman of the Young Conservatives and has, as a result, attracted informal criticism from the current Labour government, but his predecessor Andrew Marr faced similar claims from the right because he was editor of the liberal leaning Independent newspaper before his own appointment in 2000.

Hutton Inquiry

BBC News was at the centre of one the largest political controversies in recent years. Three BBC News reports (Andrew Gilligan's on *Today*, Gavin Hewitt's on *The Ten O'Clock News* and another on *Newsnight*) quoted an anonymous source that stated the British government (particularly the Prime Minister's office) had embellished the September Dossier with misleading exaggerations of Iraq's weapons of mass destruction capabilities. The government denounced the reports and accused the corporation of poor journalism.

In subsequent weeks the corporation stood by the report, saying that it had a reliable source. Following intense media speculation, David Kelly was named in the press as the source for Gilligan's story on 9 July 2003. Kelly was found dead, by suicide, in a field close to his home early on 18 July. An inquiry led by Lord Hutton was announced by the British government the following day to investigate the circumstances leading to Kelly's death, concluding that "Dr. Kelly took his own life."

In his report on 28 January 2004, Lord Hutton concluded that Gilligan's original accusation was "unfounded" and the BBC's editorial and management processes were "defective". In particular, it specifically criticized the chain of management that caused the BBC to defend its story. The BBC Director of News, Richard Sambrook, the report said, had accepted Gilligan's word that his story was accurate in spite of his notes being incomplete. Davies had then told the BBC Board of Governors that he was happy with the story and told the Prime Minister that a satisfactory internal inquiry had taken place. The Board of Governors, under BBC Chairman Gavyn Davies' guidance, accepted that further investigation of the Government's complaints were unnecessary.

Because of the criticism in the Hutton report, Davies resigned on the day of publication. BBC News faced an important test, reporting on itself with the publication of the report, but by common consent (of the Board of Governors) managed this "independently, impartially and honestly." Davies' resignation was followed by the resignation of Director General Greg Dyke the following day, and the resignation of Gilligan on 30 January. While doubtless a traumatic experience for the corporation, an ICM poll in April 2003 indicated that it had sustained its position as the best and most trusted provider of news.

Israeli-Palestinian Conflict

The BBC has faced accusations of holding both anti-Arab and anti-Israel biases, and being anti-semitic. For example, Douglas Davis, the London correspondent of *The Jerusalem Post*, has described the BBC's coverage of the Arab-Israeli conflict as "a relentless, one-dimensional portrayal of Israel as a demonic, criminal state and Israelis as brutal oppressors [which] bears all the hallmarks of a concerted campaign of vilification that, wittingly or not, has the effect of delegitimizing the Jewish state and pumping oxygen into a dark old European hatred that dared not speak its name for the past half-century."

Noam Chomsky, and David Edwards of Medialens.org tend to criticize the BBC through differences in terminology sometimes used to describe Israeli and Palestinian actions. Israeli shootings are usually described as "security sweeps" or "incursions", while Palestinian shootings are described as "terrorist killings" committed by "gunmen." Such differences are said to indicate the common institutional bias typical of Western thinking, which is neutral, so seen by racists and fanatics as biased against their side.

An independent panel was set up in 2006 to review the impartiality of the BBC's coverage of the Israeli-Palestinian conflict. The panel's assessment was that "apart from individual lapses, there was little to suggest deliberate or systematic bias." While noting a "commitment to be fair accurate and impartial" and praising much of the BBC's coverage the independent panel concluded "that BBC output does not consistently give a full and fair account of the conflict. In some ways the picture is incomplete and, in that sense, misleading." Writing in the FT, Philip Stephens, one of the panelists, later accused the BBC's director-general, Mark Thompson, of misrepresenting the panel's conclusions. He further opined "My sense is that BBC news reporting has also lost a once iron-clad commitment to objectivity and a necessary respect for the democratic process. If I am right, the BBC, too, is lost." Mark Thompson published a rebuttal in the FT the next day.

The report listed examples of how the BBC could be said to be biased in favour of Israel in section 4.7. The Guardian too has noted that "The BBC has had a difficult time over its coverage of Israel, with regular accusations of bias coming from both the Israeli and Palestinian sides." The description by one BBC correspondent reporting on the funeral of Yassir Arafat that she had been left with tears in her eyes led to other questions of impartiality, particularly from Martin Walker in a guest opinion piece in *The Times*, who picked out the apparent case of Fayad Abu Shamala, the BBC Arabic Service correspondent, who told a Hamas rally on 6 May, 2001, that journalists in Gaza were "waging the campaign shoulder to shoulder together with the Palestinian people."

Walker argues that the independent inquiry was flawed for two reasons. Firstly, because the time period over which it was conducted (August 2005 to January 2006) surrounded the Israeli withdrawal from Gaza and Ariel Sharon's stroke, which produced more positive coverage than usual. Furthermore, he wrote, the inquiry only looked at the BBC's domestic coverage, and excluded output on the BBC World Service and BBC World.

The View of Foreign Governments

BBC News reporters and broadcasts are now and have in the past been banned in several countries primarily for reporting which has been unfavourable to the ruling government. For example, correspondents were banned by the former apartheid régime of South Africa. The BBC is currently banned in Zimbabwe, whose government has proscribed it as a terrorist organization. The BBC has been banned in Myanmar (Burma) since the anti-government protests there in September 2007. Other cases have included Uzbekistan, China and Pakistan. The BBC online news site's Persian version was recently blocked from the Iranian internet.

CNN

Cable News Network, usually referred to by its initialism CNN, is a major English language television network founded in 1980 by Ted Turner. The network is now owned by Time Warner and the news network is a division of the Turner Broadcasting System. CNN was the first station to provide 24-hour television news coverage. It is now second only to Britain's BBC News in the number of employed news journalists and worldwide news bureaus.

In terms of unique viewers (Nielsen Cume Ratings), CNN rates as America's number one cable news network, and is ranked number two behind Fox News in total audience Nielsen ratings. While the news network has numerous affiliates, CNN primarily broadcasts from its headquarters at the CNN Center in Atlanta, the Time Warner Center in New York City, and studios in Washington, D.C. As of June 2008, the network is available in 93 million US households and more than 890,000 American hotel rooms. The U.S version of their broadcast is also shown in Canada. Globally, CNN airs through CNN International and has combined branded networks and services that are available to more than 1.5 billion people in over 212 countries and territories.

Launched	June 1, 1980
Owned by	Turner Broadcasting System, Inc. (a Time Warner company)
Picture format	480i (SDTV) 1080i (HDTV)
Slogan	"The Most Trusted Name in News", "CNN = Politics", "The Best Political Team on Television", "CNN = Money"
Country	United States
Language	English
Headquarters	Atlanta, Georgia, United States
Sister channel(s)	CNN Airport Network CNN en Español CNN International Headline News
	Availability
	Satellite
DirecTV	Channel 202 (SD/HD) Channel 1202 (VOD)
Dish Network	Channel 200 SD & 9436 HD
Bell TV	Channel 500
Star Choice	Channel 500
	Cable
Available on most cable systems	Check local listings
	Satellite Radio
Sirius	132
XM	122
	IPTV over ADSL
TELUS TV (Canada)	Channel 94

History

The Cable News Network was launched at 5:00 p.m. EST on Sunday June 1, 1980. After an introduction by Ted Turner, the husband and wife team of David Walker and Lois Hart anchored the first newscast. Since its debut, CNN has expanded its reach to a number of cable and satellite television networks, several web sites, specialized closed-circuit networks (such as CNN Airport Network), and two radio networks. The network has 36 bureaus (10 domestic, 26 international), more than 900 affiliated local stations, and several regional and foreign-language networks around the world. The network's success made a bona-fide mogul of founder Ted Turner and set the stage for the Time Warner conglomerate's eventual acquisition of Turner Broadcasting.

Despite its domestic standing, CNN remains a distant second in international news coverage, reaching just over half of the audience of the older BBC World News. Unlike the BBC's network of reporters and bureaus, CNN International makes extensive use of affiliated reporters that are local to, and often directly affected by, the events they are reporting. The effect is a more immediate, less detached style of on-the-ground coverage. This has done little to stem criticism, largely from Middle Eastern nations, that CNN International reports news from a pro-American perspective. This is a marked contrast to domestic criticisms that often portray CNN as having a "liberal" or "anti-American" bias.

A companion network, Headline News (originally called CNN2) was launched on January 1, 1982 and featured a continuous 24-hour cycle of 30-minute news broadcasts. Headline News broke from its original format in 2005 with the addition of *Headline Prime*. Current programmes feature confrontational personalities like radio talk-show host Glenn Beck and former Fulton County, Georgia prosecutor Nancy Grace. CNN HD was launched September 1, 2007, and was first nationally distributed by DirecTV on September 26, 2007.

The Gulf War

The first Persian Gulf War in 1991 was a watershed event for CNN that catapulted the network past the "big three" American networks for the first time in its history, largely due to an unprecedented, historical scoop: CNN was the only news outlet with the ability to communicate from inside Iraq during the initial hours of the American bombing campaign, with live reports from the al-Rashid Hotel in Baghdad by reporters Bernard Shaw, John Holliman, and Peter Arnett.

The Gulf War experience brought CNN some much sought-after legitimacy and made household names of previously obscure (and infamously low-paid) reporters. Many of these reporters now comprise CNN's "old guard." Bernard Shaw became CNN's chief anchor until his retirement in 2001. Others include the then-Pentagon correspondent Wolf Blitzer (now host of *The Situation Room* and *Late Edition with Wolf Blitzer*) and international correspondent Christiane Amanpour. Amanpour's presence in Iraq was caricatured by actress Nora Dunn as the ruthless reporter "Adriana Cruz" in the film *Three Kings* (1999). Time Warner later produced a television movie, *Live from Baghdad*, about the network's coverage of the first Gulf War, which aired on HBO.

The CNN Effect

Coverage of the first Gulf War and other crises of the early 1990s (particularly the infamous Battle of Mogadishu) led officials at the Pentagon to coin the term "the CNN effect" to describe the perceived impact of real time, 24-hour news coverage on the decision-making processes of the American government.

Fig. 8.7: CNN Breaking the News about the September 11, 2001 Attacks

CNN was the first network to have broken news of the September 11 attacks. Anchor Carol Lin was on the air to deliver the first public report of the event. She broke into a commercial at 8:49 a.m. ET and said:

"This just in. You are looking at obviously a very disturbing live shot there. That is the World Trade Center, and we have unconfirmed reports this morning that a plane has crashed into one of the towers of the World Trade Center. CNN Center right now is just beginning to work on this story, obviously calling our sources and trying to figure out exactly what happened, but clearly something relatively devastating happening this morning there on the south end of the island of Manhattan. That is once again, a picture of one of the towers of the World Trade Center."

Daryn Kagan and Leon Harris were live on the air just after 9 a.m. ET as the second plane hit the World Trace Center and through an interivew with CNN correspondent David Ensor, reported the news that U.S. officials determined "that this is a terrorist act." Later, Aaron Brown anchored through the day and night as the attacks unfolded. Brown had just come to CNN from ABC to be the Breaking News anchor.

Sean Murtagh, CNN vice-president for finance and administration, was the first network employee on the air in New York.

Experiments

CNN launched two specialty news channels for the American market which would later close amid competitive pressure: CNNSI shut down in 2002, and CNNfn shut down after nine years on the air in December 2004. CNN and Sports Illustrated's partnership continues today online at CNNSI.com. CNNfn's former website now redirects to money.cnn.com, a product of CNN's strategic partnership with *Money* magazine. Money and SI are both properties of Time Warner, along with CNN.

Online

CNN debuted its news website CNN.com (then known as *CNN Interactive*) on August 30, 1995. Initially an experiment, interest in CNN.com grew steadily over its first decade and today CNN.com is now one of the most popular news websites in the world. The wide spread growth of blogs, social media and user-generated content have influenced the site, and blogs in particular have focused CNN's previously scattershot online offerings, most noticeably in the development and launch of CNN Pipeline in late 2005.

CNN pipeline was the name of a paid subscription service, its corresponding website, and a content delivery client that provided streams of live video from up to four sources (or "pipes"), on-demand access to CNN stories and reports, and optional pop-up "news alerts" to computer users. The installable client was available to users of PCs running Microsoft Windows. There was also a browser-based "web client" that did not require installation. In July 2007 the service was discontinued and replaced with a free streaming service.

The now-defunct topical news-programme *Judy Woodruff's Inside Politics* was the first CNN programme to feature a round-up of blogs in 2004. Blog coverage was expanded when *Inside Politics* was folded into *The Situation Room*. In 2006 CNN launched CNN Exchange and CNN iReport, initiatives designed to further introduce and centralize the impact of everything from blogging to citizen journalism within the CNN brand. CNN iReport which features user-submitted photos and video, has achieved considerable traction, with increasingly professional-looking reports filed by amateur journalists, many still in high school or college. The iReport gained more prominence when observers of the Virginia Tech Shootings sent-in first hand photos of what was going during the shootings.

As of early 2008, CNN maintains a free live broadcast. CNN International is broadcasted live, as part of the RealNetworks SuperPass subscription outside US. CNN also offers several RSS feeds and podcasts. On April 18, 2008 CNN.com was targeted by Chinese hackers in retaliation for the network's coverage on the 2008 Tibetan unrest. CNN reported that they took preventative measures after news broke of the impending attack. The company was honoured at the 2008 Technology and Engineering Emmy Awards for development and implementation of an integrated and portable IP-based live, edit and store-and-forward digital newsgathering system.

Criticism and Controversies

CNN has been accused of perpetrating media bias for allegedly promoting both a conservative and a liberal agenda based on previous incidents. Media Matters for America has documented several hundred separate instances of what it sees as conservative editorializing during CNN broadcasts. Accuracy in Media and MRC have claimed that CNN's reporting contains liberal editorializing within news stories.

In 2002, Honest Reporting spearheaded a campaign to expose CNN for pro-Palestinian bias, citing public remarks in which Ted Turner equated Palestinian suicide bombing with Israeli military strikes.

Several prominent former CNN personalities have come to criticize certain aspects of the news network. Aaron Brown has said that CNN has committed "huge mistakes" and frames CNN as an "organization that is trying to figure out if it can be all things to all people." However, he also praised CNN's journalistic superiority, saying, "[...] CNN's a better journalism organization." Bernard Shaw has expressed that he is "very very disappointed with the way the news management" has handled his favourite network. He criticized the effects of Fox News' "commentary [and] personal analysis" on the news reporting of CNN, saying that "CNN continues to ape many of the on-air mannerisms of the Fox News Network, and I don't like that." As said by Ted Turner, founder of CNN, "There really is not much of a point getting some Tom, Dick or Harry off the streets to report on when we can snag a big name whom everyone identifies with. After all, it is all part of the business." However, in April 2008, Turner criticized the direction CNN has taken.

A Chinese website, anti-cnn.com, has accused CNN and western media in general of biased reporting against China, with the catch-phrase "Don't be so CNN" catching on in the Chinese mainstream as jokingly meaning "Don't be so biased." Pictures used by CNN are allegedly edited to have completely different meanings from the original ones. In addition, the network was accused of largely ignoring pro-China voices during the Olympic Torch Relay in San Francisco. Though these allegations exist, none have been proven to be true.

On April 24, 2008 beautician Liang Shubing and teacher Li Lilan sued commentator Jack Cafferty and CNN $1.3 billion damages ($1 per person in China), in New York, for "violating the dignity and reputation of the Chinese people." This was in response to an incident during CNN's "The Situation Room" on April 9, where Cafferty stated his opinion that "[the USA] continue to import their junk with the lead paint on them and the poisoned pet food" despite his view that "[the Chinese leaders were] basically the same bunch of goons and thugs they have been for the last 50 years." Further, amid China's Foreign Ministry demand for an apology, 14 lawyers filed a similar suit in Beijing.

CNN has also been accused of pro-georgian coverage of Southossetian conflict. Allegedly, it stole Rusiya Al-Yaum records from Tskhinvali and represented them as shots from Gori.

CNN in Popular Culture

- CNN has been parodied many times. Many movies outside of the Turner Broadcasting Network also mention CNN in their storylines. Several television shows (*i.e.* Seven Days, JAG, and NCIS) use a parody of CNN known as *ZNN*. In the movie *Mr. Bones* appears a news network with the name "CCN", its logo being in the same font as CNN's. In the video game *Desert Strike*, the in-game news station is called *EANN*, with the EA standing for the video game company's name, Electronic Arts. The movie *Batman Forever* shows a newscast on "GNN" (presumably standing for Gotham News Network). The logo is very similar to the "CNN" logo. GNN also appears on the Nolan series of Batman films. Other parodies or references include *Command and Conquer: Generals—Zero Hour*'s American campaign, featuring updates on missions with a correspondent from BNN, the rapper Eminem included a similar alteration in his song "Without Me", where, dressed up as Osama Bin Laden he was reported on by ENN, due to his name being Eminem.
- CNN's most famous station ID is a five-second musical jingle with James Earl Jones' simple but classic line, *"This is CNN."* Jones' voice can still be heard today in updated station IDs. The line has also been referenced in other programming, including The Simpsons.
- Australian satirist group The Chaser produced 12 half-hour episodes of CNNNN, a show that parodied the logo and slogan, with taglines such as "We report,

You believe." The show ended after CNN threatened to sue. The Chaser was shown on CNN in July 2007 after their APEC 2007 stunt on their show The Chaser's War on Everything created considerable controversy.

CNN HD

CNN HD is a 1080i High definition simulcast of CNN. Since most of CNN's programme are not produced in HD, stylized pillarboxing is used. However, during special events such as election day coverage, the areas on the sides show extra information, such as poll numbers (percentages) for each candidate and state. These are not seen on the SD channel.

Current Shows

Weekdays

ET	*Programme*	*Host(s)*	*Description*
6a-9a	American Morning	John Roberts and Kiran Chetry	The network's morning news programme.
9a-12p	CNN Newsroom	Tony Harris and Heidi Collins	A daily look at what's making news, airing live from the headquarters in Atlanta.
12p-1p	Issue #1	Ali Velshi and Gerri Willis	Live coverage of the economy, currently pre-empts an hour of Your World Today.
1p-4p	CNN Newsroom	Don Lemon and Kyra Phillips	A daily look at what's making news, airing live from the headquarters in Atlanta.
4p-7p	The Situation Room	Wolf Blitzer	A fast-paced look at the day's top stories, focusing on politics and homeland security.
7p-8p	Lou Dobbs Tonight	Lou Dobbs	A nightly news and discussion programme.
8p-9p	CNN Election Center	Campbell Brown	Discussion of the day's top political news and issues that matter to voters.
9p-10p	Larry King Live	Larry King	A nightly talk programme.
10p-12a	Anderson Cooper 360	Anderson Cooper	A fast-paced, nightly news programme. The second hour is typically a repeat of the first.

Weekends

ET	Saturday Programme	Saturday Hosts	Saturday Description	Sunday Programme	Sunday Hosts	Sunday Description
7a-830a	CNN Saturday Morning	Betty Nguyen and T.J. Holmes	The network's weekend morning news programme.	CNN Sunday Morning	Betty Nguyen and T.J. Holmes	The network's weekend morning news programme.
830a-9a	House Call	Dr. Sanjay Gupta	Medical news programme.	House Call	Dr. Sanjay Gupta	Medical news programme.
9a-930a	CNN Saturday Morning	Betty Nguyen and T.J. Holmes	The network's weekend morning news programme.	CNN Sunday Morning	Betty Nguyen and T.J. Holmes	The network's weekend morning news programme.
930a-10a	Open House	Gerri Willis	A personal finance show with a focus on the housing market.			
10a-11a	CNN Newsroom	Betty Nguyen and T.J. Holmes/Fredricka Whitfield (for 12p hour).	A daily look at what's making news, airing live from the headquarters in Atlanta.	Reliable Sources	Howard Kurtz	A weekly talk programme focusing on a critical look at the media.
11a-1p				Late Edition	Wolf Blitzer	CNN's political talk show, similar to CBS' Face the Nation or NBC's Meet the Press.
1p-2p	Your $$$$	Ali Velshi and Christian Romans	A weekend business news programme.	Fareed Zakaria GPS	Fareed Zakaria	A weekly talk show focused on international issues
2p-3p	CNN Special Investigations Unit	Various	Investigative reports.	This Week in Politics	Tom Foreman	Weekly look at political news.

(Contd.)

(*Contd.*)

ET	Saturday Programme	Saturday Hosts	Saturday Description	Sunday Programme	Sunday Hosts	Sunday Description
3p-4p	CNN Newsroom	Fredricka Whitfield/Rick Sanchez (for 5p hour)	A daily look at what's making news, airing live from the headquarters in Atlanta.	Your $$$$	Ali Velshi and Christian Romans	A weekend business news programme.
4p-6p				CNN Newsroom	Fredricka Whitfield	A daily look at what's making news, airing live from the head-quarters in Atlanta.
6p-7p	This Week in Politics	Tom Foreman	Weekly look at political news.	CNN Newsroom	Rick Sanchez	A daily look at what's making news, airing live from the head-quarters in Atlanta.
7p-8p	Lou Dobbs This Week	Lou Dobbs	Weekly edition of Lou Dobbs Tonight	Lou Dobbs This Week	Lou Dobbs	Weekly edition of Lou Dobbs Tonight
8p-9p	CNN Special Invistigations Unit/CNN Presents/Other specials	Various	Various special programming	CNN Special Invistigations Unit/CNN Presents/Other specials	Various	Various special programming
9p-10p	Larry King Live	Larry King	A nightly talk programme.	Larry King Live	Larry King	A nightly talk programme.
10p-11p	CNN Newsroom	Rick Sanchez	A daily look at what's making news, airing live from the headquarters in Atlanta.	CNN Newsroom	Rick Sanchez	A daily look at what's making news, airing live from the head-quarters in Atlanta.

Former Shows

- *Both Sides with Jesse Jackson*: A political talk show, hosted by civil rights leader and two-time presidential candidate Jesse Jackson, that aired Sundays. The show ran from 1992 to 2000.
- *The Capital Gang*: One of cable news' longest running programmes, focusing on discussion of the political news of the week. The original panelists were Pat Buchanan, Al Hunt, Mark Shields, and Robert Novak. When Buchanan left the network to run for president, Margaret Warner, Mona Charen, and later Margaret Carlson and Kate O'Beirne became regular panelists. *The Capital Gang* aired Saturday nights at 7 p.m. ET from 1988 to 2005.
- *Crossfire*: A political "debate" programme, anchored by hosts from left-wing and right-wing ideologies, that aired during prime time and daytime until mid-2005. Originally hosted by Tom Braden and Pat Buchanan, other hosts included , Michael Kinsley, John H. Sununu, Bill Press, Geraldine Ferraro, Mary Matalin, Tucker Carlson, James Carville, and Paul Begala. *Crossfire* was discontinued in 2005.
- *Evans and Novak*: Saturday night political interview programme with Rowland Evans and Robert Novak. The name changed to *Evans, Novak, Hunt and Shields* in 1998 when Al Hunt and Mark Shields became permanent panelists. When Evans died in 2001, the name changed to *Novak, Hunt, and Shields* for its final year on CNN.
- *Next@CNN*: A scientific and technology oriented programme hosted by Daniel Sieberg. Aired on weekends. Despite its cancellation on CNN in the US, the show continues to air new episodes on CNN International.
- *Inside Politics*: A political programme that aired from 3:30–5 p.m. ET weekdays. Replaced by *The Situation Room* in 2005.
- *Wolf Blitzer Reports*: A daily look at the day's stories that aired live from Washington at 5 p.m. ET. Replaced by *The Situation Room* in 2005.

- *NewsNight with Aaron Brown*: A hard-news programme anchored by Aaron Brown which took an in-depth look at the main US and international stories of the day. Was axed from CNN's schedule on November 5, 2005, leading to Brown's immediate resignation from the network.
- *CNN Daybreak*: A first look at the day's stories that aired live from New York City at 5 a.m. ET.
- *CNN Sports Sunday*: Co-anchored by Bob Kurtz and Nick Charles.
- *Connie Chung Tonight*: Hosted by Connie Chung. Cancelled in March 2003.
- *Freeman Reports*: One of the original programmes from 1980. Host Sonja Freeman interviewed guests and took live telephone call-ins regarding current news events and other topics of interest. For a brief period the programme featured a live audience in Atlanta. Freeman's former time slot is now occupied by Larry King.
- *People Now*: Another original programme. Host Lee Leonard interviewed celebrities and discussed entertainment news in a one hour programme live from the CNN Los Angeles bureau. Leonard was replaced by Mike Douglas, who himself was replaced by Bill Tush in December 1982.
- *Computer Connection*
- *Future Watch*
- *Your Health*
- *Style with Elsa Klensch*: Weekly half hour on Saturday mornings featuring news on style and fashion.
- *Talk Back Live*: A call-in talk show with a live audience hosted most recently by Arthel Neville. Aired from 1994 to 2003.
- *On the Story' '—CNN's interactive "week-in-review" series featuring an in-depth look at the story behind some of the week's biggest stories. Anchored by Ali Velshi. However, the show was suspended in June 2006, later cancelled in July.*
- *Burden of Proof*: A show that discussed legal issues of the day, hosted by Greta Van Susteren and Roger Cossack.
- *Newsstand*
- *Newshour*

- *Sonya/Sonya Live in LA: A weekday call-in show airing at 1 p.m. Eastern in the late 1980's and Early 1990s hosted by Dr. Sonya Friedman.*
- *CNN Live Today*: Was a daily look at what's making news, airing live from Atlanta at 10 a.m. ET on weekdays. Anchored by Daryn Kagan.
- *Live From...*: A lively look at the day's stories airing live from Atlanta at 1 p.m. ET. Anchored by Kyra Phillips.
- *CNN Live Saturday/CNN Live Sunday*: A look at what's making news on the weekends, airing live from Atlanta. Anchored by Fredricka Whitfield 12:00–6:00 p.m. and Carol Lin 6:00–11:00 p.m. Replaced in 2006 by CNN Newsroom Weekend.
- *CNN Saturday Night/CNN Sunday Night*: The network's weekend evening news programme, airing at 6 p.m. ET and 10 p.m. ET. Anchored by Carol Lin. Replaced in 2006 by CNN Newsroom Weekend.
- *People in the News*: CNN's feature-format programme with PEOPLE magazine profiling newsmakers from politics, sports, business, medicine, and entertainment. The programme aired on the weekend and has hosted by Paula Zahn.
- *Diplomatic License*: Weekly programme on CNNI hosted by Richard Roth, focusing on the United Nations. The show ran from 1994 to 2006.
- *Paula Zahn Now*: Was a look at the current issues affecting the world, with former CBS and Fox News anchor Paula Zahn. Last broadcast was on August 2, 2007.
- *Greenfield at Large*: Anchored by Jeff Greenfield in New York (aired at 10 p.m. ET weeknights).
- *CNN NewsSite*: Anchored by Joie Chen from Atlanta (aired at 4 p.m. ET weekdays: integrated the news and internet).
- *The Point with Greta Van Susteren*

Specialized Channels

- CNN.com Live
- CNN Airport Network
- CNN en Español
- CNN Headline News

- CNN HD (High-definition edition of the network, launched September 1, 2007)
- CNN International
- CNN Pipeline (24-hour multi-channel broadband online news service).
- CNN+ (a partner network in Spain, launched in 1999 with Sogecable).
- CNN TÜRK: A Turkish media outlet.
- CNN-IBN: An Indian news channel.
- CNNj: A Japanese news outlet.
- CNN Chile: A Chilean news channel to be launched in mid-2008.
- CNN Italia: A Italian news website launched in partnership with Gruppo editoriale l'Espresso and after with Il Sole 24 Ore, launched November 15, 1999 and closed in September 12, 2003.
- CNNfn (Financial network, closed in December 2004)
- CNN Sports Illustrated (also known as CNNSI), the network's all-sports channel, closed in 2002.

CNN Bureaus

United States

- Atlanta (Headquarters)
- Boston
- Chicago
- Dallas
- Los Angeles
- Miami
- New Orleans
- New York City
- San Francisco
- Washington, D.C.
- Columbus
- Denver
- Houston
- Las Vegas
- Minneapolis
- Orlando
- Philadelphia
- Phoenix

- Raleigh-Durham
- Seattle

Worldwide

- Baghdad, Iraq
- Bangkok, Thailand
- Beijing, China
- Beirut, Lebanon
- Berlin, Germany
- Bogotá, Colombia
- Cairo, Egypt
- Dubai, United Arab Emirates
- Havana, Cuba
- Hong Kong (Asia/Pacific regional headquarters)
- Islamabad, Pakistan
- Istanbul, Turkey
- Jakarta, Indonesia
- Jerusalem, Israel
- Johannesburg, South Africa
- Lagos, Nigeria
- London, United Kingdom (European regional headquarters)
- Madrid, Spain
- Mexico City, Mexico
- Moscow, Russia
- Nairobi, Kenya
- New Delhi, India
- Paris, France
- Rome, Italy
- Rio de Janeiro, Brazil
- São Paulo, Brazil
- Seoul, South Korea
- Sydney, Australia
- Tokyo, Japan

CNN.COM

The international edition of CNN.com is constantly updated to bring the top news stories from around the world. It is produced by dedicated staff in London and Hong Kong, working with colleagues at CNN's world headquarters in Atlanta, Georgia, and with bureaus worldwide. CNN.com relies heavily on CNN's global team of almost 4,000 news professionals.

Viewer Opinions

Help us make your comments count. Use our viewer comment page to tell us what you think about our shows by clicking on: http://www.cnn.com/feedback/

Help Page

If you have questions about how to use CNN.com or wish to request transcripts or videotapes, visit: CNN.com/feedback/help

CNN: What's On

The full rundown of all CNN programmes wherever you live CNN.com/CNNI

Services

E-Mail Newsletters

Be the first to know with a variety of e-mail news services. CNN.com/EMAIL

Subscription Video Services

CNN video is available with a subscription to CNN NewsPass or through RealOne SuperPass. If you are already a member of either CNN NewsPass or RealOne SuperPass and are having problems accessing your account, visit our FAQ for answers to frequently asked questions or go to https://account.real.com/acct/login.html for a Web-based customer service. You can also e-mail your comments directly to Customer Service.

Order CNN Video Tapes

To buy video tapes of CNN shows click here, or go to https://orion.fdch.com/forms/orcnn.html

Advertise on CNN.com

Send an e-mail and a CNN representative will provide information about advertising on the CNN Websites, or go to http://www.cnnmedia.com/cnncorp.

Business Development

Companies interested in partnering with CNN should contact CNN Business Operations by sending an e-mail to bizops@cnn.com.

Job Search

For information about job opportunities with CNN, visit www.turnerjobs.com

Send Us Your Feedback

Do you have a question, comment, suggestion or news tip to pass along to CNN? If you have a question or comment, please select the CNN network you would like to contact. If you have information or photos about a news story, please select News Tips. This page features a selection of comments sent in by CNN.com users about news coverage and other issues related to the site.

About Us

To learn more about CNN.com, including information about our programmes and anchors, our services, taking a studio tour, or to explore career opportunities with CNN.

Help Page

Visit our extensive FAQs for answers to all of your questions, from CNN TV programming to RSS to the CNN member center.

ABC NEWS

ABC News is a division of American television and radio network ABC, owned by The Walt Disney Company. Its current president is David Westin.

Fig. 8.8: ABC News Logo

Fig. 8.9: ABC News Special Report Ident, Circa 2006

Current Programmes

- *America This Morning*
- *Good Morning America*
- *Good Morning America Weekend Edition*
- *This Week with George Stephanopoulos*
- *ABC World News with Charles Gibson*
- *ABC World News Saturday & Sunday*
- *20/20*
- *Nightline*
- *ABC World News Now*

ABC News Radio distributes, through ABC Radio Networks, newscasts on the hour, live feeds and speciality news programming to some 2,000 local affiliates. *ABC NewsOne* is ABC News's affiliate news service. It gathers and feeds regional, national and international news material to ABC affiliates around the country and foreign networks. *ABC News Now* is the ABC's 24/7 news channel available online and other sources such as mobile phones. A 30 second "ABC News Brief" is broadcast weekdays at 2:58 p.m. ET, between One Life to Live and General Hospital. ABC News Briefs used to appear during many programmes, and also had sponsorships as well (similar to NBC News Digest).

A news brief containing information relevant to college students is shown every hour on MtvU, and ABC News segments are packaged or customized for broadcast over Wal-

Mart's in-store television network. ESPN, also owned by Disney, provides sports bulletins and video for some of ABC's newscasts, especially the overnight programmes. ABC News shows Primetime during the summer months along with i-CAUGHT.

Specials

- *ABC 2000 Today*
- *Peter Jennings Reporting*
- *The Century*
- *Give Me a Break* (*20/20* spinoff)

International Broadcasts

ABC News programming is shown daily on the 24-hour news network Orbit News in Europe and the Middle East. This includes several shows from ABC News. It is also available online at ABC News Now.

ABC's World News appears regularly at 1.30 a.m. local time on BBC News Channel in the UK, which itself may be simulcast on BBC One or Two during the overnight period. Commercials are removed as the BBC's UK services are financed by a license fee. ABC and the BBC also share video and reporters as needed in producing their newscasts.

In Australia, ABC World News airs at 10:30 a.m. daily and Nightline airs at 1:30 a.m. daily on Sky News Australia. Primetime airs at 2 p.m. Saturdays (Extended Edition) and 1.30 p.m. Thursdays. The 20/20 programme airs at 2 p.m. Sundays (Extended Edition) and Wednesdays at 1.30 p.m.

History

Throughout the 1960s and early 1970s, ABC News was not a major news player compared to CBS News and NBC News. It was not until Roone Arledge became the President of ABC News in 1977 that the network finally became a major player in news. Arledge, known for experimenting with the broadcast "model," created many of ABC News' most popular and enduring programmes, including *20/20*, *World News Tonight*, *This Week*, *Nightline*, and *Primetime Live*.

ABC News gained respect in the early 1980s by covering the Iran Hostage Crisis and, later, for covering the 1989 Loma Prieta earthquake in the San Francisco Bay Area live.

Arledge turned ABC News into a broadcasting titan, regularly defeating rivals NBC and CBS. ABC would remain dominant for over two decades.

ABC News' slogan, *More Americans get their news from ABC News than from any other source,* refers to the number of people who watch, listen, and read to ABC News programming on television, radio, and the Internet.

CNBC

CNBC (an abbreviation for the "Consumer News and Business Channel", its official name until 1991) is a cable and satellite television business news channel in the US, owned and operated by NBC Universal. The network and its international spinoffs cover business headlines and provides live coverage of financial markets. The combined reach of CNBC and its siblings is 390 million viewers around the world. The network is currently ranked as the 19th most valuable cable channel in the US, worth roughly $4 billion.

History of CNBC

The CNBC channel originally had its beginnings around 1980 as The Satellite Programme Network (SPN), showing a low-budget mix of old movies, instructional and entertainment programmes, and infomercials. The channel later changed its name to Tempo Television. After initially signing a letter of intent to acquire Tempo, NBC eventually opted for a deal to lease the channel's transponder in June 1988. On this platform, the channel was relaunched on April 17, 1989 as the Consumer News and Business Channel. NBC and Cablevision initially operated CNBC as a 50-50 joint venture, choosing to headquarter the channel in Fort Lee, New Jersey.

CNBC had considerable difficulty getting cable carriage at first, as many providers were skeptical of placing it alongside the longer-established Financial News Network. By the winter

Launched	April 17, 1989
Owned by	NBC Universal
Picture format	480i (SDTV) 1080i (HDTV)
Slogan	"First in Business Worldwide" "America's Business Channel"
Country	United States
Broadcast area	United States, Canada
Headquarters	Englewood Cliffs, New Jersey, U.S.
Website	CNBC.com
	Availability
	Satellite
DirecTV	Channel 355
Dish Network	Channel 208
C-Band	AMC-10, Channel 101 (Transponder 13)
Orbit Network	Channel 46
	Cable
Available on most cable systems	Check local listings for channels
	Satellite Radio
Sirius	Channel 129
XM	Channel 127
	IPTV over ADSL
TELUS TV (Canada)	Channel 99
	Internet Television
CNBC Plus	(US$9.95/month or US$99.95/year)

of 1990, CNBC was only in 17 million homes—less than half of FNN's potential reach—despite having the muscle of NBC standing behind it.

However, around this time, FNN encountered serious financial difficulties. After a protracted bidding war with a Dow Jones-Westinghouse Broadcasting consortium, CNBC acquired FNN for $154.3 million on May 21, 1991 and immediately merged the two operations, hiring around 60 of FNN's 300-strong workforce. The deal increased the distribution of the newly enlarged network to over 40 million homes. Cablevision sold its 50 per cent stake to NBC upon completion of the deal. With the full name "Consumer News and Business Channel" dropped, the network's business programming was at first branded "CNBC/FNN," although this was phased out before the mid-1990s.

CNBC began to grow during the 1990s, launching Asian and European versions of the channel in 1995 and 1996 respectively. In 1997, CNBC formed a strategic alliance with Dow Jones, including content sharing with Dow Jones Newswires and The Wall Street Journal and the rebranding of the channel as "a service of NBC and Dow Jones". CNBC's international channels were then merged into a 50-50 joint venture with their Dow Jones-owned rivals, London-based EBN (European Business News) and Singapore-sited ABN (Asia Business News) in 1998, while ratings grew on the US channel until the new millennium's dot-com bubble burst in 2000.

The new millennium also brought changes to the network, moving its world headquarters from Fort Lee to Englewood Cliffs, New Jersey in 2003, which features completely digital video production and studios made by PDG Ltd of Beeston, Nottinghamshire and the FX Group of Ocoee, Florida.

NBC Universal reacquired full control of loss-making CNBC Europe and CNBC Asia from Dow Jones at the end of 2005. The licensing agreement between Dow and CNBC U.S. remained intact, however.

Today, CNBC provides business news programming from 4 a.m. to 8 p.m., Eastern Time, while broadcasting talk shows, investigative reports, documentaries, infomercials, repurposed NBC game shows, and other programmes during the evening and early morning. A rolling ticker provides real-time updates on share prices on the NYSE, NASDAQ, and AMEX, as well as market indices, news summaries, and weather updates by NBC

Weather Plus (prior to March 27, 2006, all of CNBC's weather reports were provided by AccuWeather). A rotating top band of the screen rotates provides real-time updates on index and commodity prices from world markets.

CNBC is the only NBC network whose abbreviation, while containing NBC, stands for another name: the Consumer News and Business Channel. The moniker was simply shortened to CNBC when the former was dropped.

Programming

Present Shows

CNBC provides a variety of programmes throughout the business day presenting reports on U.S. businesses, updates of stock market indices and commodities prices, interviews with CEOs and business leaders, and commentary from many investment professionals. The following is the usual "business day" (term used by CNBC hosts and announcers) lineup (as of August 4, 2008, all times Eastern) is discussed in table.

Since 17 September 2007 the network has also run hourly *CNBC.com News Now* update segments during business day programming. These short bulletins, which are around 30 seconds in length (similar to ESPN's *SportsCenter Right Now*), air before the start of the network's programmes from *Squawk on the Street* through *Kudlow and Company*.

CNBC has experimented with non-business programming during primetime hours with a mixed record of success. The channel has at times rebroadcast several NBC programmes, including *Late Night with Conan O'Brien, Deal or No Deal, The Apprentice, The Apprentice: Martha Stewart,* and *1 vs. 100*. CNBC's current primetime lineup features *The Big Idea with Donny Deutsch,* re-airs of NBC programmes *The Apprentice, Deal or No Deal* and *1 vs. 100,* along with its own documentaries and talk shows including *Mike on America, American Greed* and *Conversations with Michael Eisner*. Prior to 2006-04-20, programmes in primetime hours were shown with a 'scroll' featuring news headlines and weather updates at the bottom of the screen.

ET	Programme	Hosts	Description
4a-6a	Worldwide Exchange	Brian Shactman, Ross Westgate, Christine Tan	First word on movements on futures exchanges and trading in Europe and Asia
6a-9a	Squawk Box	Joe Kernen, Carl Quintanilla, Rebecca Quick	Provides a mix of business news and commentary
9a-11a	Squawk on the Street	Mark Haines, Erin Burnett (both live from NYSE), David Faber	Broadcasts live from above the New York Stock Exchange trading floor
11a-12p	The Call	Dylan Ratigan, Trish Regan, Melissa Francis (Ratigan live from NYSE)	Focuses on real-time market coverage
12p-2p	Power Lunch	Bill Griffeth, Sue Herera	Examines the companies, people, and trends influencing Wall Street, plus real-time market coverage at the midway point of the trading day
2p-3p	Street Signs	Erin Burnett	Focuses on trends, world events affecting stock markets, and real-time market coverage
3p-5p	Closing Bell	Maria Bartiromo, co-hosted with Dylan Ratigan for the 3-4 p.m. hour (Ratigan live from NYSE)	Covers the close of the trading day and real-time market coverage
5p-6p	Fast Money	Dylan Ratigan	Fast-paced roundtable discussion of stocks for short-term trades
6p-7p	Mad Money	Jim Cramer	A fast-paced show offering stock advice to callers
7p-8p	Kudlow & Company	Lawrence Kudlow	provides market, economic and political commentary and Interviews
8p-9p	On the Money	Carmen Wong Ulrich	Features personal finance advice to viewers, similar to The Suze Orman Show (unlike the original incarnation of the programme that aired from 2005-07)

Infomercials are typically aired from 2 a.m. to 4 a.m. ET and throughout most of the day at the weekend. Since the September-October 2008 financial crisis, the network has begun to place a *paid programming* tag on the top right corner of the screen during all airings of infomercials. On January 24, 2007, the network launched a long-anticipated monthly news magazine called *Business Nation*, which is anchored by award-winning journalist David Faber. Each edition of the programme covers three stories; a mixture of profiles, investigative pieces and features. The format of the show is structured similarly to HBO's *Real Sports*.

CNBC's breakout hit among its original series is *Mad Money*. Hosted by money manager Jim Cramer, the hour-long show gives stock advice to viewers who call to the programme. The show also has a popular segment called "The Lightning Round." In August 2007, Cramer's on-air tirade about the weakening economy, which was seen during the "Stop Trading" segment on *Street Signs*, received national attention and helped galvanize widespread support for the Federal Reserve Board to cut interest rates. Other special or weekend programming includes *CNBC on Assignment* (for example, *The Age of Wal-Mart*), *Cover to Cover*, *The Suze Orman Show*, and *The Wall Street Journal Report with Maria Bartiromo*.

Past Shows

Among the shows that have been cancelled are:

Weekdays

Weekly, Weekend and Other Programming

- *National Geographic Explorer* (moved to MSNBC and then to the National Geographic Channel)
- *Louis Rukeyser's Wall Street* (ended its run on New Year's Eve 2004 at Louis Rukeyser's request)
- *Market Week with Maria Bartiromo* (renamed *After Hours with Maria Bartiromo* and then *Special Report with Maria Bartiromo*—cancelled in 2004)
- *Tim Russert* (moved to MSNBC)
- American Le Mans Series races (inaugural 1999 season only, as part of agreement with NBC Sports)

- PGA Champions Tour
- *Management Today*
- *How to Succeed in Business*
- *Strictly Business*
- *Weekly Business*
- *Inside America's Courts*
- *CNet News.com*
- *Ushuaia*
- *Weekend Squawk Box*
- *Topic [A] with Tina Brown*
- *World Business Reports*
- *Consumer News*
- *Smart Money*
- *Media Biz*
- *Business Wrapup*
- *Business View*
- *Media Beat*
- *Your Portfolio*
- *Money Talk*
- *Money Shack*
- *Money Today*
- *Opinions*
- *McLaughlin*
- *Real Story*
- *Real Life*
- *Real Personal*
- *The Dick Cavett Show*
- *Tom Snyder*
- *Outside the Box*

Personalities and Coverage

Much of CNBC's on-air talent has been with the network for some time: Sue Herera and Scott Cohn joined CNBC at its inception, and remain on the air co-hosting *Power Lunch* and as senior correspondent respectively. Some personalities who joined CNBC from FNN in 1991, such as Ron Insana, Bill Griffeth and Joe Kernen, are also still with the channel. The network has of late sought to increase the profile of its on-air team with the launch of rival business station Bloomberg Television and Fox Business Network—although CNBC's best known personality, *Closing Bell* host, Maria Bartiromo, has for some time made regular appearances on other NBC News broadcasts such as *The Today Show* as well as anchoring the syndicated *Wall Street Journal Report*, other CNBC hosts such as Jim Cramer and Erin Burnett have also been used increasingly across NBC's output.

In addition to its roster of programme anchors, CNBC employs a team of reporters who contribute across the network's business day programming, the majority of whom are based at CNBC's global headquarters in Englewood Cliffs. In addition, CNBC has staff permanently based at bureaux in Midtown Manhattan, Chicago, Washington, D.C., Los Angeles and San Jose (the latter referred to on air as "CNBC Silicon Valley"). Cost-cutting at NBC Universal's news divisions has seen some of these offices merged with those of NBC owned-and-operated stations: the Silicon Valley facility was moved from Palo Alto to the KNTV (NBC 11) newsroom in San Jose in January 2007 (occasionally KNTV reporters Scott Budman and Scott McGrew will now correspond for CNBC), while the Chicago bureau now shares a home with WMAQ (NBC 5). The network also has reporters posted at the New York Stock Exchange (where CNBC also has a set used for broadcasting *Squawk on the Street, The Call* and *Closing Bell*), NASDAQ MarketSite, NYMEX and the Chicago Board of Trade and Chicago Mercantile Exchange each day.

Ratings

There is a fairly clear correlation between the performance of global stock markets and the audience ratings of CNBC. The network had a difficult time attracting viewers in the first half of the decade, although current viewership is significantly up from its 2005 bottom. CNBC continues, however, to possess the wealthiest audience (in terms of average income) of any television channel in the United States.

During the late 1990s and early 2000s, CNBC's ratings were increasing sharply along with the stock market. In fact, CNBC often beat CNN during the daytime. In 2000, daytime viewership at the network peaked at 343,000, around the time the Nasdaq Composite crossed 5000. However, when the dot-com bubble began to burst later that year, CNBC's viewing figures declined in tandem. The network's ratings steadily fell quarter after quarter, year after year, until bottoming in Q1 2005, with an average viewership of 134,000 during the day. From the bottom, the network, along with the markets, have rebounded significantly—average daytime viewership (6 a.m. to 6 p.m.) stood at around 278,000 (as of the third quarter of 2007), and has rebounded to a 7-year high of 310,000 viewers in the first quarter of 2008. Even though that pales in comparison to what Fox News and CNN draw in today, it is still a very healthy 135 per cent increase in viewership since the beginning of 2005. Despite the viewership slump since the turn of the decade, CNBC is extremely profitable: average revenues top $510 million while profits for the network exceeded $333 million in 2007, making CNBC a cash cow for NBC Universal and its parent company, General Electric. CNBC is the second most profitable of NBC Universal's thirteen cable channels in the United States, behind only the USA Network.

The network often sees large spikes in viewership on days of major market moves. In the week of 27 February 2007, when the Dow Jones Industrial Average had its 7th largest loss ever, CNBC's continuing coverage of events resulted in its best ratings week since the market crash after the September 11, 2001 terrorist attacks, with *Kudlow and Company*, *Mad Money*, and *Fast Money* recording their best ratings ever in the coveted 25-54 demographic. When the financial crisis wrecked havoc in the worldwide equity markets, CNBC recorded some of the highest ratings in the network's two-decade history. For the week ended September 19, 2008, the network averaged 502,000 viewers during the "business day" (defined by the network as 5 a.m. to 7 p.m.). During this week, *Squawk Box*, *Closing Bell*, *Fast Money*, *Mad Money* and *Kudlow and Company* recorded their best viewership figures ever. On September 29, 2008 when the markets faced their worst single day performance since the crash of 1987, CNBC notched its best ratings day ever; a whopping 726,000 viewers tuned into the network during the business day.

While daytime viewership has rebounded from its 2005 lows, primetime ratings remain weak relative to those of other news networks and CNBC continues to try and rejuvenate its evening lineup. Along with developing new programme formats such as *Fast Money* and *Mad Money*, the network operates a "checkerboard" programming approach, airing various genres of shows including documentaries, town-hall style discussions and repeats of some NBC output.

When discussing the network's ratings, CNBC management and press releases regularly suggest that considerable viewership, particularly during the daytime, is done "out of home" in places such as offices and hotel rooms. As this demographic is not covered by Nielsen Media Research ratings, CNBC claims that the network's true viewership is considerably higher than what is measured.

On-Air Presentation

Graphics

CNBC is well-known today for its flashy and ostentatious graphics package, complete with accompanying animations and animation-sounds. Previous graphics packages put together by the network since the early 1990's have gradually increased the "wow" factor—likely in order to catch a casual viewer's eye, as cable news competition has increased dramatically since the late 1980's (when the network was launched).

On 2006-11-15, CNBC's 'crystal' gray logo bug was changed to colour revealing the rainbow's peacock's normal NBC colours. On 2006-11-28, the new smaller CNBC colour bug (similar to the one used in the revamped ticker) began to show up on CNBC's non-business related primetime programming (where the ticker is not shown, except *Mad Money* and *Fast Money*), replacing the much bigger 'crystal' bug.

On 2007-03-01, CNBC's *Squawk on the Street* and *Closing Bell* both started using a new countdown clock (shown in minutes:seconds:tenths-of-a-second format) on the graphics' lower-third of the screen. On 2007-07-27, it moved to the lower right of the screen, where the CNBC colour bug is usually seen. The countdown clock is used for the "Opening Bell Countdown" segment on *Squawk on the Street*, and for the "Closing Countdown" segment on *Closing Bell*, along with the announcement of some monthly consumer indices and Federal Reserve Bank interest rate changes.

On 2007-05-02, CNBC's *Mad Money* revamped its own on-air graphics package, replacing what was used—including its opening animation sequence—since the programme's 2005-03-14 debut. In November 2007, the CNBC colour bug in the ticker on the lower right of the screen started rotating (and morphing) between the network logo and the CNBC.com logo and back. This is seen only during the network's "Business Day" programming.

First Generation Graphic

Used from 1989-04-17 to 1994-12-31. The bottom band of the ticker displayed various indices (such as the *Value Line Arithmetic Index*, shown). The network did not have a live bug tracking the various indices, nor did they have their logo fixed on the screen. Instead, camera shots of the anchors at the main desk were positioned in a way to show the "CNBC" lettering at all possible times. The studio in the picture, right, is located in the original Fort Lee, New Jersey building. This was later completely rebuilt as part of changes introduced by the network's then president Roger Ailes.

1995 Revamp

Used from 1995-01-01 to 1997-12-31.

1998 Revamp

This was used from January 1998 to May 1999. Majority of the lower-thirds and the live bug was coloured blue with the left side of the lower thirds and upper part of the live bug coloured red. The background for its charts was animated with majority of the background being blue and a narrow green strip running at the right side of the screen resembling a stock ticker. When the major maker indexes hit a new record, the green strip is tweaked to reflect "DOW RECORD", "S&P RECORD" or "NASDAQ RECORD." It is also tweaked during the holiday season. (Note: The image rightward does not contain the ticker part.)

Fig. 8.10

1999 Revamp: "Red" Turns "Green"

The 1998 graphics scheme was slightly tweaked in May 1999 where the once red parts of the lower thirds (seen on the left of the blue strip of the lower thirds) and the "LIVE" bug's upper part turned green. The font was also modified. The green strip at this time is also tweaked during earnings season. Graphs also started having the CNBC logo was behind them and included grids. On 3 April 2000, CNBC Asia has used this scheme only for its charts but a month later CNBC Europe used it for its charts and lower thirds as well. This package was in place until 29 September 2000 on CNBC, until 31 December 2000 on CNBC Asia and until mid-January 2001 on CNBC Europe. Show titles however remained the same as the 1998 package.

Fig. 8.10(a)

2000 Revamp

Used from 2000-10-02 to 2002-09-13. In January 2001, CNBC Asia and CNBC Europe both followed up to use the same graphic package, making some changes to the lower thirds and the charts respectively (for example, removing the animation on and off screen). This marked the first time that the three main CNBC channels had used the same graphics scheme in their entirety for all daytime shows. In February 2002 however, while most programme titles largely remained the same on the CNBC US channel, two new shows, *Morning Call* and *Closing Bell* used the titles which were originally for *Street Signs* and *Market Watch* respectively (the latter two were cancelled at the same period as well).

Fig. 8.11

2002 Revamp

Used from 16 September 2002 to 10 October 2003. This package saw an evolution of the graphics introduced in 2000, with programme titles and chart formats remaining the same. The lower thirds were, however, completely revamped with the lower half of it coloured red and text was centre-justified, and a new background animation and colour scheme was introduced for charts and other on-screen data. The font was also tweaked. The titles in the lower thirds were centre-justified. CNBC Asia used a similar lower thirds effective 2 January 2003 except that the lower thirds was entirely light blue and the text was still aligned to the left. CNBC Europe adopted the same chart backgrounds in use by CNBC US later in 2003 as well but used a different lower-thirds.

Fig. 8.12

2003 Revamp

Used from 2003-10-13 to 2005-12-16. In this revamp, CNBC added an independent space to the lower thirds to show the "topic title" to indicate the subject being discussed (*i.e.* "money to burn" in the rightward photo). This formerly shared space with the programme logo on the left-hand side of the lower thirds.

Fig. 8.13

CNBC also added another animation to the lower thirds: when showing stock charts, the lower thirds would move down vertically, keeping just the "topic title" visible above the ticker. When charts were removed from the screen, the whole lower thirds would move vertically up again.

The "LIVE" sign was also moved from the left-top corner to the right-top corner, along with the location (which was formerly included on the lower thirds) at this time. CNBC Asia adopted this graphics scheme in 2004 but on CNBC Europe's next graphics revamp in the same year, it chose to create its own graphics scheme for charts, lower-thirds and titles.

Dec. 2005 Revamp: From 2D to 3D

Used from 2005-12-19 to 2006-05-12. On 2005-12-19, CNBC unveiled a new on-air look, replacing that which had been used since October 2003. This included a new look for all the graphics, new logos for all business day programmes, and the relocation of the index and commodity prices from the stacked bug in the bottom right-hand corner of the screen to the bug bar across the top of the screen.

Fig. 8.14

Since then, the ticker has shown full company names (and full commodity names used in the commodity summary, which runs at the 1s of each hour) instead of just ticker symbols. The "LIVE" and location graphics were moved back to the top-left of the screen from the top-right corner at this time. This graphic package was created by Randy Pyburn of Pyburn Films (that also designed the WNBC's 2003 graphic package) and also designed earlier CNBC graphic packages. The estimated cost of the 2005-06 package was about $2,000,000.

Mid 2006: Revamped Bug and Lower Thirds

- On 2006-05-15, CNBC made a slight change to its lower thirds, adding a blue block to the right-hand side. Occasionally this space was used to display the title of the topic being discussed. This format was abandoned on 2006-12-18.

Fig. 8.15

- On 2006-09-06, CNBC unveiled a revamped bug, which now has a similar resemblance to that of CNBC Europe. On the same day, the network launched a slightly modified ticker with a narrower font (to allow more quotes to stream by within a period of time). CNBC Asia adopted a revamped bug of its own on 2007-03-26 as part of its graphics package revamp.

Dec. 2006: New Lower Thirds

Used from 2006-12-19 to present. On 2006-12-19, exactly one year after its relaunch, CNBC revamped its on-air graphics package, replacing the old lower thirds that were previously used from 12/19/2005-12/18/2006. The current graphic package was created in house. In this revamp, CNBC cancelled the independent space for the "topic title", which once again shares space with the programme logo on the left-hand side of the lower thirds.

Fig. 8.16

CNBC Asia adopted the similar lower thirds on 2007-03-26, but unlike its US version, the "topic title" does not share the space with the programme logo. Its European sibling (CNBC Europe) finally debuted its own lower thirds on 2008-01-07, and like its US version, the "topic title" shares space with the programme logo on the left-hand side.

- On 2007-04-23, the data bug was slightly tweaked, with the titles of the securities now displayed in yellow and the numbers still being displayed in white.

Fig. 8.17

- On 2007-07-26, the Dow Jones Industrial Average lost more than 300 points, CNBC stayed on the story and put a live shot of the trading board in the NYSE to show the status of Dow above the lower thirds during the *Closing Bell* to track the markets.
    - (Note: The screenshot rightward comes from CNBC Asia, so the style of the top bug and the ticker are different from the package of CNBC US.)
- On 2008-02-28, the chart was slightly tweaked, when showing session is more than two days, CNBC put up the per cent of the session performance, just like CNBC Europe.

Ticker

The CNBC Ticker is a computer simulation of ticker tape shown on the lower part of the screen during the network's live business programming, containing security and index symbols along with movements in their value. At the top of the screen, a rotating band, partitioned into three segments, provides index and commodity prices.

History

When CNBC first aired in 1989 until approximately 1991, the original CNBC Ticker only had one band, displaying NYSE stocks. After a 20 minute period when the ticker was off-air one day, as announced by anchor Ted David, did CNBC finally decide to include the NASDAQ in a new format at the time, creating the two-band system used ever since. FNN did use a two-line ticker design (with white and blue bands, quotes listed during trading without price changes and a market summary on the bottom band during trading) prior to the merger with CNBC in 1991, and many of these features were subsequently adopted by the newly-merged channel. Here is an example of FNN ticker circa 1987.

Fig. 8.18: CNBC Ticker, 1995 to 1997

CNBC had another ticker format, mainly a font variation on the ticker, for a short time before the 1995-97 photo on this page. During special events (for example, the Dow Jones Industrial Average passing 6000, 7000, etc. or another extremely impactful market event), the CNBC Ticker showed mutual funds on the NYSE band while leaving the NASDAQ band unchanged. This convention has been discontinued. In 1998, CNBC's ticker became more colourful with green indicating a stock price increase and red indicating a stock price decrease. The ticker now shows full company names (and full commodity names used in the Commodity Summary, which runs at the 1s of each hour) instead of just the ticker symbols, as seen before December 2005 but only the arrows remain coloured green or red.

Current Graphic Formats

The bug bar, at the top of the screen, which stays on-screen during the business day (4 a.m. ET to 6 p.m. ET), will give viewers a real-time snapshot of the general stock market (Dow Jones, Nasdaq S&P 500 indices and Russell 2000 index, along with the DJ Utilities, DJ Transports and NYSE indices), international markets and futures (between 4 a.m. ET and 9:30 a.m. ET only), currencies, bond prices/yields and commodities. The stock market indices, global markets, currencies, bonds, yields, and commodities are displayed in yellow, with the numbers displayed in white. This data stays on for 5-7 seconds, before refreshing to the new set of data.

Fig. 8.19: Typical On-Air screen Appearance during the Business Day

The bottom two lines, called the ticker, gives viewers real-time NYSE quotes (on the top band) and Nasdaq/AMEX quotes (bottom band) throughout the trading day (ticker symbols are 1, 2, or 3 letters long for the NYSE stocks; Nasdaq uses 4- and 5-letter symbols; 3-letter ticker symbols are used at the AMEX). A commodity summary is shown on the top band during market hours (every 10 minutes at 0:01, 0:11, 0:21, 0:31, 0:41, 0:51 past the hour), along with a market summary (which is shown every 20 minutes at 0:01, 0:21, 0:41 past the hour). A Nasdaq/AMEX market summary is shown on the bottom band every 20 minutes at 0:06, 0:26, 0:46 past the hour. The ticker now also provides the size of each trade (the volume, or number of shares traded), a feature which was reinstated on July 12, 2006 after it was dumped during the relaunch in December 2005.

Also, PowerShares ETF symbols, which are traded along the lower band of the ticker, are highlighted in orange for sponsorship reasons.

Before and after-market hours (8:00 a.m. ET 9:30 a.m. ET and 4:00 p.m. ET 6:30 p.m. ET respectively), the ticker gives viewers extended hours trading quotes (after-hours quotes are symbolized with gold text). Between the hours of 5:00 a.m. ET 8:00 a.m. ET and 6:30 p.m. ET 8:00 p.m. ET, viewers are shown an alphabetical recap of the closing prices of S&P 500 stocks on the top band, while latest news headlines as well as weather projections for selected cities are displayed on the bottom band.

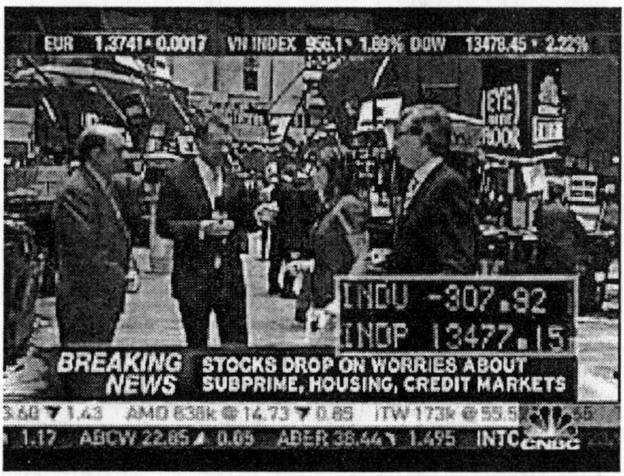

Fig. 8.20

CNBC's "Breaking News mode" (Note: The screenshot comes from CNBC Asia, so the style of the top bug and the ticker are different from the package of CNBC US.)

Above the ticker, the left-hand side graphic will provides the logo for the specific programme that is currently on-air (*i.e.* "MORNING CALL"). The middle block gives viewers either a caption of the topic being discussed (*i.e.* "MIKE HUCKMAN") or information about the correspondent on the screen. Additionally, the left block is also replaced by logos indicating general subjects (*i.e.* "BEHIND THE WHEEL") or the network's "Breaking News" (red), "CNBC Alert" (green) or "CNBC Exclusive" (orange) logo when required.

Taglines

- "A Service of NBC Universal and Dow Jones" (2004-05-17—2005-12-31, 2007-present)
- "Fast, Accurate, Actionable, Unbiased" (2007-present)
- "America's Business Channel" (2005 or earlier—present)
- "First in Business Worldwide" (2006-06-12—present)
- "The World Leader in Business News" (2004-06-06-11)
- "Make It Your Business" (2002-04)
- "Business for the New World" (2002)
- "Profit from It" (1998-2002)
- "First in Business, Worldwide" (1996-97)
- "First in Business, First in Talk" (1995)
- "Information that hits home" (1992-95)

Music

The music used from October 2003 to December 2005 was produced by 615 Music of Nashville, Tennessee. This music (though only edited versions of the arrangements for Squawk Box, Street Signs, and Closing Bell) continues as of October 2008 to be used by CNBC Europe, although CNBC Asia ceased using it in March 2007. CNBC Europe continued also to use a theme previous to this, composed by Edd Kalehoff (The theme package name: "Bold and Grand") used by CNBC US between 2000-02, for its main channel ident until a relaunch on 30 September 2008—however, it is still used for its "Europe Update" segments during US programming. The current music package is composed by James Ryan of Rampage Music. Ryan also composed the network's 2002 music package. Willie Wilcox composed the themes for *The Big Idea, Mad Money, Conversations with Michael Eisner* and currently *Fast Money*.

Fig. 8.21: CNBC News Store at Detroit Metropolitan Wayne County Airport

Fig. 8.22: CNBC News Store at Raleigh-Durham International Airport

CNBC's main voice-over announcer is Jim Birdsall, who has also worked for NFL Films.

Partnerships

Dow Jones and Company

Since December 1997, the network has held a strategic alliance with the publishing and financial information firm Dow Jones and Company. Under the agreement, CNBC has extensive access to the journalism of such outlets as MarketWatch, *The Wall Street Journal*, Dow Jones Newswires and *Barron's*, with their reporters and editorial staff making frequent appearances on the channel. Some former CNBC programmes have included Dow Jones branding, while the network currently produces and syndicates the weekly *Wall Street Journal Report* with Maria Bartiromo. CNBC's current deal with Dow Jones expires in 2012, and its continuation has been the subject of some uncertainty following the 2007 acquisition of Dow by News Corporation, parent company of rival financial network Fox Business. News Corp CEO Rupert Murdoch has stated that the current agreement "covers actual news and access to reporters on *business* news" only, and that Fox and Dow Jones are free to cooperate on other issues.

Other Content Partnerships

CNBC has also held a content deal with the *The New York Times* since January 2008, which has widely been seen as an attempt by both parties to take on increased competition from News Corporation. Under the agreement, CNBC has access to the business coverage of the *Times,* while video from CNBC.com is featured on the *Times'* website. The station's video clips and other content are also distributed through Yahoo! Finance and, as of May 2008, AOL Money and Finance.

The network's live market prices, economic data and other statistics are largely provided by Thomson Reuters (Reuters and Thomson Financial prior to their 2008 merger). Since September 2006 CNBC has operated its own stock market index in conjunction with London's FTSE Group. The FTSE CNBC Global 300 includes the fifteen largest companies from each of the sectors of the Industry Classification Benchmark as well as the thirty largest companies from emerging markets. Calculated continuously from 9 p.m. through to 4:10 p.m. ET each trading day, the index is referenced throughout the network's live programming, particularly on *Worldwide Exchange.* The channel also maintains the "CNBC Investor Network", a series of webcam connections to the trading rooms of various independent financial institutions across the United States. The scheme was launched on October 22, 2007 and allows participating traders and strategists to appear on the network during the business day.

International Channels

CNBC has operated international versions of its channel since 1995, when CNBC Asia originally launched. CNBC Europe followed in 1996. On 1997-12-09, Dow Jones and Company and NBC announced the merger of their international business news channels. This resulted in a merger of CNBC Europe with Dow Jones' European Business News, and likewise of CNBC Asia with Asia Business News. From then (until January 2006) the international CNBC services carried the tagline "A Service of NBC (Universal) and Dow Jones" (or depending on other local partners, a variation of this tagline). Correspondents from Dow Jones Newswires contribute to the channels. CNBC Europe is headquartered in London, and CNBC Asia is headquartered in Singapore. On 2005-12-31, the sale by Dow Jones of its interests in the international CNBC channels took effect. From 2006-01-01, the "A Service of NBC Universal and Dow Jones" tagline was removed from the international CNBC channels, in line with this. In 2007, CNBC Asia dropped the word "Asia" from its channel idents, on 30 September 2008, CNBC Europe similarly dropped the word "Europe" from its logo. This means the big three CNBC channels—US, Europe, and Asia—are all on-screen known as simply CNBC.

Besides CNBC Europe and CNBC Asia, the network also operates a number of local business news channels in association with other companies. These channels include Class CNBC in Italy, CNBC-e in Turkey, CNBC Arabiya in the UAE, Nikkei CNBC in Japan, CNBC-TV18 and CNBC Awaaz in India, CNBC Pakistan in Pakistan and TVN CNBC Biznes in Poland.

CNBC Europe and CNBC Asia are rebranded in some parts of the world with tickers containing local financial information. Examples include CNBC Nordic, CNBC Singapore, CNBC Hong Kong and CNBC Australia. In North America, CNBC World airs business programming from CNBC Europe and CNBC Asia, as well as weekly magazine programmes provided by CNBC-TV18 and the United Nations. In Central America and the Caribbean, CNBC Latin America retransmits live programmes from CNBC and CNBC World.

In Canada, CNBC can be seen with most of the programming identical to the US counterpart. However, due to Canadian programming rights, the 9 p.m. slot which shows television programming such as *Deal or No Deal, The Apprentice, 1 vs. 100* and *Heads Up Poker*, as well as any and all Olympic Games coverage, are replaced by CNBC World programming. However, documentaries are shown in Canada. This had the making of a major problem, as a highlight episode of *The*

Apprentice 5 that aired April 23, 2006, was assumed to not be available anywhere for Canadians due to these blackouts. While the first airing at 9:00 p.m. ET was blacked out, the second airing at 12:00 a.m. ET was accidentally shown. Blackouts on episodes that originally air on NBC and Global are likely to continue. However, occasionally, the television shows are shown and are not blacked out, possibly due to a mistake in transmission. The television series *The Apprentice UK*, now airing on CNBC, which has never aired on Canadian television and does not have a Canadian rightsholder, has also been replaced without merit. The Apprentice UK airs in Canada on Showcase, which would seem to explain the fact that it does not air on CNBC in Canada.

CNBC's most recent international spinoff is CNBC Africa. With roughly $600 million spent on advertising in South Africa alone, the network sees great potential in grabbing a potential share of that pot. Initially, CNBC Africa has bureaus in Kenya, Nigeria and South Africa and produces 9 hours of local programming per business day. The network was launched on 2007-06-01.

CNBC.com

CNBC.com is the companion website to the financial network. It was launched in 1996 with minimal content, other than show programme grids, host biographies and basic network images (on the internet, business news then was handled by the website of CNBC's sister channel, MSNBC). The site gradually progressed alongside internet technology, giving investors more useful information such as stock quotes, news bulletins, in-depth programming information and a whole host of other data.

In August 2001, CNBC.com merged with MSN's Moneycentral.com, creating "CNBC on MSN." This new partnership allowed the two parties to meet two objectives: (1) provide richer content to visitors, with expanded news offerings, a wider array of stock tools (including interactive charting, free online portfolio managers) plus more in-depth market coverage, and (2) more effectively compete with other finance related websites, such as Marketwatch.com and Yahoo! Finance.

During this period the editorial content on the CNBC.com site was controlled by Microsoft Corporation. CNBC.com officially disbanded its relationship with MSN in mid-November 2006. CNBC.com was relaunched on 2006-12-04. The website provides new online tools for investors and better integration of the website with daytime programming. Some of the new features include:

- Exclusive online interviews (the first being with Chicago Fed President Michael Moskow).
- Live market updates from CNBC personalities 3 times per day during the trading day (discontinuing the "Market in a Minute" updates in June 2007).
- A streaming desktop ticker, real-time data and the network's "tick-by-tick" charts (for major indices).
- Themed blogs by various correspondents (*i.e.* "Tech Check" with tech reporter Jim Goldman).
- Unedited, full-length interviews from CNBC specials or other on-air interviews.
- Free video of recent on-air segments, interviews, features etc.
- An exclusive "CNBC.com" set built at CNBC's U.S. headquarters where the market update segments (among other things) are taped from.
- Blogging from on-air personalities about the various "goings-on" within the network.
- An original show to air exclusively online with Maria Bartiromo, Bill Griffeth and Joe Kernen (yet to debut).
- Top-of-the-hour summary of business news entitled *CNBC.com News Now* which is also seen during the trading day on CNBC TV.

Content on the new website is edited 24 hours a day during the business week. CNBC U.S. updates the content from 6 a.m. to 7 p.m. ET, CNBC Asia then takes over from 7 p.m. to 2 a.m. and CNBC Europe handles the (North American) overnight hours from 2 a.m. to 6 a.m.

In April 2007, the site was able to attract 662,000 unique visitors to the website, ranking it #22 amongst all financial news websites.

CNBCplus

"CNBCplus" is a subscription-based service (similar to the now-defunct CNN Pipeline) which allows users to have 24-hour, commercial-free access to three individual CNBC feeds—CNBC US, CNBC Europe, and CNBC Asia—along with access to an archive of over 40,000 VOD clips, updated with up to 200 clips daily. It also offers a search feature allowing the user to find video clips using keywords. The service is available to PC Windows users running Internet Explorer 6.x or 7.x. The CNBC US stream offers most television broadcast programming, including the popular shows, *Mad Money* and *Fast Money*.

Since its inception, the service has offered a free seven-day trial for people who register. After that, individuals who register will be required to pay a monthly fee to continue their subscription. The 'introductory offer' (still in effect) is $9.95 per month, although the fee will eventually go up to $14.95 per month. As of March 2008, CNBCplus has only signed up 15,000 regular subscribers to its service.

Million Dollar Portfolio Challenge (2007)

CNBC.com's *Million Dollar Portfolio Challenge*, a virtual stock-picking contest, ran from 2007-03-05 to 2007-05-25. CNBC hosted a similar contest the previous year, called the *Squawk Box Fantasy Portfolio Challenge*.

Contest "Multiple Accounts" Controversy

The *Million Dollar Portfolio Challenge*, which was sponsored by OptionsXpress, became embroiled in controversy after just its first week when it was revealed that one participant, Nancy Beaumont from California, registered 800 separate portfolios in the contest, exponentially increasing her probability of winning the $1,000,000 first prize, and leading to her occupying no fewer than nine places in the Top 25 Leader Board.

The express terms of the Rules, however, provided in material part:

> *Description of the Contest:* The contest is a stock trading game that provides participants with *a fictional trading account, One Million (1,000,000) fictional dollars* ("CNBC Bucks") and

the fictional ability to trade individual stocks on the NYSE, NASDAQ and/or AMEX exchanges.

The Rules further stated:

Trading: Each *participant* begins the contest with *one million (1,000,000)* CNBC Bucks to create *a fictional portfolio* of the NYSE, NASDAQ and/or AMEX-traded stocks... Each *participant* can make a *maximum of fifty (50) trades per day,* based on the time the trade is entered by the *participant.*

As a result of Nancy Beaumont's registration of 800 accounts, she had $800,000,000 CNBC Bucks available to her in the contest, spread over 800 separate accounts, and the ability to make a total of 40,000 trades per day. Other participants who registered one account per the express terms of the rules, by comparison, had $1,000,000 CNBC Bucks available to them and could only make 50 trades per day. As a result, the probability of Nancy Beaumont winning the contest was dramatically skewed in her favour.

After Hours Trading Controversy

A June 8, 2007 *BusinessWeek* article entitled *CNBC's Easy Money* detailed another massive flaw in the network's fantasy portfolio challenge. Traders were able to open their browsers, enter various stocks into the trading module, but execute the trade after hours (assuming the browser and module were still open). This allowed traders to profit off of after-hour market movements in stocks that, for example, reported better than expected earnings. CNBC issued a statement on the same day on their website, stating the network was "investigating whether one or more finalists wrote and executed computer programme scripts to bypass the contest's security measures. CNBC retained two leading consultants in the information security industry to investigate these two computer programming related issues."

Winner of Portfolio Challenge

After a lengthy investigation which resulted in numerous disqualifications, on July 13, 2007 CNBC announced Mary Sue

Williams of St. Clairsville, Ohio as the winner of the portfolio challenge and of the $1 million cash prize.

Million Dollar Portfolio Challenge (2008)

The 2008 version of this contest ran for 10 weeks, from May 12, 2008 to July 18, 2008. CNBC announced Edward Burke of Shippensburg, Pennsylvania as the winner of the $500,000 cash prize on July 28, 2008.

CNBC HD+

CNBC HD+ is a high definition enhanced simulcast of CNBC which was initially announced at an upfront analysts meeting in New York in September 2007. CNBC programming shown on CNBC HD+ is not actually in high definition, but is an upconversion of the SD feed. The feed is pushed to the left of the screen, with the extra room used for additional content, such as statistics and charts, and a wider ticker with more room. A window in the corner also displays video content from CNBC.com, which can be switched to using the SAP function on the television. It was initially launched on October 10, 2007 on DirecTV, to be followed by other carriers.

Fig. 8.23: CNBC HD+ Screen Layout

Airport "Stores" or "Bureaus"

CNBC holds stores (can be called bureaus) in many airports across the nation. The stores sell limited CNBC merchandize, along with newspapers, magazines and a small selection of snacks and drinks. Some examples would be:

- Tulsa, Oklahoma
- Salt Lake City, Utah
- Oklahoma City, Oklahoma
- San Francisco, California

Competitors:

- Bloomberg Television
- CNN International
- BBC World News
- Fox Business Network

CBS NEWS

CBS News is the news division of American television and radio network CBS. Its current president is Sean McManus who is also head of CBS Sports. Don Hewitt was the original creator of "60 Minutes" and former executive producer of CBS News. Rick Kaplan, a multiple award-winning news producer and executive whose career in broadcast journalism spans more than 35 years, is the executive producer of the CBS Evening News with Katie Couric.

Fig. 8.24

Current CBS News Broadcasts

- *CBS Morning News*
- *The Early Show*
- *The Saturday Early Show*
- *CBS News Sunday Morning*
- *Face the Nation with Bob Schieffer*
- *CBS Evening News with Katie Couric*
- *CBS Evening News* (Saturday edition, reported by Jeff Glor or other rotating anchors)
- *CBS Evening News with Russ Mitchell* (Sunday edition)

- *60 Minutes*
- *48 Hours Mystery*
- *Up to the Minute*
- *Newsbreak* (twice-daily 90 second daytime broadcast)
- *CBS News MoneyWatch* (60 second business news break, reported by Alexis Christoforous, Anthony Mason, Russ Mitchell, Alison Harmelin or Claire Leka).

Five Minute News Programme History

- Charles Collingwood with the News (1956, 61-62)
- Walter Cronkite with the News (1956-60)
- Charles Kuralt with the News (1960)
- Ron Cochran with the News (1960-61)
- Stuart Novins with the News (1961)
- Harry Reasoner with the News (1961-62)
- CBS News with Harry Reasoner (1962-63)
- CBS News with Douglas Edwards (1962-63)
- CBS Mid-Morning News with Douglas Edwards (1979-80)
- CBS Midday News with Harry Reasoner (1963)
- CBS Midday News with Robert Trout (1963-65)
- CBS Midday News with Mike Wallace (1965-66)
- CBS Midday News with Joseph Benti (1966-69)
- CBS Midday News with Douglas Edwards (1969-79)
- CBS Afternoon News with Douglas Edwards (1963-69)

Saturday Afternoon/Evening Network News History (15 and 30 Minute Programmes)

- The Week in Review (1950)
- Saturday News Special (with Don Hollenbeck) (1950-51)
- Douglas Edwards and the News (1951)
- News with Edward P. Morgan (1951)
- Up To The Minute (Walter Cronkite) (1951-52)
- The Saturday News with Robert Trout (1959)
- The Saturday News with Harry Reasoner (1959-62)
- CBS News with Robert Trout (1962-63)
- CBS News with Roger Mudd (1962)
- CBS News with Mike Wallace (1963)
- CBS Saturday News with Robert Trout (1963-66)
- CBS Saturday News with Richard C. Hottelet (1964)
- CBS Saturday News with Martin Agronsky (1964-65)

- CBS Saturday News with David Schoumacher (1965)
- CBS Saturday News with Dave Dugan (1965)
- CBS Saturday News with Charles Kuralt (1965)
- CBS Saturday News with Stuart Novins (1965)
- In February 1966, the "CBS Evening News" premiered on weekends as 30 minutes. The named to "CBS Weekend Evening News." In 1976, it was renamed to "CBS Saturday Evening News" in Saturday broadcasts, and "CBS Sunday Evening News" in Sunday broadcasts.
- CBS Weekend Evening News with Roger Mudd (1966-72)
- CBS Weekend Evening News with Dan Rather (1972-76)
- CBS Saturday Evening News with Bob Schieffer (1976-96)
- CBS Saturday Evening News with Paula Zahn (1996-99)
- CBS Saturday Evening News with Russ Mitchell (1999-07) or Thalia Assuras (2002-07) (anchors rotated every other Saturday); Mika Brzezinski (substituted in 2005-06)

Sunday Late Afternoon/Early Evening News History

- The Week in Review (1948)
- News Programme (Edward P. Morgan) (1951)
- Shape of the News (Edward P. Morgan) (1951)
- Sunday News (Ron Cochran) (1951)
- The American Week (commentary and analysis by Eric Sevareid) (1954-55)
- CBS Sunday News (Eric Sevareid) (1956)
- World News Roundup (Eric Sevareid, Robert Trout) (1957-58)
- Robert Trout with the News (1958)
- Harry Reasoner with the News (1959-60)
- CBS Sunday Evening News with Morton Dean (1976-85)
- CBS Sunday Evening News with Susan Spencer (1985-89)
- CBS Sunday Evening News with Connie Chung (1989-93)
- CBS Sunday Evening News with John Roberts (1993-07); Giselle Fernández (substituted in 1993) or Deborah Norville (substituted in 1993-94)

CBS Sunday Late News History (All 15 Minute Programmes)

- The Week in Review (1949-50)

- John Daly and the News (1950)
- Sunday News Special (Don Hollenbeck, Winston Burdett) (1951-61)
- Walter Cronkite with the News (1961-62)
- CBS Sunday Night News with Eric Sevareid (1962-63)
- CBS Sunday Night News with Harry Reasoner (1963-70)
- CBS Sunday Night News with Dan Rather (1970-72)
- CBS Sunday Night News with Bob Schieffer (1972-76)
- CBS Sunday Night News with Ed Bradley (1976-81)
- CBS Sunday Night News with Charles Osgood (1981-88)
- CBS Sunday Night News with Bill Plante (1988-96)
- Broadcasts were after late night local news and ended after 1996.

Prime Time/Evening News Programme History

- See It Now (Edward R. Murrow, Howard K. Smith) (1951-57)
- Douglas Edwards and the News (1948-62)
- The Twentieth Century (Walter Cronkite) (1957-70)
- CBS Evening News with Walter Cronkite (1962-81)
- CBS Reports (Howard K. Smith, Edward R. Murrow, Eric Sevareid, Ed Bradley) (1959-71)
- CBS Evening News with Dan Rather (1981-2005) or Connie Chung (1993-95)
- Nightwatch (Charlie Rose) (1982-92)
- West 57th (Meredith Viera, John Ferrugia) (1985-89)
- America Tonight (Dan Rather, Charles Kuralt, Lesley Stahl) (1990-91)
- Street Stories (Ed Bradley) (1992-93)
- Eye to Eye with Connie Chung (1993-95)
- Public Eye with Bryant Gumbel (1997-98)
- 60 Minutes II (Wednesday) (1999-05)
- CBS Evening News with Bob Schieffer (2005-06)

CBS Newspath

CBS Newspath is CBS News' satellite news gathering service (similar to CNN Newsource). *CBS Newspath* provides national hard news, sports highlights, regional spot news, features and live coverage of major breaking news events for affiliate stations to use in their local news broadcasts. *CBS Newspath* has a team of correspondents and freelance reporters dedicated to reporting for affiliates and offers several different national or international stories fronted by reporters on a daily basis. *CBS Newspath* also relies heavily on local affiliates sharing content. Stations will often contribute locally-obtained footage that may be of national interest.

CBS Newspath is a part of the Network News Service, a collaborative effort between the affiliate news services of ABC, CBS and FOX. This means that, for example, the FOX affiliate could uplink footage to their affiliate network, which would then be picked up by NNS, and be available to any ABC, CBS or FOX affiliate outside of the market that the footage originated in.

CBS Radio Network News

The branch of CBS News that produces newscasts and features to radio stations is CBS Radio News, which airs on the *CBS Radio Network*. The radio network is the oldest unit of CBS News and traced its roots to the company's founding in 1927, and the news division took shape over the following 10 years. The list of CBS News correspondents (below) includes those reporting on CBS Radio News.

CBS Radio News produces the oldest daily news show on radio or television, the *CBS World News Roundup* (it first aired in 1938 and celebrates its 70th anniversary in 2008), which airs each morning and evening. Nick Young anchors the original morning broadcast, produced by Paul Farry, while Bill Whitney hosts the evening edition, produced by Greg Armstrong. The evening *Roundup*, previously known as *The World Tonight*, has aired since 1956 and has been anchored by Blair Clark, Douglas Edwards, Dallas Townsend and Christopher Glenn.

CBS Radio News produces newscasts at the top of the hour, regular updates at:31 past the hour, and the popular Newsfeeds for affiliates (including WCBS and KYW) at:35, and breaking news updates when developments warrant, often at:20 and:50 past the hour.

Public Eye

In 2005, CBS News created its own blog called *Public Eye* to act as a defacto ombudsman for CBS News and give greater transparency to the decisions being made. It occasionally invites other journalists and bloggers to give their own opinions on this site.

Present CBS News Correspondents

- Serena Altschul—Correspondent
- Wyatt Andrews—Supreme Court Correspondent
- Howard Arenstein—Correspondent, CBS Radio News
- Thalia Assuras—Correspondent
- Sharyl Attkisson—Investigative Correspondent
- Jim Axelrod—Chief White House Correspondent
- Barry Bagnato—Correspondent, CBS Radio News
- Dave Barrett—Correspondent, CBS Radio News
- Robert Berger—Correspondent, CBS Radio News
- John Blackstone—Correspondent
- Jerry Bowen—Correspondent
- Cynthia Bowers—Correspondent
- Rita Braver—Senior Correspondent, *CBS News Sunday Morning*
- Joel Brown—Correspondent, CBS Newspath
- Karen Brown—Correspondent, CBS Newspath
- Jerry Browning—Producer, former correspondent in Los Angeles
- Harley Carnes—Anchor, CBS Radio News
- Julie Chen—Anchor, *The Early Show*
- Pauline Chiou—Correspondent, CBS Newspath (freelance)
- Alexis Christophorus—Business Correspondent, CBS Newspath
- Elaine Cobbe—Correspondent, CBS Radio News (freelance)
- Kelly Cobiella—Correspondent
- Nancy Cordes—Transportation and Consumer Safety Correspondent
- Katie Couric—Anchor, *CBS Evening News*; Correspondent, *60 minutes*

- Lucy Craft—Correspondent, CBS Radio News (freelance)
- Charlie D'Agata—Correspondent, CBS Newspath
- Priya David—Correspondent
- Seth Doane—Correspondent
- Harold Dow—Correspondent, *48 hours*
- Kimberly Dozier—Correspondent
- Bob Fuss—Capitol Hill Correspondent, CBS Radio News
- Manuel Gallegus—Correspondent, CBS Newspath
- Bill Geist—Correspondent, *CBS News Sunday Morning*
- Michelle Gielan—Anchor, *CBS Morning News*
- Wendy Gillette—Correspondent, CBS Newspath (freelance)
- Jeff Glor—National Correspondent, *The Early Show*; Anchor (rotating), *CBS Evening News* (Saturday edition)
- Jeff Greenfield—Senior Political Correspondent
- Tony Guida—Correspondent (WCBS Radio)
- Alison Harmelin—Correspondent, *CBS News MoneyWatch*
- Steve Hartman—Assignment America Correspondent and Columnist (*CBS Evening News*)
- Celia Hatton—Correspondent, CBS Newspath (freelance)
- Sandra Hughes—Correspondent
- Hattie Kauffman—Correspondent
- Armen Kateyian—Chief Investigative Correspondent
- Mark Knoller—White House Correspondent
- Susan Koeppen—Consumer Correspondent
- Steve Kroft—Co-Editor, *60 minutes*
- Stephanie Lambidakis—Producer/Correspondent in Washington
- Josh Landis—Correspondent, CBS Newspath
- Dr. Jon LaPook—Medical Correspondent
- Claire Leka—Correspondent, *CBS News MoneyWatch* and CBS Newspath
- Drew Levinson—Correspondent, CBS Newspath
- Lara Logan—Chief Foreign Affairs Correspondent; Correspondent, *60 minutes*
- Sheila MacVicar—Correspondent
- Peter Maer—White House Correspondent, CBS Radio News

- Maureen Maher—Correspondent, *48 hours*
- Dr. Mallika Marshall—Medical Correspondent, *The Early Show*
- David Martin—National Security Correspondent
- Anthony Mason—Business Correspondent
- Cami McCormick—Correspondent, CBS Radio News
- Tara Mergener—Correspondent, CBS Newspath (freelance)
- Michelle Miller—Correspondent
- Russ Mitchell—News Anchor, *The Early Show*; Anchor, *CBS Evening News* (Sunday)
- Erin Moriarty—Correspondent, *48 hours*
- Teri Okita—Correspondent, CBS Newspath
- Meg Oliver—Anchor, *Up to the Minute*
- Bob Orr—Justice and Homeland Security Correspondent
- Charles Osgood—Anchor, *CBS News Sunday Morning*
- Elizabeth Palmer—Correspondent
- Scott Pelley—Correspondent, *60 Minutes*
- Barry Petersen—Correspondent
- Mark Phillips—Correspondent
- Randall Pinkston—Correspondent
- Byron Pitts—National Correspondent
- Allen Pizzey—Correspondent
- Bill Plante—Senior White House Correspondent
- Dave Price—Weather Anchor, *The Early Show*
- Lonnie Quinn—Weather Anchor, *The Saturday Early Show*
- Dan Raviv—National Correspondent, CBS Radio News
- Chip Reid—Capitol Hill Correspondent
- Dean Reynolds—National Correspondent
- Susan Roberts—Correspondent, CBS Newspath
- Troy Roberts—Correspondent, *48 hours*
- Maggie Rodriguez—Anchor, *The Early Show*
- Andy Rooney—Correspondent, *60 minutes*
- Charlie Rose—Contributor, *60 minutes*
- Richard Roth—Correspondent
- Morley Safer—Co-Editor, *60 minutes*
- Forrest Sawyer—Substitute Anchor, *CBS Evening News* (Saturday) (freelance)
- Bob Schieffer—Chief Washington Correspondent; Anchor, *Face the Nation*

- Richard Schlesinger—Correspondent
- Dr. Emily Senay—Medical Correspondent
- Frank Settipani—Anchor/Correspondent, CBS Radio News
- Daniel Sieberg—Science and Technology Correspondent
- Bob Simon—Correspondent, *60 minutes*
- Harry Smith—Anchor, *The Early Show*
- Tracy Smith—Correspondent, *The Early Show*
- Bianca Solorzano—Correspondent
- Susan Spencer—Correspondent, *48 hours*
- Hari Sreenivasan—Correspondent
- Lesley Stahl—Co-Editor, *60 minutes*
- Mark Strassmann—Correspondent
- Gaby Tabunar—Correspondent (freelance)
- Martha Teichner—Correspondent, *CBS News Sunday Morning*
- Ben Tracy—Correspondent
- Debbye Turner-Bell—Early Show Contributing Correspondent
- Peter Van Sant—Correspondent, *48 hours*
- Kelly Wallace—Correspondent
- Mike Wallace—Correspondent Emeritus, *60 minutes*
- Bill Whitaker—Correspondent
- Bill Whitney—Anchor, CBS Radio News
- Charles Wolfson—State Department Correspondent/ Producer
- Chris Wragge—Anchor, *The Saturday Early Show*
- Nick Young—Anchor, CBS *Radio World News Roundup*

Source: CBS News & NewsWatch Dallas

Past CBS News Correspondents

- Betsy Aaron
- Jim Acosta
- Jacqueline Adams
- Martin Agronsky
- Sharyn Alfonsi
- Ron Allen
- Bob Allison
- David Andelman
- Jose Diaz-Balart
- Griffin Bancroft
- Roberta Baskin
- Joseph Benti
- Nelson Benton
- Derrick Blakely
- Regina Blakely
- Karen Boros

- Ray Brady
- Heywood Hale Broun
- Winston Burdett
- Ned Calmer
- Sylvia Chase
- Connie Chung
- Lou Cioffi
- Michele Clark
- Ron Cochran
- Reid Collins
- Lee Cowan
- David Culhane
- Faith Daniels
- Randy Daniels
- Morton Dean
- Nancy Dickerson
- David Dow
- Terry Drinkwater
- Bruce Dunning
- Douglas Edwards
- Bob Faw
- Giselle Fernández
- Rita Flynn
- Murray Fromson
- Christopher Glenn
- Diana Gonzalez
- Fred Graham
- Bruce Hall
- Erin Hayes
- Don Hollenbeck
- Alan Jackson
- Gordon Joseloff
- Marvin Kalb
- Peter Kalischer
- Frank Kearns
- Alexander Kendrick
- Dana King
- Jeffrey Kofman
- Mitchell Kraus
- Charles Kuralt
- Ed Bradley
- Mika Brzezinski
- Karen Burnes
- Gretchen Carlson
- Joie Chen
- Wells (Ted) Church
- Blair Clark
- Jane Clayson
- Charles Collingwood
- Victoria Corderi
- Walter Cronkite
- Frank Currier
- John Daly
- Foster Davis
- David Dick
- Linda Douglass
- Bill Downs
- Dave Dugan
- Jed Duvall
- Eric Engberg
- Tom Fenton
- John Ferrugia
- Rick Fredericksen
- Monica Gayle
- Bernard Goldberg
- Liz Gonzalez
- Bryant Gumbel
- John Hart
- George Herman
- Richard C. Hottelet
- Phil Jones
- Bernard Kalb
- Elizabeth Kaledin
- H.V. Kaltenborn
- Chris Kelley
- Cinny Kennard
- Don Kladstrup
- Ted Koop
- Robert Krulwich
- Bill Kurtis

- Bill Lagattuta
- Bill Leonard
- Stan Levey
- Vicki Mabrey
- Carol Marin
- Mark McEwen
- Derek McGinty
- Bill McLaughlin
- Jim McManus
- John Meyer
- Bruce Morton
- Roger Mudd
- George Natanson
- Deborah Norville
- Mike O'Connor
- Ike Pappas
- Robert Pierpoint
- George Polk
- Deborah Potter
- Jane Bryant Quinn
- Bert Quint
- Dan Rather
- Bill Redeker
- Trish Regan
- John Roberts
- Steve Rowan
- Marlene Sanders
- Diane Sawyer
- Stephen Schiff
- Daniel Schorr
- Barry Serafin
- Bill Shadel
- John Sheahan
- William L. Shirer
- Bob Sirott
- Terrence Smith
- Mike Stanley
- Alison Stewart
- Hannah Storm
- Neil Strawser
- John Laurence
- Larry LeSueur
- Bill Lynch
- Edie Magnus
- Melissa McDermott
- Susan McGinnis
- Bob McKeown
- Marya McLaughlin
- Bob McNamara
- Edward P. Morgan
- Bill Moyers
- Edward R. Murrow
- Paul Niven
- Stuart Novins
- Bill O'Reilly
- Hampton Pearson
- Larry Pintak
- Larry Pomeroy
- Ned Potter
- Sally Quinn
- Ed Rabel
- Harry Reasoner
- Gary Reaves
- Jane Robelot
- Norman Robinson
- Hughes Rudd
- Tony Sargent
- Robert Schakne
- David Schoenbrun
- David Schoumacher
- Eric Sevareid
- Bernard Shaw
- Gary Shepard
- Maria Shriver
- Howard K. Smith
- Joan Snyder
- John Stehr
- Jim Stewart
- Bill Stout
- Kathleen Sullivan

- Rene Syler
- Lee Thornton
- Dallas Townsend
- Robert Trout
- Doug Tunnell
- Charles Von Fremd
- Hal Walker
- Don Webster
- Paula Zahn
- Lowell Thomas
- Richard Threlkeld
- Liz Trotta
- Lem Tucker
- Meredith Vieira
- Richard Wagner
- Jane Wallace
- Steve Young

Source: CBS News & NewsWatch Dallas.

International Broadcasts

CBS Evening News is shown on Sky News to viewers in Europe and Africa. In Australia, the CBS Evening News bulletin is shown at 11.30 a.m. Monday to Saturday, and at 12.30 p.m. on Sundays on Sky News Australia.

CBS is not shown outside the Americas on a channel in its own right. However, both CBS News is shown for a few hours a day on Orbit News in Europe, Africa and the Middle East. CBS News stories are a common occurrence on Australia's Ten News on Network Ten, as part a CBS programming content deal. They also air The Early Show each weekday as well.

Controversies

In 1964, Rep. Jimmy Utt (R-Cal.) filed a libel suit against CBS regarding a CBS Reports "Case History of a Rumor" programme. He claimed the defendants had "'entrapped' him into giving a television interview that turned out to be a 'cross examination' by Roger Mudd, who acted as 'prosecutor, judge, and jury.'" The case was dismissed. Utt died in office in 1970 and was succeeded by John Schmitz.

In a speech in 1971, Vice-President Spiro Agnew accused CBS News of disseminating "deceptive, self-serving propaganda." He quoted from reports by the Federal Communications Commission (FCC) and the Special Subcommittee on Investigations of the House Commerce Committee. These reports mentioned a CBS documentary called "Project Nassau", an effort to depose the Francois Duvalier regime in Haiti. "The House Subcommittee found that CBS had, in effect, financially subsidized a planned 1966 invasion of Haiti in order to make a documentary on the event." In his deposition, Tom Dunkin, journalist for the Atlanta Journal, said that producer Jay McMullen of CBS told him in November, 1966 that he had "spent a lot of time and money on this project and had nothing to show for it." (In January of 1967 the project ended with the arrest of 75 participants.)

In 1986 CBS Television sought to trim its expenses. It undertook major layoffs of the News division staff. In a September 1, 2004 CBS news commentary, titled "Vice-President Dick Agnew", CBS editorial director Dick Meyer said that Vice President Cheney "drew from a different tradition typified by Spiro Agnew" in a tradition that "uses the hired help to do the political dirty work."

NBC NEWS

NBC News is the news division of American television network NBC, a part of NBC Universal, which is majority-owned by General Electric. Its current president is Steve Capus.

Fig. 8.25: NBC News Logo, 1959-72

History

Caravan Era

The first television newscast in history was made by NBC News on February 21, 1940, anchored by Lowell Thomas and airing weeknights at 6:45 p.m. In 1949, the *Camel News Caravan* anchored by John Cameron Swayze began on NBC, continuing until 1956 when it was succeeded by the *Huntley-Brinkley Report*.

Huntley-Brinkley Era

Although the operations of CBS News have received more attention from historians of broadcast journalism, NBC's operations often received higher ratings. From 1956 through 1970, NBC's *Huntley-Brinkley Report* anchored by the team of Chet Huntley and David Brinkley consistently exceeded the viewership levels attained by CBS News and its main anchor Walter Cronkite. The pair, together with fellow correspondents Frank McGee and Jay Barbree, distinguished itself in the coverage of American manned space missions in the Project Mercury, Project Gemini and Project Apollo programmes, during an era when space missions rated continuous coverage. (An entire studio, Studio 8H, was configured for this coverage, complete with models and mockups of rockets and spacecraft, maps of the earth and moon to show orbital trackage, and stages on which animated figures created by puppeteer Bil Baird were used to depict movements of astronauts before on-board spacecraft television cameras were feasible. Studio 8H is now the home of the long-running NBC show *Saturday Night Live.*)

NBC Nightly News Era

NBC's ratings lead began to slip toward the end of the 1960s and fell sharply when Chet Huntley retired in 1970 (Huntley died of cancer in 1974). The loss of Huntley, along with a reluctance by RCA to fund NBC News at a similar level CBS was funding its news division, left NBC News in the doldrums. The network tried a platoon of anchors (Brinkley, McGee, and John Chancellor) for some months afterward. Despite the efforts of the network's eventual lead anchor, the articulate, even-toned Chancellor, NBC News did not recover its previous viewership levels until after General Electric acquired RCA. Even perennially third-place ABC would equal *Nightly News* by decade's end with its *World News Tonight* format. It was only when Tom Brokaw became sole anchor in 1983, after breifly co-anchoring with Roger Mudd, that things began to improve for *Nightly News*. In 1995, NBC finally won the top spot in the Nielsens for the first time in over 25 years.

NBC's primary news show is *NBC Nightly News*. Brian Williams assumed primary anchor duties in December 2004 upon the retirement of his predecessor, Tom Brokaw. On 22 October, 2007, NBC Nightly News moved into its new high definition studios, at Studio 3C at NBC Studios in 30 Rockefeller Plaza in New York City. The network's 24-hour cable network,

MSNBC joined the network in New York on that day as well. The new studios/headquarters for NBC News and MSNBC are now located in one area.

Current Programming

- *Early Today*
- *Today*
- *Weekend Today*
- *Meet the Press*
- *NBC Nightly News with Brian Williams*
- *NBC Nightly News with Lester Holt*
- *Dateline NBC*

Syndicated Productions

- *The Chris Matthews Show*
- *Your Total Health*

Other Productions

NBC News provides content for the Internet, as well as cable—only news networks CNBC and MSNBC. Additionally, NBC News broadcasts radio news bulletins at the top of the hour, distributed by Westwood One, a radio service owned by NBC's competitor, CBS. Listen to the latest headline bulletin by clicking here (subject to availability). In 1982, NBC News began production on *NBC News Overnight* with anchors Linda Ellerbee, Lloyd Dobyns, and Bill Schechner. That programme was cancelled in December 1983, but in 1991, NBC News aired another overnight news show called *NBC Nightside*. During its run, the show's anchors included Sara James, Bruce Hall, Antonio Mora, Tom Miller, Campbell Brown, Kim Hindrew, Tom Donavan, and Tonya Strong. *NBC Nightside* lasted until 1998 and was replaced by reruns of the *Tonight Show with Jay Leno* and *Late Night with Conan O'Brien*. In the early 1990s, NBC News produced a shortlived investigative programme called *Exposé*.

NBC News Channel is a news video and report feed service, similar to a wire service, providing pre-produced international, national and regional stories some with fronting reporters customized for NBC network affiliates. It is based in Charlotte,

North Carolina. NBC News Channel also served as the production base of *NBC Nightside.*

Noted Coverage

NBC News got the first American news interviews from two Russian presidents (Vladimir Putin, Mikhail Gorbachev), and Brokaw was the only American TV news correspondent to witness the fall of the Berlin Wall in 1989.

In the Iraq War, NBC News main anchor Brokaw covered the war extensively, in part owing to the willingness of GE to fund it. NBC newsman David Bloom pushed through the GE and US Department of Defense bureaucracies permission to construct a mobile news vehicle that could transmit live video broadcasts from the battlefield. The "Bloom-mobile" brought satellite images and videos (clear, detailed) into homes across America and Europe, live and one-on-one. Bloom did not live to accept the accolades after the armed conflict; he died of natural causes unrelated to combat during the final phase of the fighting.

Controversies

***Dateline NBC* General Motors Investigation**

In 1993, *Dateline NBC* broadcast an investigative report about the safety of General Motors (GM) trucks. GM discovered the "actual footage" utilized in the broadcast had been rigged by the inclusion of explosive incendiaries attached to the gas tanks and the use of improper sealants for those tanks. GM subsequently filed an anti-defamation lawsuit against NBC, which publicly admitted the results of the tests were rigged and settled the lawsuit with GM. As a result of the controversy, several *Dateline* producers were fired and NBC News President Michael Gartner was forced out.

Anthrax

After the September 11, 2001 attacks, a letter postmarked from Trenton, New Jersey containing anthrax was addressed to then *NBC Nightly News* anchor Tom Brokaw as part of the 2001 anthrax attacks. The third floor offices of NBC News in New York were sealed off by the FBI for an investigation. Brokaw was not harmed, although two NBC News employees sustained anthrax infection but no permanent injuries.

Mail from a Mass Murderer

On April 16, 2007, Cho Seung-hui stormed through a classroom building at Virginia Polytechnic Institute and State University at Blacksburg, Virginia and randomly shot and killed 32 people, injuring 29 others. Two hours earlier, he had slain two other people at a dormitory in another part of the campus.

Cho took time between the two shooting episodes to prepare and mail a large multimedia package to NBC News in New York containing messages about his anger at the wealthy and alluding to the slaughter that was about to take place. Although the package was sent overnight mail, it was not received until 11 a.m. on April 18 because of Cho's confusion over the zip code of NBC's headquarters at 30 Rockefeller Plaza.

The package contained a DVD showing video clips of Cho speaking and more than two dozen photos of Cho, including 11 of him thrusting pistols at the camera. A postal worker delivering the parcel to the network's Rockefeller Center offices recognized the sender and alerted NBC security personnel. They immediately reported the package to the FBI. Meanwhile, NBC made copies of the contents and aired carefully edited pieces on its evening news and cable programmes. Snippets from the package, including still photos, videos and voice narration, were also made available to competing news outlets who agreed to credit the network as the source. NBC News president Steve Capus defended use of the material but the frequency of its broadcast was cut dramatically.

Personnel

Current

- Dan Abrams Chief Legal Correspondent
- Jane Arraf
- Tom Aspell
- Peter Alexander
- Tiki Barber National Correspondent, Today
- Jay Barbree Cape Canaveral, Space Correspondent
- Robert Bazell Chief Science Correspondent

- Tom Brokaw Interim Moderator, Meet the Press; NBC News Special Correspondent
- Contessa Brewer Anchor, MSNBC
- Ned Colt
- Erin Burnett Anchor "Squawk on the Street", "Street Signs" (CNBC); Fill in Co-Anchor "Weekend Today"
- Kevin Corke
- Bob Costas
- Ann Curry Newsreader, "Today; Anchor, "Dateline"
- Lisa Daniels
- Giada De Laurentiis
- Bob Dotson National Correspondent, "Today"
- Rehema Ellis
- Richard Engel NBC News Chief Foreign Correspondent
- Martin Fletcher
- Michelle Franzen
- Dawn Fratangelo
- Jamie Gangel National Correspondent, "Today"
- Kathie Lee Gifford Co-Anchor (4th hour), "Today"
- David Gregory Chief White House Correspondent; Anchor, "Race for the White House" (MSNBC)
- Peter Greenberg Travel Editor, "Today"
- Chris Hansen Correspondent, "Dateline NBC"
- Hoda Kotb Co-Anchor, (4th Hour) "Today"; Correspondent "Dateline NBC"
- Lester Holt Co-Anchor "Weekend Today"; Anchor, Weekend Edition "NBC Nightly News"
- Michelle Kosinski
- Margaret Larson Correspondent "Dateline NBC"
- Matt Lauer Co-Anchor, "Today"
- George Lewis
- Jim Maceda
- Chris Matthews Anchor, "Hardball", "The Chris Matthews Show", and *Decision* Election coverage
- Preston Mendenhall
- Maria Menounos
- Jim Miklaszewski Chief Pentagon Correspondent
- Andrea Mitchell Chief Foreign Affairs Correspondent; Anchor, MSNBC

- Natalie Morales National Correspondent, "Today" Co-Anchor (3rd hour), "Today"
- Keith Morrison Correspondent, "Dateline NBC"
- Ron Mott
- Dennis Murphy
- Lisa Myers NBC News Senior Investigative Correspondent
- Kelly O'Donnell
- Norah O'Donnell Correspondent, NBC News; Chief Washington Correspondent, MSNBC
- Michael Okwu
- Jeannie Ohm
- Keith Olbermann Anchor, "Countdown with Keith Olbermann", and *Decision* Election coverage
- Roger O'Neil
- Carl Quintanilla Anchor, "Squawk Box" (CNBC); Alternating Newsreader, "Weekend Today"
- Amy Robach National Correspondent, "Today", "NBC Nightly News"; Co-Anchor, "Weekend Today"
- Al Roker Weatherman, "Today"
- Luke Russert NBC News Convention Correspondent
- Kerry Sanders
- Martin Savidge
- Mara Schiavocampo NBC News Digital Correspondent
- Willard Scott
- Gene Shalit
- David Shuster Anchor, MSNBC
- Dr. Nancy Snyderman Chief Medical Editor
- Alison Stewart Substitute Anchor, MSNBC; Alternating Newsreader, "Weekend Today", NBC News Contributor
- Mike Taibbi
- Don Teague
- Anne Thompson Chief Environmental Affairs Correspondent
- Kevin Tibbles
- Meredith Vieira Co-Anchor, "Today"
- Brian Williams Anchor, "NBC Nightly News"
- Ian Williams
- Pete Williams Justice Correspondent

- Jenna Wolfe National Correspondent, "Today Show"; Co-Anchor, "Weekend Today"
- John Yang

Former

- Elie Abel
- Martin Agronsky
- Piers Anderton
- Jim Avila
- Kenneth Bernstein
- Frank Blair
- Ken Bode
- David Brinkley
- Christina Brown
- Henry Champ
- Connie Chung
- Kristen Cornett
- Patty Culhane
- John Dancy
- Nancy Dickerson
- Phil Donahue
- Paul Duke
- Linda Ellerbee
- Bonnie Erbe
- Elise Finch
- Fred Francis
- Pauline Frederick
- Joe Garagiola
- Dave Garroway
- Robert Goralski
- Tony Guida
- Robert Hager
- Welles Hangen
- John Hart
- Bob Herbert
- Chet Huntley
- Bob Jamieson
- Bernard Kalb
- Floyd Kalber
- Bill Karins
- Bob Abernethy
- Lew Allison
- Jodi Applegate
- Marilyn Berger
- Jim Bitterman
- David Bloom
- Frank Bourgholtzer
- Ned Brooks
- David Burrington
- John Chancellor
- John Cochran
- Katie Couric
- Jim Cummins
- Faith Daniels
- Lloyd Dobyns
- Hugh Downs
- Rosey Edeh
- John Elloitt
- Giselle Fernandez
- Jack Ford
- Eliot Frankel
- Betty Furness
- Anne Garrels
- Alexis Glick
- Bryant Gumbel
- Peter Hackes
- Nanette Hansen
- Don Harris
- Jim Hartz
- John Hockenberry
- Gwen Ifill
- Ray James
- Marvin Kalb
- Herbert Kaplow
- Art Kent

- Arthur Kent
- Emery King
- Bob Kur
- Irving R. Levine
- Sean McLaughlin
- Robert MacNeil
- Robert McCormick
- Bill Monroe
- Merrill Mueller
- Ron Nessen
- Edwin Newman
- Soledad O'Brien
- John Palmer
- Jack Perkins
- Stone Phillips
- Gabe Pressman
- Brigitte Quinn
- Jeff Ranieri
- Chip Reid
- Brian Ross
- Tim Russert
- Bill Ryan
- Jessica Savitch
- Mike Schneider
- John Seigenthaler
- Claire Shipman
- Lawrence E. Spivak
- Melissa Stark
- John Cameron Swayze
- Lem Tucker
- Richard Valeriani
- Sander Vanocur
- Chris Wallace
- Barbara Walters
- Joe Witte
- Judy Woodruff
- Douglas Kiker
- Dan Kloeffler
- Jack Lescoulie
- Jennifer London
- Cassie Mackin
- Boyd Matson
- Frank McGee
- Roger Mudd
- Roy Neal
- Jackie Nespral
- Deborah Norville
- Don Oliver
- Jane Pauley
- Tom Pettit
- Mark Potter
- Norma Quarles
- Ed Rabel
- Milissa Rehberger
- Betty Rollin
- Ford Rowan
- Bob Ryan
- Aline Saarinen
- Chuck Scarborough
- Ray Scherer
- Scott Simon
- Maria Shriver
- Rob Stafford
- Carl Stern
- Liz Trotta
- Garrick Utley
- Charles Van Doren
- Linda Vester
- Colleen Williams
- Mary Alice Williams
- Lew Wood
- Tony Zappone

Broadcasts Abroad

NBC Nightly News is shown on CNBC Europe. MSNBC is not shown outside the Americas on a channel in its own right.

However, both NBC News and MSNBC are shown for a few hours a day on Orbit News in Europe, Africa and the Middle East. MSNBC is also shown occasionally on sister network CNBC Europe during breaking news. Some NBC News programmes are shown in the Philippines on 2nd Avenue. NBC Nightly News, along with the full programme lineup of NBC, is carried by affiliate VSB-TV in Bermuda. In Australia; the first 2 hours of Today, Weekend Today and Meet The Press are broadcast early in the morning on the Seven Network, just before their own morning show Sunrise.

Bureaus

Major Bureaus

- New York, New York—NBC News World Headquarters
- Los Angeles, California—NBC News West Coast Headquarters
- Washington, D.C.—NBC News Governmental Affairs Headquarters
- London, England—NBC News European Headquarters

Minor Bureaus (within the United States)

- Atlanta, Georgia
- Chicago, Illinois
- San Francisco, California
- Dallas, Texas
- New Orleans, Louisiana
- Miami, Florida
- Philadelphia, Pennsylvania
- Denver, Colorado
- Arlington, Virginia (The Pentagon)
- All NBC Owned and Operated Affiliates are considered NBC News Bureaus.

Foreign Bureaus (NBC Universal Affiliates)

- Johannesburg, South Africa (CNBC Africa Headquarters)

- Nairobi, Kenya (CNBC Africa)
- Abuja, Nigeria (CNBC Africa)
- Lagos, Nigeria (CNBC Africa)
- Cape Town, South Africa (CNBC Africa)
- London, England (CNBC Africa)
- Singapore (CNBC Asia Headquarters)
- Sydney, Australia (CNBC Asia)
- Tokyo, Japan (CNBC Asia)
- Hong Kong (CNBC Asia)
- Beijing, China (NBC Sports)
- Frankfurt, Germany (CNBC)
- Baghdad, Iraq (MSNBC and CNBC)
- Beruit, Lebanon (MSNBC and CNBC)
- Jerusalem, Israel (MSNBC and CNBC)
- New Delhi, India (CNBC)

Theme Music

Most of NBC's news television programmes use the "The Mission" by John Williams as their theme. The composition was first used by NBC in 1985 and was updated in 2006.

9

Indian News Channels and News Media: Select Case Studies

NDTV.COM

New Delhi Television Limited (NDTV), founded in 1988, is India's first and largest private producer of news, current affairs and entertainment television. NDTV is home to the country's best and brightest reporters, anchors and producers; 23 offices and studios across the country host India's most modern and sophisticated production and newsgathering facilities. At home, NDTV 24×7, the flagship English news channel is the market leader with an unrivalled reputation for excellence. NDTV India, the company's 24-hour Hindi news channel, is respected for its integrity and commitment to real journalism.

NDTV Profit, a 24-hour business channel, has established new standards for simple, clear and transparent reporting on the world of business. NDTV has launched its first channel outside India in partnership with Astro, a leading South East Asia media group. "Astro Awani", launched in Indonesia, is a 24-hour news, infotainment and lifestyle channel.

NDTV India is one of the leading Hindi 24-hours TV News channel in India. This is the sister channel of NDTV 24×7 and NDTV Profit. Prannoy Roy is the founder of NDTV. Vinod Dua is associated with this channel, and comes with the programme *KHABARDAR*. Its motto is *"Khabar wahi, jo sach dikhaaye"*, meaning "The news which only shows the truth." NDTV India is considered to be one of the few Hindi news channel which does not emphasize on Infotainment, along with Sahara Samay, DD News, etc.

NDTV PROFIT

NDTV Profit is a business news channel started by New Delhi Television in January 2005. Started to provide competition to the monopoly enjoyed by CNBC-TV18, the channel has managed to garner a decent market share.

NDTV PROFIT	
Launched	2005
Owned by	NDTV Ltd.
Slogan	News You Can Use.
Country	India
Headquarters	Delhi
Sister channel(s)	* NDTV 24×7 NDTV India NDTV Imagine NDTV GOOD TIMES NDTV Metro Nation NDTV Arabia
Website	http://www.ndtvprofit.com
Availability	
IPTV over ADSL	
mio TV (Singapore)	Channel 49

It has a large number of journalists covering the action from the Bombay Stock Exchange (BSE) and the National Stock Exchange (NSE). Furthermore, it also covers the latest business deals and acts as a platform for companies to give their public results, with growth rate, net profit etc. On 14 December 2006 NDTV Profit was launched a video screen at the BSE building.

Leadership Awards

The NDTV Profit Business Leadership Awards was started by NDTV Profit in July 2006. The first edition of this saw the awards being given away to entrepreneurs by the Indian Prime Minister Manmohan Singh. Nandan Nilekani of Infosys was chosen the Viewers' Choice Best Global Indian.

Programming

Present Programmes

- Value for Money
- Big Fish (Interview on NDTV Profit)
- Inside Hollywood
- Hot Property on NDTV Profit
- Business Prime Time
- One Life to Love
- Profit at Night
- Gadget Guru
- All About Ads
- Money Mantra
- Breakfast with Profit
- Countdown on NDTV Profit
- Opening Moves
- Profit Fundamentals
- Buy or Sell on NDTV Profit
- Profit Newsroom
- Power Lunch on NDTV Profit
- The 2:30 Factor
- Tomorrow's Picks
- Digital Duniya
- Cell Guru
- The Car and Bike Show
- Nasdaq Live
- Profit this Week
- Profit Palette
- Business on Course
- D Street this Week
- Boss's Day Out
- Reality of Realty
- World Business (NDTV Profit)

Personalities

Name	Title
Namrata Brar	
Siddharth Vinayak Patankar	Editor, NDTV and Anchor of The Car and Bike Show
Shweta Rajpal Kohli	
Aunindyo Chakravarty	
Nikunj Dalmia	
Shaili Chopra Aroor	
Shivnath Thukral	Managing Editor

NDTV 24×7

NDTV 24×7 is a premier English language news channel in India that is owned by New Delhi Television Ltd. It is the largest private producer of news and current affairs programming. NDTV 24×7 is widely considered the best 24-hour English news channel in India. It won the Asian Television Award for *Best News Channel* in 2005.

NDTV 24×7 is home to a team of award winning journalists who spearhead the news campaign. Some of them are Dr. Prannoy Roy, Barkha Dutt. The news channel also has many other extra-news programmes like "The Big Fight", "We the People", which are highly popular. The channel continues to produce original content such as documentaries and special reports. NDTV 24×7 is also available outside of India, broadcasting in the UK on the Sky Digital platform, in the US on the DirecTV platform, in Canada on the ATN platform, in Australia on the Vision Asia platform, in Europe on the WorldTV platform, and in Singapore on the mio TV platform.

Programming

The channel airs one of India's most successful opinion-based shows: We the People with Barkha Dutt. The show has received critical acclaim and has won several key awards. Another very popular show is hosted on NDTV 24×7 called 'The Big Fight' hosted by Vikram Chandra (the show was earlier hosted by Rajdeep Sardesai, who quit NDTV in 2005). 'The Car and Bike Show' with Siddharth Vinayak Patankar is also a very avidly watched and followed programme.

NDTV 24x7

Launched	2003
Owned by	NDTV Ltd.
Slogan	Experience. Truth First.
Country	India
	NDTV India
Sister channel(s)	NDTV Profit
	NDTV Imagine
Website	http://www.ndtv.com
Availability	
Satellite	
Bell TV (Canada)	Channel 727
DirecTV (U.S.)	Channel 2007
Dish TV (India)	Channel 603
Sky Digital (UK and Ireland)	Channel 511
Tata Sky (India)	Channel 532
Telus TV (Canada)	Channel 524
Vision Asia (Australia)	Channel ???
WorldTV (Europe)	Channel 16
Cable	
Rogers Cable (Canada)	Channel 586
Shaw Cable (Canada)	Channel 241
IPTV over ADSL	
mio TV (Singapore)	Channel 48
Telus TV (Canada)	Channel 524

In October 2007, the channel started a new series—'Documentary 24×7' that features path-breaking documentaries that explore contemporary issues.

The channel is also popular amongst the youth, and regularly features educational series such as GetAhead in June 2007, Exam Guru and Cat Scan as well as shows for young professionals such as Show Me the Money, Cell Guru and 'The Car and Bike Show.'

Awards

- Best English News Channel of Asia in 2005 at the Asian Television Awards.
- Best English News Channel in 2005 at the Indian Television Academy Awards.
- Best English News Channel in 2006 at the Indian Television Academy Awards.

STAR NEWS

STAR News is the Hindi language entertainment channel of STAR TV. The channel presents a mix of rolling entertainment bulletins and specialized shows covering topics from crime to cricket.

Launched	1998
Owned by	STAR TV
Country	India
Sister channel(s)	STAR Ananda, STAR Majha
Website	Official Site
Availability	
Satellite	
DirecTV (U.S.)	Channel 2002
Dish TV (India)	Channel 569
One B (New Zealand)	Channel ???
Sky Digital (UK and Ireland)	Channel 808
Sun Direct TV (India)	Channel 118
Tata Sky (India)	Channel 502
Big TV (India)	Channel 2760
Cable	
First Media (Indonesia)	Channel 175
SkyCable Premium (Philippines)	Channel 68, Channel 76 with addressable boxes
Virgin TV (UK)	Channel 802
IPTV over ADSL	
Now TV (Hong Kong)	Channel 795
World on Demand (Japan)	Channel 114

A lot of programming on Star News is very opinionated. They are also thought to sensationalize and exaggerate entertainment content, this channel is a good example of the growing culture of tabloid Hindi entertainment channels.

History

When STAR News launched in 1998, it was at first a Bilingual English/Hindi News Service, and was initially run in partnership with NDTV. But when the agreement, with the NDTV expired, STAR News was transformed into a Hindi entertainment service. It also has its own DTH service which is running successfully.

Operating Channels

- STAR News India
- STAR News India (US Feed)
- STAR News Europe
- STAR News India (Hong Kong Feed)

Other STAR News Channels

- *STAR Ananda*—A Bengali entertainment channel. For more information about the channel and the new website itself, see under external links.
- *STAR Majha*—A 24-hour National Marathi entertainment channel. For more information about the channel and the new website itself, see under external links.

Ratings

- STAR News claims that "... attracting a 25 per cent market share in six major metros. (*Source*: TAM, All Adults, C&S, 15+, 6 metros, Week 34 and 35)..."

Broadcasts Outside India

The international feeds of STAR News differ somewhat from the Indian version.

Europe

The old STAR News logo is still used in Europe despite the

change in India. The text of the entertainment ticker is in English and also featured is Star News Asia, a 30-minute English language entertainment bulletin that is shown in Asia on STAR World.

Philippines and Hong Kong

In the Philippines and Hong Kong, the programmes are similar to India. The new STAR News logo is used and the entertainment ticker is written in English.

United States

In the United States, the word "India" is incorporated in the logo to denote the Indian origin of the channel and the news ticker is in English. The programmes are broadcast live from India, excluding Star News Asia, which is telecast in weekdays over repeat programming.

HT MEDIA

HT Media found its beginning in 1924 when its flagship newspaper, Hindustan Times was inaugurated by Mahatma Gandhi. HT Media (BSE, NSE) has today grown to become one of India's largest media companies. Produced by an editorial team known for its quality, innovation and integrity, Hindustan Times (English) and Hindustan (Hindi), have a combined daily circulation of 2.25 million copies and a readership base of 12.4 million readers to their credit. Both dailies enjoy a strong brand recognition among readers as well as advertisers. To cater to the large readership base, HT Media operates 19 printing facilities across India with an installed capacity of 1.5 million copies per hour.

In addition to Hindustan Times and Hindustan, HT Media also publishes a national business newspaper, Mint. Mint is a one-of-its-kind newspaper in the sense that the company has an exclusive agreement with the Wall Street Journal to publish Journal-branded news and information in India. Mint is today the second-largest business newspaper in India with presence in the key markets of Delhi, Mumbai and Bangalore.

HT Media, through its subsidiary HT Music and

Entertainment Company Ltd., has made its foray into electronic media. Diversifying its ambit of operations, the company in a consulting partnership with Virgin Radio, has launched the FM radio channel—Fever 104. Currently available in Delhi and Mumbai, Fever 104 has established a strong presence as being one of the most vibrant channels on air. In a short span of two years, the channel's rise has been meteoric considering its position in Delhi as the No. 2 station on the popularity charts.

Internet businesses of HT Media, incorporated under Firefly e-ventures, operate leading web portals Hindustantimes.com and livemint.com in the general and business news categories respectively. The company has recently launched Shine.com, a job portal which has received high appreciation from consumers and industry for its innovative design and usability.

HT Media reported FY 2007 annual revenue of $245 million. For the fiscal third quarter ended March 31, 2007, the company reported a 13 per cent increase in revenue to $82 million and a 10 per cent increase of profit after tax (PAT) to $9 million from the year-ago quarter. "The FM radio space in India is showing tremendous promise. I am very happy with the progress that Fever 104 FM has made. Virgin and HT Media have worked together successfully to create a differentiated and compelling brand and business in Fever 104 FM" Richard Branson (on Virgin Radio's relationship with Fever 104 FM).

Latest Press Releases

- Shine.com hits the One Million Mark
- HT Media FY 2008-09 Q1 Results
- Outcome of Postal Ballot for passing of Resolutions
- Sixth Annual General Meeting convened on Friday, the 1st August, 2008
- Firefly eVentures, an HT Media company, launches Shine.com, the newest and innovative Job portal.
- HT Media scoring high: All About Newspapers
- HT Media, BURDA announce joint venture to tap media services market
- HT Media FY 2007-08 Q4 Results

- Outcome of Postal Ballot for amendment in HTML Employee Stock Option Scheme
- HT Media FY 2007-08 Q2 Results

History

The *Hindustan Times* was the brainchild of the Akalis who felt that a newspaper in English would enable them to reach an audience other than the Punjabi-reading one. This was in the year 1922. From the outset the newspaper was set up to oppose the British. The *Hindustan Times* finally came into being on September 1924 and was inaugurated by Mahatma Gandhi. The newspaper was to become a premier nationalist newspaper of the capital in the turbulent years preceding independence. From a humble beginning in a three-storey building, the company has expanded its operations from print to other media channels like radio, internet, events and marketing, and strategic partnerships, as part of its endeavour to establish itself as a giant media conglomerate in the present times.

September 26, 1924

This date marked the August beginnings of *Hindustan Times* with Mahatma Gandhi, the Father of the Nation inaugurating the newspaper.

1927: *Hindustan Times*, was reborn as *Hindustan Times Ltd.*, a limited liability company.

1936: The Hindi daily *Hindustan* was launched, which remains the dominant newspaper in the core Hindi belt of northern India.

1937: Devdas Gandhi was appointed the Managing Editor of the newspaper and remained the managing editor till his death in 1957.

1942: The *Hindustan Times* was one of the few newspapers that stopped publishing the newspaper for four and a half months as it refused to accept the British imposition of censorship on all newspapers.

1947: The year India gained its freedom, was also the year *Hindustan Times* attained the status of being the dominant newspaper in Delhi.

1957: The newspaper circulation grew from 58,693 copies to 144,287 in 1970 after KK Birla took over the mantle from GD Birla.

1960: The Hindi literary magazine *Kadambini* was launched.

1964: The group started actively targeting the youth of India and launched the *Nandan* magazine.

1991: At the start of liberalization of India, *Hindustan Times* moved to becoming an autonomous power centre in a mature democracy.

1999: The *Hindustan Times* celebrated its platinum anniversary.

2000: With a focus on localization, five new editions from Calcutta, Bhopal, Ranchi, Chandigarh and Jaipur were launched.

2003: The media business of was de-merged and incorporated under *HT Media Ltd.*

2004: *HT Media Ltd* was listed as a public company and attracted external funding.

2005: *Hindustan Times* successfully entered the Mumbai market with a refreshingly new product and content mix.

2006: *Fever 104 FM* is launched, in technical collaboration with the Virgin Group. *Hindustan* was relaunched re-establishing the company's prominent presence in the regional news space.

2007: *Mint,* the business paper in partnership with the *Wall Street Journal* was launched in Delhi and Mumbai. In the internet space, *Hindustantimes.com* was relaunched and *Livemint.com* was introduced.

2008: Firefly e-Ventures, an HT Media Company launched its first portal for job seekers, Shine.com

Vision and Values

HT Media—A rich heritage to live upto the solid edifice on which HT Media stands tall today was built on high ideals and values.

Values

HT Media "A rich heritage to live up to! Organizational values are the foundation stones on which the organization" image is built. These help the company realize its organizational goals and in turn transform lives. These values are intended to infuse an infectious energy, professionalism and a sense of true empowerment to the workplace. The solid edifice on which HT Media stands tall today was built on high ideals and values. The company has its roots in the independence movement in the first half of the twentieth century, a cause to empower the nation. We are adaptive to the changing times, while remaining steadfast to the values rooted in our culture.

Our values drive us towards our goals of expansion, diversification and excellence. These values define our philosophy of operations, guide our important decisions and determine our commitment and achievement.

The values personified by HT Media are:

- *Courage*: To encourage the ability that meets opposition with skill, competence and fortitude.
- *Responsibility*: Be accountable for results in line with the company's objectives, strategies and values.
- *Empowerment*: Support our people and give them the freedom to perform and to provide our readers with information to influence their environment.
- *Continuous Self Renewal*: Determination to constantly re-examine and re-invent ourselves for further innovation and creativity.
- *People Centric*: People are our greatest asset. We invest in them expect a lot and know that the rest will follow.
- *Vision*: HT Media strives to be a visionary organization and not an organization with a vision. In our endeavour to have a shared understanding, alignment and commitment, we have derived our company's vision that sets the course and empowers people to take action.

    - BHAG: By 2020, HTML will be the #1 Indian media and entertainment company - all the while staying true to our values. We will measure our success through market capitalization.
    - CORE PURPOSE: We endeavour to improve the quality of people's lives by empowering them through information, entertainment and education.

- CORE VALUES: Courage, Responsibility, Empowerment, Continuous Self-Renewal, People Centric.

EXPRESS GROUP

The Express Group are the publishers of the *Indian Express* newspapers in India.

Delivering Quality for Years

The Indian Express Group was the unifying voice behind India's struggle for independence. *The Indian Express* began its journey in 1932. Since then, the Group has grown from strength to strength. From a single edition to 35 national editions, 14 publication centres and 7 language dailies that reach over 19 million people across the country.

For the millions of readers, the name "*Indian Express*" evokes a feeling of trust. Published from 21 centres across the country, the newspaper has been identified with credible and fiercely independent journalism in India. One of the most influential newspapers of the Indian subcontinent, The Indian Express has been the watchdog for the Indian people, treading the terrains of investigative and proactive journalism.

Current Openings

The Indian Express Group of Publications launched a state-of-the-art printing press in Aurangabad, as part of its ongoing expansion plans.

Express Events

Screen Photo Exhibition

The Photo Exhibition will enable the visitors at the Express Gallery to relive unforgettable moments from 12 years of the Screen Awards. A Red Carpet atmosphere will be created at the Express Towers.

Pharma Excellence Awards

These are exciting times of change for the Indian pharmaceutical industry, and never before has there been a stronger case for benchmarking.

RNG—India Press Photo Awards 2006

Press Photos are an integral part of journalism. The India Press Photo Awards instituted by The Indian Express Group are an initiative to identify, promote and reward the Press photographer and the Photojournalist.

THE HINDU

India's National Daily

- *News Update*: Breaking News and Updates
- *Sunday Magazine*: Published on Sundays
- *Open Page*: Published on Sundays
- *Literary Review*: Published once in a month
- *Business Review*: Published on Mondays
- *Metro Plus*: Published on Mondays, Tuesdays, Wednesdays, Thursdays and Saturdays
- *Education Plus*: Published on Mondays with an update on Tuesdays
- *Book Review*: Published on Tuesdays
- *Young World*: Published on Tuesdays
- *Opportunities*: Published on Wednesdays
- *SciTech*: Published on Thursdays

- *NXg*: Published on Thursdays
- *Friday Review*: Published on Fridays
- *Cinema Plus*: Published on Fridays
- *Retail Plus*: Published on Fridays and Sundays
- *Property Plus*: Published on Saturdays
- *Quest*: Newspaper in Education—Published once in a month
- *Events 1997-07*: Summary of Events under National, International, Sport and Obituary

Ceased Features

- *Life*: Feature Published daily
- *Folio*: Special feature with Sunday Magazine once in six weeks

Business Line

- *Business Line*: Financial daily from THE HINDU Group of publications
- *News Update*: Round the week
- Investment World: Weekly News Round up and Investment Analysis
- *e-World*: Weekly Information Technology News with weekly features
- *Brand Line*: Weekly Marketing news with weekly features
- *Life*: Weekly Feature
- *Smartbuy*: Weekly lifestyle magazine
- *Ships in Ports*: Movements of Ships in various Ports of India
- *Stock Exchange Quotes*: Share Prices at different Stock Exchanges
- *Stock Exchange Diary*: List of notifications from the Stock Exchanges
- *Scoreboard*: Performance of Listed Stocks
- *Brand Quest*: A Weekly Quiz on Advertising and Marketing
- *Canvas*: A monthly Executive Guide
- *Praxis*: BL's Management Journal

- *Urban* Pulse: A market research-based Journal

Magazines

- *Frontline*: Fortnightly Features Magazine
- *Sportstar*: Weekly Sports Magazine

Annuals

- *Industry*: Survey of Indian Industry—2008
- *Agriculture*: Survey of Indian Agriculture—2007
- *Environment*: Survey of The Environment—2007
- *Cricket*: Indian Cricket—2004 (Discontinued)

Compilations: The Hindu Speaks on Series

- *Scientific Facts Vol II*: 226 selective questions and answers under 10 major heads
- *Scientific Facts*: 365 selective questions and answers under 10 major heads
- *Management Vol I*: 85 articles under five major heads
- *Education*: 80 articles under five categories
- *Religious Values*: 500 articles under 25 headings
- *Music*: 125 articles under 10 chapters
- *Management Vol II*: 65 articles under four broad categories
- *Libraries*: a compilation of news, views, editorials etc. covering the period 1918 to 1992
- *Information Technology*: 140 items of news and features under five categories

Compilations: From the pages of The Hindu Series

- Mahatma Gandhi: The Last 200 days: Diary of events starting on the 15th of July 1947 to 30th January 1948

The Hindu eBooks

Categories

- Cartoons
- Health
- InfoTech
- Management
- Development
- Humour
- Investment
- Marketing

- Music
- Sportstar
- Sports
- Travel

THE PRINTERS (MYSORE) PVT. LTD.

Dream of a Visionary

Mr. K.N. Guruswamy had a dream. The year was 1948. The heady days just after the nation's independence. Mr. Guruswamy had dedicated his life to truth and impartiality and he would not rest till his vision took concrete form. The result was The Printers (Mysore) Private Limited and its publications—Deccan Herald, Prajavani, Sudha and Mayura. An institution that has completed 50 glorious years of chronicling the joys and sorrows of the people of Karnataka, India and the world.

Over the years, the group has not forgotten what provides value to readers. Therefore, along with core competency, it satisfies the aesthetic needs of its readers with innovative layout and design in all its publications. Its well-designed publications achieve high communication impact by helping the reader cut through all the information clutter. The Group's strong identity is, therefore, the starting point, and not the residue, of any effort to win and keep readers. While cementing its traditional strengths, the Group is also geared to face new challenges and enhance emotional contact with its readers. As the Group believes that 'change is the only constant', it treats critical thinking as a dynamic process and keeps pace with the rapid change in the newspaper and magazine publishing industry.

Corporate Philosophy

The Printers (Mysore) Private Limited continues to give shape to the founder's ideals, acting as an instrument of service to the people. Here, everybody shares in the pursuit of excellence. And today's widening geopolitical compulsions only make the job more challenging. A band of hardcore professionals bonded together by team spirit, the people at The Printers (Mysore) Private Limited are passionate about growth and compassionate about people.

Computerization

From manual operations to computerized systems, the Group focuses on Electronic News Transmission and processing. Hence its facility at Bangalore is completely computerized, right from front end up to billing. It was the first Indian publication to provide notebook computers to all its State correspondents. Moreover, all district correspondents have desktops and modems and are connected over I-Net. Since November 1989, Hubli has been a facsimile office—the latest in news publishing the world over.

The Printers (Mysore) Private Limited was the first Indian publication group to introduce colour in the main issue. Deccan Herald and Prajavani evolved to colour in 1987 with colour supplements. Today both newspapers have special sections on every single day of the week and colour on all days of the week. Both magazines also offer high quality colour forms for both editorial as well as advertisements.

As Karnataka prepares to be the business nucleus of the 21st century, The Printers (Mysore) Private Limited is also preparing to keep pace with a sophisticated expansion and integration programme designed to make each of its publications reflect the true essence of the new Karnataka. With this objective, the Group is now focusing on making its publications superior, not just in terms of the reading material but also in technology and quality.

Technological Superiority

When it started publication in 1948, Deccan Herald was produced on printing equipment that was comparable to the best in this part of the country at the time. From stereo rotary machines to linotype composing machines to fully computerized editing and page production systems and web offset colour printing, it has been striding along the steady path of modernization. The automation extends today to counting, packaging and strapping of the printed copies rolling out of the rotary machines. Side by side advances in newspaper concepts, content, design and layout have helped Deccan Herald keep pace with the rapidly expanding interests of its readers.

Welfare

The blueprint for rapid growth is appreciation, excellent infrastructure and a healthy and safe work environment that ensures job satisfaction. The Group cares for its people. So it has several comprehensive programmes designed to change attitude and behaviour and home strategic decision making and problem solving skills.

Encouragement received from the Group has helped the DHPV Lalitha Kala Sangha's troupes to win many major awards and shields in cultural contests at the State level. The Group's sports squads too have fared well in sports meets and tournaments organized for the media. A unique feature is the counselling service offered to employees facing crises of diverse kinds.

Redefining Excellence

Fifty spectacular years of growth, multi-faceted and on target. Fifty years of active interaction with Karnataka, its people, their aspirations, and the history they have made. Today, the Group is poised to stand tall among the newspaper giants of the country.

Commitment to Quality—ISO 9002

As the first step towards total quality, the Group changed its quality control processes from 'reactive' to 'proactive.' And installed a quality system ISO 9001:2000—model for quality assurance in production, installation and servicing. With this, the Group has become the first publishing house in the country to receive this prestigious certification for all its facilities. The functions covered in the quality system include advertisement, editorial, materials, production and training.

Total Quality Management (TQM)

The Group believes in Total Quality Management (TQM) which is an effective system of integrating quality improvement efforts so as to provide a product that ensures customer satisfaction. Every section of the organization is therefore geared to face challenges. A common vision, a common mission and common goals bind people together here. Not content with streamlining its day-to-day functioning, the Group is constantly integrating quality into its corporate strategic planning process.

Deccan Herald

Every day Deccan Herald touches the lives of the people of Karnataka. Today the daily shapes the opinions and directs their actions. Deccan Herald was born 54 years ago when the first edition hit the streets on June 16, 1948. The newspaper was a reflection of the optimism, and a voice of the aspirations of a newly independent nation.

Proud of its regional moorings and responsive to global changes, Deccan Herald is Karnataka's guide to the times we live in. Karnataka and Bangalore hold a special place in the newspaper's scheme of things, but its coverage of national and world happenings is equally comprehensive and analytical. Deccan Herald is also the voice of the poor and the underprivileged. On its agenda is a relentless campaign against corruption and advocacy of pro-environment economic development.

The very analytical opinion/policy page presents a variety of views on national, state and international issues. Regular columnists and experts in various fields place the latest events in perspective. The well-written editorials are known for their unbiased and informed commentary on events and developments. The newspaper's human-interest reports and profiles of interesting personalities give the reader not only news and views, but also the emotions and the drama behind the happenings. Special sections like Miscellany, On the Beat and Around the City encapsulate offbeat happenings in a short and snappy manner.

Special Supplements

To each his own—that is the rationale behind Deccan Herald's multi-faceted special supplements. Each Sunday morning the reader finds various special colour sections waiting on his doorstep.

1. *Sunday Herald* is a supplement with strong thought-provoking and mainstream concerns, as well as regular features on consumer issues, green subjects, animal welfare, gardening, bridge, crossword and offbeat travelogues. The Entertainment section of the Sunday magazine tells the reader about all that's hot and happenings in showbiz.
2. *Articulations* is devoted to literature and art, with in-depth interviews, quality fiction and book reviews. Articulations also includes debates on education.
3. *Economy and Business* is the weekly round-up of the country's industry, trade and commerce. Using interview based articles and features on international developments from foreign publications, it also brings in a global perspective on money matters. The COMMENT column analyzes issues like policy decisions, mergers, takeovers and other corporate events.
4. *Science and Technology* carries articles on science, industry, agriculture, development, health, information technology, ecology and research, and development. Articles are written by experts for the specialist as well as the lay person.
5. *Avenues* is a weekly supplement that focuses on careers, personnel and corporate management issues. In-depth features on aspects of human resource development and organizational behaviour by management veterans are the section's highlights. Also included here are appointment advertisements.
6. *Sportscene* reviews and previews the sporting action of the week past and the week ahead. It covers sports personalities, keeps track of developments in sports and profiles regional talent. The supplement unravels controversies and at regular intervals brings to light malpractices and corruption in the sporting arena. Sportscene also has the OPINION column which comments on sports related issues. The RESPONSE section gives readers an opportunity to express their opinions on sports matters.

7. *Metrolife* your bond with Bangalore, was started on November 28, 2002. This eight page tabloid size supplement captures the happenings in and around Bangalore and contains lively articles on civic issues in the city, eating out, weekend getaways around Bangalore, shopping, fashion, real estate and crime file.
8. *Spectrum* carries a wide range of articles on the people of Karnataka. Profiles of personalities and development stories from the districts are also included.
9. *Living* concentrates on the home and family with a look at contemporary life and forays into the realms of nostalgia. It features changes in lifestyle, dress codes, home decor, gardening, child rearing, relationships, attitudes, table manners and home remedies.
10. *Open Sesame* is a fun-filled eight page tabloid for kids packed with some of the the best children's writing from India, do-it-yourself columns, nature notes, riddles, serial stories that are specially commissioned, everyday science, reflections of school teachers and the occasional comic strip. And of course the reader-friendly page of letters from the young readers responding to the messages and queries of Sesame Seed, the section's mascot.
11. *The World Wide Web*: On April 15, 1996, Deccan Herald launched its Internet edition. Today Deccan Herald reaches out to the world and its innovative and easy to navigate web site is a big hit with netizens.

Zoned Editions

Deccan Herald's several zoned editions serve to cover local news in greater detail and to highlight the developments in these areas, thus being in touch with readers in every region of Karnataka.

1. *Hubli Printing*: Karnataka, the land of culture, also happens to be the land of distances. With the increase in technological sophistication, The Printers (Mysore) Private Limited has found a solution to this problem. The facsimile edition of Deccan Herald and Prajavani

was launched on November 1, 1989. Edited in Bangalore, the news is sent through high speed telecommunication lines to Hubli-Dharwad where the paper is printed and distributed.

By using the cutting-edge of technology, like total digital workflow, to its advantage, The Printers (Mysore) Private Limited has made sure that its publications reach readers in this region on time. The Group challenged basic assumptions like the problem of distance and came up with specific strategies to tap resources using technology as a tool. Three 64 KB lines enable quick transmission of data. Offset printers like Newsline 45 and Coroset which run on state-of-the-art technology can print up to 40,000 copies per hour. As a result, circulation has increased and the Group is constantly expanding its market in this region. Readers in the districts of Dharwad, Karwar, Shimoga, Davangere, Bijapur, Bellary and Belgaum welcome the day with Deccan Herald and Prajavani.

2. *Hyderabad-Karnataka Edition*: In addition to Bangalore and Hubli printing, Deccan Herald and Prajavani started printing a separate Hyderabad-Karnataka edition in Hyderabad on June 15, 1999 to facilitate the readers of the northern Karnataka districts of Gulbarga, Bidar and Raichur getting their papers well in time. The printing was shifted to Gulbarga on March 11, 2001
3. *Mangalore Edition*: To serve the interests of the readers in coastal Karnataka and to ensure that they get their favourite newspaper at the crack of dawn, the Group set up a printing plant at Mangalore and started printing a separate edition on August 25, 2000. The number of editions, districts served and copies printed from these centres are as follows.
4. *Belur Plant*: Four editions. Serves districts of Bellary, Koppal, Raichur, Bijapur (part), Bagalkot, Davangere, Shimoga (part), Uttara Kannada, Belgaum, Haveri, Gadag and Dharwad Mangalore plant: Two editions. Serves the districts of Chikmagalur, Shimoga (part),

Kodagu, Udupi and Dakshina Kannda besides Kasargod

5. *Gulbarga Plant*: Two editions. Serves the districts of Raichur, Bidar, Bijapur (part) and Gulbarga.

GEMINI NEWS

Gemini News is a 24×7 News Channel from Sun Network. Though the channel was launched in May 2004 with much hype and publicity, it failed to attract the viewers. Poor technical standards are the main drawback of this channel. Now the sun network is planning to renew the image of Gemini news channel. They appointed Satish Babu who once elevated Maa TV's news bulletins to popularity, as the channels new chief.

SUNTV NETWORK

Holding a bouquet of Twenty top-rated channels in its clutch, SunTV Network has got a reach, frequency and patronage that other groups covet but cannot compete with. SunTV Network believes in giving you wholesome fare. Be it news or entertainment, we are there first. If it is happening South of Vindhyas, its on SunTV Network. And you are a part of it. With Twenty channels in four Indian languages and Forty One FM Radio stations, we are able to connect India, erasing geographical distances.

The response to our programmes and the viewership of our news has been phenomenal. The fact that we touch so many hearts gives us great pleasure. Every single South Indian channel that boasts of a No. 1 slot among its viewers belongs to the SunTV Network. Crores of people all over the world watch a channel of SunTV Network. With every programme a sell-out, every single transmission digitized, every serial a hit, for millions of viewers all over the world every day is indeed a Sunday. SunTV Network believes in giving you wholesome fare. Be it news or entertainment, we are there first. If it is happening South of Vindhyas, its on SunTV Network. And you are a part of it.

We have come a long way. And its heartwarming to know that you were, and are, with us every step of the way. The response to our programmes and the viewership of our news has been phenomenal. The fact that we touch so many hearts gives us great pleasure.

Awards

1. CNBC "Business Excellence Award" in 2005—Kalanithi Maran, CMD, SunTV Network
2. Outstanding Businessman Award in the Entertainment and Information Sector in 2004—Kalanithi Maran, CMD, SunTV Network
3. World's Young Achiever for Creativity in 1999—Kalanithi Maran, CMD, SunTV Network
4. India's Best Entrepreneur Award in 1999—Kalanithi Maran, CMD, SunTV Network
5. Indian Televison Academy Award for the best Tamil TV Channel for the year 2001—Sun TV
6. Indian Televison Academy Award for the best Malayalam TV Channel for the year 2001—Surya TV
7. Indian Televison Academy Award for the best Kannada TV Channel for the year 2001—Udaya TV
8. Indian Televison Academy Award for the best Telugu TV Channel for the year 2001—Gemini TV

CNN-IBN

CNN-IBN is an English-language Indian TV news channel. The network is a partnership between Global Broadcast News (GBN) and Turner International (Turner) in India (a Division of Time Warner). Rajdeep Sardesai is the Editor-in-Chief of the network. The Indian company GBN runs the channel completely but uses the CNN brand name, in return giving Time Warner a 26 per cent stake. The network broadcasts 24 hours a day. The network models most of its programming on that of CNN in the United States, with current-event talk programmes mixed with news reports. The flagship evening programme, *India at 9*, is usually broadcast daily on CNN Pipeline, although it is not simulcast (except during breaking news events, such as the 11 July 2006 Mumbai train bombings).

It is one of the first news channels in India to use the concept of "citizen journalist," whereby any person can send in a report that is aired in a separate section.

Type	Tabloid Journalism based News
Branding	CNN-IBN
Country	India
Availability	India, online
Slogan	"Whatever it takes"
Owner	Global Broadcast News/Turner International India/Time Warner launch_date — December 16, 2005
Key people	Rajdeep Sardesai, Chief Editor, Anchor
Website	www.ibnlive.com

Quite recently, CNN-IBN expanded the Citizen Journalism Segment by including Mobile Citizen Journalism. Indian citizens are now able to take photos from mobile phones which can be send via MMS to the news desk of CNN-IBN. The technology for the same powered by Mobshare as per official website. Launched in 2005, CNN-IBN's name comes from CNN, Time Warner's flagship network in the United States, and IBN (which stands for India Broadcast News), which is GBN's flagship news channel brand.

Stance

This channel has been accused of sharing the general leftist bias of English news channels in India. It has also been accused of "sensationalizing" content.

AAJ TAK

Till Today is a 24-hour Hindi news television channel run by TV Today Network Ltd. Aaj Tak loosely translates as "Till

Today" or "Up to the Minute." Watched by some 45 million viewers in India's cable and satellite universe, Aaj Tak is India's largest privately owned news channel. Aaj Tak is a free-to-air channel in India, while it is being offered as a pay channel in the overseas market. In the United States, it is available on EchoStar's DISH Network.

सबसे तेज़

Type	Cable Television Network
Branding	Aaj Tak
Country	India
Availability	India, worldwide
Founded	TV Today Network
Slogan	"Sabse Tez"
Owner	India Today Group
Key people	Aroon Purie (CMD)
Launch date	31 December 1999

Despite serving Infotainment, Aaj Tak has been awarded Indian Television Academy's Best News Channel award for six consecutive years. In a recent BBC/Reuters/Media Center Poll, Aaj Tak was voted the most trusted and most important news source in India surpassing even the Government sponsored channel Doordarshan and expansively beating news sources like Star News, Dainik Jagran, Sun TV, NDTV, AIR (All India Radio) and The Times of India.

GHANTA

24 Ghanta (literally meaning 24 hours) is a popular 24×7 infotainment Bengali channel, owned by the Zee Aakash News division of Zee News Ltd. of the Zee Entertainment Enterprises.

24 Ghanta

Launched	2006
Owned by	Zee Aakash News Private Limited
Country	India
	Availability
	Satellite
Insat	4A (India)
Dish	TV (India)

ZEE 24 TAAS

Zee 24 Taas (झी २४ तास, *zee chovis taas*) is Marathi news channel owned by Zee Network. *Chovis taas* literally means twenty four hours. This is first Marathi news channel. In a very short span of time it has made an impact.

ZEE ENTERTAINMENT ENTERPRISES

Channels

Zee Entertainment Enterprises Ltd. television network consists of the following channels:

1. *Zee TV*—Hindi General Entertainment Channel
2. *Zee Next*—New Hindi General Entertainment Channel
3. *Zee Cinema*—Hindi Movie Channel
4. *Zee Music*—Hindi Music Channel
5. *Zee Sports*—A Sports Channel
6. *Ten Sports*—50 per cent in the Sports Channel
7. *Zee Premiere*--Hindi New Movie Channel
8. *Zee Action*—Hindi Action Movie Channel
9. *Zee Classic*—Hindi Old Movie Channel
10. *Zee Smile*—Hindi Comedy Channel
11. *Zee Jagran*—Hindi Religious Channel
12. *Zee Trendz*—A Fashion Channel
13. *Zee Café*—English General Entertainment Channel
14. *Zee Studio*—English Movie Channel
15. *Zee Arabiya*—Arabic Music Channel

Besides that, Zee News Ltd. (ZNL) is also a part of the Essel Group, which operates news and regional entertainment channels and is listed on the stock exchange. It was demerged from Zee Entertainment Enterprises Ltd. in 2006 , and following are the list of channels that Zee News Ltd. operates:

1. *Zee News*—Hindi News Channel
2. *Zee Business*
3. *Zee Marathi*—Marathi General Entertainment Channel
4. *Zee Bangla*—Bengali General Entertainment Channel
5. *Zee Gujarati*—Gujarati General Entertainment Channel
6. *Zee Tamil*—Tamil General Entertainment Channel
7. *Zee Telugu*—Telugu General Entertainment Channel
8. *Zee Kannada*—Kannada General Entertainment Channel
9. *Zee Punjabi*—Punjabi General Entertainment Channel
10. *Zee 24 Taas*
11. *24 Ghanta*
12. *Zee Talkies*

TV9 KANNADA NEWS CHANNEL

TV9 Kannada is a 24-hour news channel in Kannada. This is owned by hylab (abcl) group from Hyderbad. This channel already have news channel in Andra Pradesh, Karnataka and Kerela and also expands to Madhya Pradesh, Uttar Pradesh, Maharashtra and other states also. This news channel slogan is FOR BETTER SOCIETY. This is special for 24-hour news channel with live news. Recently this broadcast company started spiritual channel in Telugu that is called SAMSKRUTHI is esspecially for spiritual programmes like bhajanas, prathnas etc., by Rohithjayaram.

TV5 (INDIA)

TV5 is a 24-hour Telugu language news channel in India. It was launched on October 2, 2007 by Chiranjeevi,

Y.S. Rajasekhara Reddy and Chandra Babu Naidu. The channel's CEO is Siva Rama Prasad. It telecasts 24 hourly news bulletins, 30 special news bulletins, with the support of 294 special reporters in every constituency of the state of Andhra Pradesh, 8 OB vans, and 6 metro bureaus.

NEWSX

NewsX is an English-language Indian TV news channel. The channel is part of the INX Network which headed by Indrani Mukerjea.

NewsX	
Launched	2008
Owned by	INX Network
Slogan	Clarity in a Complex World
Country	India
Sister channel(s)	9X 9XM
Website	http://newsx.com/

MANORAMA NEWS

MM TV or Manorama News is a 24-hour Malayalam news channel owned and operated by the Malayala Manorama news house. The company is headquartered in Kottayam. The channel, based at Aroor near Kochi, was launched on August 17, 2006, which coincides with the Malayalam New Year. The channel was launched with the assistance of media consultanting company Mediaguru Consultants Pvt. Ltd. The thirty minute simultaneous newscast of regional news, the *Nattuvartha,* from three regions of Kerala, viz. Malabar region, Central Kerala and Thiruananthapuram was done for the first time in the country. Also, the exclusivity includes separate persons for daily programmes, which include entertainment, business and crime which is new in Malayalam. The Chief Editor of the channel is Johny Lukose and he also anchors a programme "Nere Chove."

manorama NEWS

Type	Cable Television Network
Branding	MM TV or Manorama News
Country	India
Availability	Indian sub-continent, Middle East
Website	www.manoramanews.com

HEADLINES TODAY

Headlines Today is a premier 24-hour English language Indian news and information television channel sponsored by TV Today Network Ltd. which is a part of the well-known India Today Group. The channel was launched in the year 2003 is a sister channel of the Hindi Aaj Tak news channel and is one of the four niche news channels from the TV Today Network stable.

Headlines Today

Type	Broadcast television network
Country	India
Availability	National
Owner	TV TODAY NETWORK

Headlines Today has many popular extra-news programmes such as "Wheel Spin", "EQ", "The Big Ticket", "Grand Stand" and "Sports Quarter." Some of its prime time anchors are Avantika Singh, Rashim Sharma, Arjun Bhagat, Rahul Kanwal and Zakka Jacob.

Early morning 7O'clock it starts with the programme namely, HEADSTART. The programme is about giving fresh news and information with an interesting discussion among three of the newsreaders of this channel. They are:

- Avantika Singh for *National* and *International* news
- Rashim Sharma for *Sports* news
- Mandeep Beivi for *Entertainment* news

KOLKATA TV

Kolkata TV (Bengali: 'Kolkata Tibhi) is a 24×7 news Bengali channel, launched by SST Media, formerly a company of the Rs. 627 crore Xenitis Group, March 27, 2006.

- Kolkata TV launch on March 27.

Bibliography

"A Radio Giant Moves to Limit Commercials", by Nat Ives: The New York Times, Monday, July 19, 2004.

Aaron Brown Talks About... "CNN's Struggle" and The Competition From Fox. TVNEWSER, 6 July 2007.

"ABOUT BBC NEWS—Timeline of events—1950s." Retrieved on 2007-04-11.

"ABOUT BBC NEWS—Timeline of events—1970s." Retrieved on 2007-08-25.

"About CNBC U.S." *CNBC*. Retrieved on 2007-11-14.

"About the Ten O'Clock News." Retrieved on 2007-08-15.

"Afrol News: Broadcasting of BBC in Zimbabwe Stopped." Retrieved on 2007-04-11.

"Ailes on Fox Business Channel and the Battle with CNBC", *The Wall Street Journal* (October 8, 2007). Retrieved on 2007-10-14.

Al Roker: Weather and Feature Reporter, "Today"—Today Show—MSNBC.com

"Alexandra Palace: A History of the Palace." Retrieved on 2007-04-03.

Alison, Stewart: Meet the faces of MSNBC—MSNBC.com

Allan; M. Siegal and William G. Connolly. *The New York Times Manual of Style and Usage: The Official Style Guide Used by the Writers and Editors of the World's Most Authoritative Newspaper,* (2002).

American Public Media: News Archive for October 7, 1996.

American Television News: *The Media Marketplace and the Public Interest* by Steve Michael Barkin, M.E. Sharpe, 2003.

Amy, Robach: TODAY, WEEKEND EDITION (Co-Anchor, Saturday Edition of "Today"; News National Correspondent).

Anderson & Coate: Market Provision of Broadcasting: A Welfare Analysis. Review of Economic Studies. October 2005. http://www.blackwell-synergy.com/doi/full/10.1111/0034-6527.00357.

Anderson & Coate: Market Provision of Public Goods: The Case of Broadcasting. National Bureau of Economic Research. January 2000. http://www.nber.org/papers/w7513.pdf.

Andrea, Mitchell: Nightly News with Brian Williams—MSNBC.com

Andrea, Sutcliffe: *New York Public Library Writer's Guide to Style and Usage,* (1994).

Ann, Curry BIO: Dateline NBC—MSNBC.com

Anne, Thompson: Nightly News with Brian Williams—MSNBC.com

"Annual Report 1995: Business Review: NBC." *General Electric*. Retrieved on 2007-07-16.

"AP Watched Different Speech Last Night" (August 29, 2008): Retrieved on 2008-08-29.

April 2005 Competitive Programme Ranker (M-F 6a-11p programmes), TV Newser.

"April 2007 Weekday Ranker" (PDF): TV Newser.

"Asia Media: CHINA: Censor blocks sensitive issues in BBC series." Retrieved on 2007-04-11.

Associated Press (2005-01-31): "19th-century papers shed new light on origin of The Associated Press." Press release.

"At the new Fox News Channel, the buzzword is fairness, separating news from bias."

BAFTA 1980—p. 2 British Academy of Film and Television Arts (PDF).

BAFTA 1982—p. 10 British Academy of Film and Television Arts (PDF).

BAFTA 1982—p. 12 British Academy of Film and Television Arts (PDF).

Bangkok Post. "Teaching feature stories." Retrieved on September 6, 2006.

"BBC cuts back programmes and jobs", BBC News Online (2007-10-18): Retrieved on 2007-10-25.

"BBC cuts: look on the bright side", The Guardian (2007-10-22): Retrieved on 2007-10-25.

"BBC delays London HQ work", The Guardian (2007-08-13): Retrieved on 2008-06-20.

BBC Guide to Comedy TW3.

"BBC NEWS—Entertainment—BBC 'must improve Mid-East view.'" Retrieved on 2007-04-11.

"BBC NEWS—Entertainment—BBC News Interactive's new editor." Retrieved on 2007-04-11.

"BBC NEWS—Entertainment—TV and Radio—BBC Iraq war coverage criticised." Retrieved on 2007-04-11.

"BBC NEWS—Entertainment—TV and Radio—BBC report 2004: At a glance." Retrieved on 2007-04-11.

"BBC NEWS—Entertainment—TV and Radio—Fifty years of TV news." Retrieved on 2007-04-03.

"BBC NEWS—Entertainment—TV and Radio—From royal dramas to wartime: 1922-46." Retrieved on 2007-04-03.

"BBC NEWS—Help—Your guide to the BBC News Player." Retrieved on 2007-04-11.

"BBC NEWS—New era for BBC radio news." Retrieved on 2007-08-18.

"BBC NEWS—Programmes—Breakfast—Breakfast's new look." Retrieved on 2007-04-03.

"BBC NEWS—Programmes—From our own correspondent—Uzbeks banish BBC after massacre reports." Retrieved on 2007-04-11.

BBC NEWS—*The Editors Blog*—New News.

"BBC ON THIS DAY—17-1983: BBC wakes up to morning TV." Retrieved on 2007-04-03.

"BBC one gets extra news bulletin." BBC News. Retrieved on 2007-07-11.

"BBC refurbishment £20 m over-budget and a 'waste of money'—the Daily Mail." Retrieved on 2007-04-03.

BBC Urdo taken off Pakistan radio—BBC News: 15 November 2005.

"BBC versus British government", News 24 (2003-07-21).

"BBC World dropped for al-Jazeera English in Israel—Israel and the Middle East—Guardian Unlimited." Retrieved on 2007-04-11.

"BBC's coverage of Israeli-Palestinian conflict 'misleading'—Israel and the Middle East—Guardian Unlimited." Retrieved on 2007-04-11.

Becker, Anne (2006-12-04): "CNBC's New Online Splash", *Broadcasting & Cable*. Retrieved on 2007-07-17.

Bekken, Jon. "Community Radio at the Crossroads: Federal Policy and The Professionalization of a Grassroots Medium" in Sakolsky, Ron and S. Dunifer (eds.) Seizing the Airwaves: A Free Radio Handbook. (also available online)

Ben, Bova. "*The Writer's Craft*: No. 5."

Benen, Steve (August 23, 2008): "Fournier is at it Again", *Political Animal*, Washington Monthly. Retrieved on 2008-08-23.

"Berry & Waldfogel: Public radio in the United States: does it correct market failure or cannibalize commercial stations? Journal of Public Economics. February 1999. http://www.sciencedirect.com/science?_ob=ArticleURL&_udi=B6V76-3VM0P4Y-2&_user=99318&_rdoc=1&_fmt=&_orig=search&_sort=d&view=c&_acct=C000007678&_version=1&_urlVersion=0&_userid=99318&md5=60e2570a7bf90273ba06284ab7756fb5

"Bill, Griffeth". *CNBC*. Retrieved on 2007-11-14.

Bill, Walsh. *The Elephants of Style: A Trunkload of Tips on the Big Issues and Gray Areas of Contemporary American English* (2004).

Bob, Dotson—Today Show—MSNBC.com

Boyer, Peter J. (June 10, 1988): "The Media Business; NBC Cable Deal is off, but Lease Accord is Set", *The New York Times*. Retrieved on 2007-10-19.

Brady, Ray (June 2003): "CNBC Fell from Grace when the Bubble Burst. How Does it Look Now?", *Columbia Journalism Review*. Retrieved on 2008-07-21.

Braxton, Greg (April 6, 1997): Chicago Sun-Times, *How Fox broke from the pack to become cutting-edge network.*

"Broadcasting Public Notice CRTC 2004-45—Call for comments on proposals for the addition of Fox News and NFL Network." Retrieved on 2007-01-25.

"Broadcasting Public Notice CRTC 2004-88—Requests to add Fox News and NFL Network from the Canadian Cable Telecommunications Association." Retrieved on 2007-01-25.

Brown. Economics, Public Service Broadcasting, and Social Values. The Journal of Media Economics. http://www.leaonline.com/doi/pdfplus/10.1207/s15327736me0901_2.

Bryan, A. Garner. *The Winning Brief: 100 Tips for Persuasive Briefing in Trial and Appellate Court* (1999).

Buck, Ryan and Michael, O'Donnell. *The Editor's Toolbox: A Reference Guide for Beginners and Professionals* (2001).

"Business Models on the Web" by Dr. Michael Rappa, North Carolina State University.

Cable TV: Content Analysis, The State of the News Media 2005.

Calderone, Michael (2008-07-14): "Is Fournier saving or destroying the AP?", *Politico*. Retrieved on 2008-08-23.

Calderone, Michael (2008-07-30): "One of Fournier's job options: McCain", *Politico*. Retrieved on 2008-08-23.

Canada News Centre—Centre des nouvelles du Canada.

Carl Quintanilla Profile, Biography, About—CNBC.com

Carl, Schreck. "Proletarian Bloggers Celebrate a Milestone", Moscow Times. Retrieved on 2007-11-14.

Carter, Bill (April 10, 1989): "THE MEDIA BUSINESS: Television; NBC Walks Into a Cable Minefield", *The New York Times*. Retrieved on 2007-10-19.

Casagrande, June: Grammar Snobs Are Great Big Meanies: A Guide to Language for Fun and Spite. Penguin, 2006.

Catts, Tim (2007-06-07): "CNBC's Easy Money", *BusinessWeek*. Retrieved on 2007-07-17.

CBONLINE Culture, Commitment, Community: The Australian Community Radio Sector: Susan Forde, Micahel Meadows and Kerrie Foxwell [1]. Retrieved 3 January 2007.

Charles, Bierbauer: CNN senior Washington correspondent, discusses his 19-year career at CNN. (May 8, 2000). CNN.com. Accessed 2007-06-18.

Chicago Tribune (July 17, 1986): *Turnaround for fox films* Section: Business; p. 1.

Chris, Hansen: Dateline NBC—MSNBC.com

"Chronomedia: 1950." Retrieved on 2007-10-08.

"City Hall Threatens Action if Time Warner Rejects Channel."

Claburn, Thomas: "CNN Faces Cyberattack Over Tibet Coverage," *Information Week*, 2008.

CNBC (2006-06-08): "CNBC PROGRAMMING SCHEDULE CHANGES." Press release. Retrieved on 2007-07-17.

CNBC (2007-08-31): "CNBC Has Best August in Five Years." Press release. Retrieved on 2007-10-19.

CNBC (2007-09-27): "CNBC Announces New After-Market Hours Programming Line-Up." Press release. Retrieved on 2007-09-27.
"CNBC and The New York Times make content deal", *Associated Press*, International Herald Tribune (7 January 2008). Retrieved on 2008-03-31.
CNBC Europe (18 September 2006): "FTSE and CNBC Team up to create FTSE CNBC Global 300 Index." Press release. Retrieved on 2008-03-31.
"CNBC looking to distinguish itself", *USA Today* (October 30, 2006): Retrieved on 2007-07-16.
"CNBC redesigns its Website", *International Herald Tribune* (December 04, 2006): Retrieved on 2007-07-17.
CNBC Sets Up Trading Floor Webcams", *TV Newser* (22 October 2007): Retrieved on 2008-03-31.
CNBC. "CNBC Plus." Retrieved on 2007-07-16.
CNBC. "Million Dollar Contest Rules." Retrieved on 2007-07-17.
CNBC. "Million Dollar Portfolio Challenge." Retrieved on 2007-07-17.
CNBC's 10-year anniversary documentary.
"CNBC's Best Day Ever." *TV Newser* (October 1, 2008): Retrieved on 2007-10-01.
CNBC's Erin Burnett Signs On For Three More Years, Adds NBC Duties—mediabistro.com: TVNewser.
CNN and the Liberal Propaganda Machine.
CNN blamed for using misleading war video.
CNN chief accuses Israel of terror.
"CNN website targeted", April 18, 2008.
CNN.com (September 11, 2001): Available at archive.org. Accessed 2007-06-18.
"Conflict in Plane Sight", *Broadcasting and Cable* (2007-02-05): Retrieved on 2007-11-14.
"Consolidated Financial Statements, The Associated Press and Subsidiaries: Years ended December 31, 2005 and 2004." Associated Press (2006-03-07): Retrieved on 2006-10-13.
Contessa, Brewer: Meet the faces of MSNBC—MSNBC.com
Coyle, Jake (July 19, 2004): Advocacy Groups Challenge Fox News Slogan. Associated Press.
Crum, Rex (20 May 2008): "AOL announces new content deal with CNBC", *MarketWatch*. Retrieved on 2008-05-21.
Dan, Abrams: Meet the faces of MSNBC—MSNBC.com
"Dave, Barry": *The Miami Herald*.
David, Lodge: *The Art of Fiction*.
David, Shuster: Meet the faces of MSNBC—MSNBC.com
Davis, Douglas: "Hatred in the air: The BBC, Israel and Antisemitism" in Iganski, Paul and Kosmin, Barry (eds): *A New Anti-Semitism?*

Debating Judeophobia in 21st century Britain. Profile Books, 2003, p. 130.

Dawn, Fratangelo: Nightly News with Brian Williams—MSNBC.com

De Moraes, Lisa (August 12, 2003): Three Little Words: Fox News Sues. *Washington Post.*

Dean on President Clinton Standing Up To Right-Wing Propaganda On Fox News Sunday, The Democratic Party, September 25, 2006.

"Decision CRTC 2000-565—Registration with CRTC for Fox News Canada." Retrieved on 2007-01-25.

Dennis, Murphy: Dateline NBC—MSNBC.com

Dickson, Glen (2007-09-17): "CNBC To Throw HD Switch", *Broadcasting & Cable*. Retrieved on 2007-09-17.

"Digital Dilemma: Will new royalty fees kill Web radio?" by Michael Roberts 2002, Westword.

"Digital, DTV, Internet, Mobile phone and MP3 Listening"—December 2006, RAJAR.organisation.

Don, Teague: Nightly News with Brian Williams—MSNBC.com

"Dow, Jones: Completes Acquisition of Full-Ownership of Factiva", dowjones.com (2006-12-15).

"Dow, Jones: To carry Agence France-Presse, drop AP." Reuters (2008-03-18): Retrieved on 2008-08-27.

Early Satellite Broadcasts, 1960s & 1970s, British TV History.

Eric, Boehlert: "33 internal FOX editorial memos reviewed by MMFA reveal FOX News Channel's inner workings." Retrieved on 2008-09-19.

Erin, Burnett: Profile, Biography, About—CNBC.com

Fabrikant, Geraldine (1991-02-27): "THE MEDIA BUSINESS; Surprise Pact By G.E. Unit To Buy FNN", *The New York Times*. Retrieved on 2007-10-19.

"Factiva, a Dow Jones & Reuters Company." factiva.com.

Félix, Guattari: "Plan for the Planet." In Molecular Revolution. Psychiatry and Politics. London: Penguin Books, 1984. p. 269.

"Fib, Newton:" Slate.com (October 29, 2002): Retrieved on 2008-04-16. "The Associated Press accused Washington bureau reporter Christopher Newton of journalistic fraud last month and sacked him. The AP alleges that in at least 40 of the many hundred stories Newton wrote for the wire service between January 13, 2000, and September 8, 2002, Newton quoted sources who appear not to exist."

Fishman, Charles (May 2000): "The Revolution Will Be Televised (on CNBC)", *Fast Company*. Retrieved on 2007-07-17.

"Five More Ws for Good Journalism." *COPY EDITING, InlandPress*. Retrieved on September 12, 2008.

"Five Ws and H." *Creativity Techniques*. Retrieved on September 12, 2008.

FNC's 25-54 Prime "Downward Spiral", TVNewser.

"Form 10-K submitted by Dow Jones and Company for the fiscal year ended December 31, 1997." Dow Jones and Company, United States Securities and Exchange Commission (1998-03-17): Retrieved on 2007-07-16.

"Four more Newspapers Intend to Drop AP Over Rates." Editor and Publisher (2008-08-20): Retrieved on 2008-08-27.

Fournier, Ron (August 23, 2008): "Analysis: Biden pick shows lack of confidence", Associated Press. Retrieved on 2008-08-23.

"Fox Business Network gets ready to battle CNBC", *San Francisco Chronicle* (October 14, 2007): Retrieved on 2007-10-14.

Fox News Channel Leads in 2007 Cable News Ratings.

Fox News Channel to Take HD Leap—4/29/2008 3:12:00 PM—Broadcasting and Cable.

FOX News Mobile website.

Friedman, Jon (2006-08-09): "CNBC's Maria Bartiromo outgrows the 'Money Honey' label", *MarketWatch*. Retrieved on 2007-11-14.

Fritz, Spiegl: *What The Papers Didn't Mean to Say,* Scouse Press, Liverpool, 1965.

George, Lewis: Nightly News with Brian Williams—MSNBC.com

Girard, Bruce (ed): "A Passion for Radio: Radio waves and community."

"Giuliani Pressures Time Warner to Transmit a Fox Channel."

Goldman, Jim (2007-01-29): "The View on Vista", *CNBC*. Retrieved on 2007-10-22.

"Google News Becomes A Publisher", Information Week (August 31, 2007): Retrieved on 2008-04-26. "Because the Associated Press, Agence France-Presse, U.K. Press Association and the Canadian Press don't have a consumer Website where they publish their content, they have not been able to benefit from the traffic that Google News drives to other publishers," Josh Cohen, Business Product Manager for Google News, explained in a blog post. "As a result, we're hosting it on Google News."

Google's cache of http://www.unification.net/1996/960102.html as retrieved on Feb. 7, 2008 16:16:19 GMT.

Greg, Sandoval (July 30, 2006): "CNN snatching page out of YouTube's book", C/Net. Retrieved on 2007-11-13.

Greppi, Michele (2007-10-07): "Q&A: CNBC President Mark Hoffman", *TV Week*. Retrieved on 2007-10-19.

Guy, Pat (1991-02-27): "NBC Wins FNN; Dow Jones Jilted", *USA Today*. Retrieved on 2007-10-19.

Harold, Evans: *News Headlines* (Editing and Design: Book Three) Butterworth-Heinemann Ltd. (February 1974).

Hau, Louis (8 August 2007): "Murdoch Plots Course for Dow Jones", *Forbes*. Retrieved on 2008-03-29.

HEARINGS before the special subcommittee on investigations of the committee on interstate and Foreign Commerce House of representatives, 91st Congress, 1st and 2nd sessions, Serial No. 91-55: U.S. Government Printing Office, Washington.

Hempel, Jessi (31 March 2008): "CNBC Feels Your Pain...", *Fortune*. Retrieved on 2008-03-31.

Hinckley, David (1999-11-26): "Joe Franklin: Truth in Packaging", *New York Daily News*. Retrieved on 1 January 2008.

History of the BBC—key dates p. 4 BBC Heritage 1960s.

History of the BBC—key dates p. 4 BBC Heritage 1970s.

Hoda, Kotb: Today Show—Today.msnbc.com

"House of Commons Hansard Debates for 15 February 1996 (pt 22)." Retrieved on 2007-04-03.

How the Liberal Media Stonewalled the Edwards Chicago Daily Observer, August 18, 2008.

"Illinois Television Stations": Record Information Services. Retrieved on 2007-10-22.

"Impartiality Review: Israeli-Palestinian Conflict—BBC Governors" (PDF): Retrieved on 2007-05-14.

"Internet Radio: This Year's Business Models"—2004 Streaming Media West Conference session.

Interview transcript: Rupert Murdoch and Roger Ailes, The Financial Times, October 6, 2006.

"Iran bloggers test regime's tolerance—The Boston Globe." Retrieved on 2007-04-11.

"Iraq threatens arrest of police officer" Associated Press, 4 January 2007.

Jack M. Bickham, *The 38 Most Common Fiction Writing Mistakes and How to Avoid Them.*

Jamie, Gangel: National Correspondent, NBC News 'Today'—Today Show—MSNBC.com

Jane, Arraf: Nightly News with Brian Williams—MSNBC.com

Jaques, Steinberg (October 20, 2006): "NBC Says Viewers Won't Notice Cuts in News Staff", New York Times. Retrieved on 2007-11-12.

Jeannie, Ohm: Meet the faces of MSNBC—MSNBC.com

Jesse, Walker: *Rebels on the Air: An Alternative History of Radio in America* (New York University Press, 2001), pp. 147-49.

Jim, Maceda: Nightly News with Brian Williams—MSNBC.com

Jim, Miklaszewski: Nightly News with Brian Williams—MSNBC.com

Joe, Kernen: *CNBC*. Retrieved on 2007-11-14.

John, Yang: 1 Named NBC News Correspondent.

John, Moody: "Moody Memos Set the Stage for the Fox Effect." Retrieved on 2008-09-19.

John, Moody: "Fox News internal memo" (PDF).

Johnson, Bridget (2008-02-03): "New Washington Times Editor Alters Loaded Style." *About.com*. Ed. Michael Daecher. New York, New York: About, Inc. The New York Times Company. Retrieved on 2008-03-07." "The church is the mind and the media is the body, to reach the external world. We should begin that movement and activity in the United States, because the Washington Times and UPI are headquartered there. Once we establish our organization in the United States, it can be expanded to the world without much alteration."

Kahn, Frank J., ed. *Documents of American Broadcasting*, fourth edition (Prentice-Hall, Inc., 1984).

Kathie, Lee: Gifford returns to morning TV—Today Show—MSNBC.com

Keith, Morrison: Dateline NBC—MSNBC.com

"Keith, Olbermann on Charles Babington's analysis" (August 28, 2008): Retrieved on 2008-08-29.

Kelly, O'Donnell: Nightly News with Brian Williams—MSNBC.com

"Kerbango AM/FM/IM Radio moves us toward The Broadcast Internet From the Ether" by Bob Metcalfe 2000, InfoWorld.

Kerry, Sanders: Nightly News with Brian Williams—MSNBC.com

Kevin, Corke: Nightly News with Brian Williams—MSNBC.com

"Key Facts: BBC News and Current Affairs", BBC Press Office (October 2006): Retrieved on 2007-10-25.

"Knowing What's What and What's Not: The Five W's (and 1 "H") of Cyberspace." *Media Awareness Network*. Retrieved on September 12, 2008.

Learmonth, Michael (2005-02-07): "CNBC on a road bound for revamps", *Variety*. Retrieved on 2007-10-19.

Learmonth, Michael (2006-06-18): "Biz net builds buzz", *Variety*. Retrieved on 2007-07-17.

Learmonth, Michael (2006-10-29): "NBC News braces for the ax", *Variety*. Retrieved on 2007-10-22.

Lenzner, Robert (May 5, 1985): Boston Globe *Murdoch, partner plan 4th network*. Section: National/Foreign; p. 1 (the six stations cover many of the nation's major markets—New York, Chicago, Los Angeles, Dallas, Houston and Washington).

Lichty, Lawrence W., and Topping Malachi C., eds.: *American Broadcasting: A Source Book on the History of Radio and Television* (Hastings House, 1975).

Linda, Jorgensen: *Real-World Newsletters* (1999).

Lisa, Daniels: Nightly News with Brian Williams—MSNBC.com

Lisa, Myers: Nightly News with Brian Williams—MSNBC.com

Loades-Carter, Jonathan (2005-07-21): "Dow Jones pulls out of joint venture with CNBC", *Financial Times*. Retrieved on 2007-11-28.

London This Week had started in early 1969 as a once per week "opt out" replacing the Friday edition of *Town and Around*" TV and Radio Bits: BBC South East: History." Retrieved on 2007-06-21.

Lowell, Thomas: *So Long Until Tomorrow*. New York: Wm. Morrow and Co., 1977, pp. 17-19.

M.L. Stein, Susan Paterno, and R. Christopher Burnett, *The Newswriter's Handbook Introduction to Journalism* (2006).

"Managing the Digital Enterprise", by Dr. Michael Rappa.

Many others however dismiss this as as a convenience to get Company Management off the hook of poor performance. Aussie guardian for agency's ethics—The Australian.

Margaret, Larson: Dateline NBC—MSNBC.com

Mark, Levin: *The Reporter's Notebook: Writing Tools for Student Journalists* (2000).

"Market Selloff: CNBC's Best Week Since '01". *TV Newser* (March 6, 2007). Retrieved on 2007-07-17.

Martin, Fletcher: Nightly News with Brian Williams—MSNBC.com

Martin, Savidge: Nightly News with Brian Williams—MSNBC.com

Matt, Lauer: Today Show—MSNBC.com

Media and War—The Falklands Conflict Imperial War Museum.

Media Matters for America Results: Tagged with CNN, Media Matters for America.

Media Research Center CyberAlert—02/17/1999--slant of CNN's Tuesday night town meeting.

Meet the candidates' kids—The Daily Nightly—msnbc.com.

Meredith, Vieira: Today: It's a New Day Today—Today.msnbc.com

Meyrowitz, Joshua: Mediating Communication: What Happens? Ch. 3.

Michael, Okwu: Nightly News with Brian Williams—MSNBC.com

Michelle, Kosinski: Nightly News with Brian Williams—MSNBC.com

Mike, Shields (October 29, 2007): "CNN To Launch Bureau in Second Life Virtual World", Media Week. Retrieved on 2007-11-14.

Mike, Taibbi: Dateline NBC—MSNBC.com

"Milosevic attacks BBC 'bias'", BBC News (2002-08-22).

Moon, Sun Myung (2000-12-06): "Rev. Sun Myung Moon; Talks Given on His South American Tour, November 29-December 6, 2000". Retrieved on 2008-03-07.

"MoveOn.org: Targets AP's Fournier for Alleged Pro-McCain Bias", *Editor & Publisher*, August 23, 2008, <http://www.editorandpublisher.com/eandp/news/article_display.jsp?vnu_content_id=1003842038>

"MSNBC Host Rips AP Reporter's Analysis of Obama Speech", *Editor & Publisher* (August 29, 2008). Retrieved on 2008-08-29.

"Multimedia News": BBC News Online (2007-11-12). Retrieved on 2007-12-19.

Nancy, Kress: *Beginnings, Middles & Ends.*
Nancy, L. Snyderman: NBC Nightly News with Brian Williams (Chief Medical Editor, NBC ws).
Natalie, Morales: Today Show—MSNBC.com
NBC, Dow Jones & Company (9 December 1997): "NBC and Dow Jones to form Global Business Television and Internet Alliance." Press release. Retrieved on 2008-03-29.
NBC, News Continues its Expansion in Asia with Bangkok Bureau.
NBC/MSNBC Announce Convention Plans—mediabistro.com: TVNewser.
Ned Colt—Nightly News with Brian Williams—MSNBC.com
New York Times (July 11, 1985) *$55.9 Million Fox Film Loss.* Section: D; p. D19.
"New-Media Focus Splits Associated Press Members." The Wall Street Journal (2008-06-26). Retrieved on 2008-08-27.
News Corporation denies Fox News bias Australian Associated Press, October 26, 2004.
"News Corporation: FOX News Channel." News Corporation (2008-04-18). Retrieved on 2008-04-21.
News World Communications UPI.
"News World Communications; "Media Arm of Reverend Sun Myung Moon's Unification Church"." *The Colombia Journalism Review* (2003-11-24). Retrieved on 2008-02-02.
"NewsWatch—About BBC News—This is BBC News." Retrieved on 2007-04-03.
Norah O'Donnell—Nightly News with Brian Williams—MSNBC.com
"Northern Echo: Archive." Retrieved on 2007-08-17.—*Robert Dougall was even less flattering about the first set, and is quoted as saying that the tiling was "grey and lavatorial" together with "a huge round thing" in the background—referring to the new rotating clockface logo and CSO screen.*
Official Documentation of Petitioned Cancellation of "Fair and Balanced" trademark phrase, Trademark Trial and Appeal Board Inquiry System
"Oh No They Didn't!." On The Media (2008-04-25). Retrieved on 2008-08-27.
Olga Kharif, The Last Days of Internet Radio?, March 7, 2007, Downloaded March 7, 2007.
"Our Company Independence and Trust Principles." reuters.com. Retrieved on 2008-03-03.
"Pan Global TV Japan."
Pete Williams—Nightly News with Brian Williams—MSNBC.com
Peter Alexander—Nightly News with Brian Williams—MSNBC.com
Peter Mukherjee's NewsX channel slated for major launch—Yahoo! India News.

Pfanner, Eric (2006-10-01): "CNBC pushes hard to fend off rival Fox", *International Herald Tribune*. Retrieved on 2007-07-17.

Philip Gerard, Creative Nonfiction: Researching and Crafting Stories of Real Life (1998).

Philip Stephens: BBC is losing public service plot, FT June 20, 2006.

Poynter Online: Katie Couric/CBS Timeline (1975-2008).

Preston, Mendenhall: Nightly News with Brian Williams—MSNBC.com

"Radical reform to deliver a more focused BBC", BBC Press Office (2007-10-18). Retrieved on 2007-10-25.

"RadioValve: Local radio station uses fiber-optics instead of FM waves", by Heather Morgan 1998, Boulder Daily Camera.

Read, Donald (1992): *The Power of News. The History of Reuters 1849-1989*. Oxford, Oxford University Press.

Reese Schonfeld Bio. (January 29, 2001) *MeAndTed.com*. Accessed 2007-06-18.

Rehema, Ellis: Nightly News with Brian Williams—MSNBC.com

Retired anchor Shaw laments effects of Fox on his beloved CNN. *Chicago Sun-Times*. 5 June, 2007.

Reuters admits altering Beirut photo, Ynetnews, Retrieved on June 3, 2008.

"Reuters opens virtual news bureau in 'Second Life'", USA Today (October 10, 2006). Retrieved on 2007-11-14.

"Reuters to Acquire European Fund Research Specialist", news.taume.com (2007-06-29).

Rev. Jesse Jackson. (October 2001): *RainbowPush.org*. Accessed 2007-06-18.

Rev. Sun Myung Moon: LET US GO OVER THE HILL.

Rev. Sun Myung Moon: Our Mission During the Time of World Transition.

Richard, Engel: Nightly News with Brian Williams—MSNBC.com

Richard, Katz (1996-05): "Bold grab for subs: Murdoch offers $11 to carry Fox News". BNET. Retrieved on March 2, 2008.

Robert, Bazell: Nightly News with Brian Williams—MSNBC.com

Robins, J. Max (2006-09-25): "A Modified MSNBC?", *Broadcasting and Cable*. Retrieved on 2007-07-17.

Roger, O'Neil: Nightly News with Brian Williams—MSNBC.com.

Roma-Atlanta via web Parte CNN Italia *la Repubblica* (Italian).

"Ron Insana." *CNBC*. Retrieved on 2007-11-14.

Ron Mott: Nightly News with Brian Williams—MSNBC.com.

"RTS Hall of Fame—p. 46." Retrieved on 2007-04-11. (PDF)

Samuel Chinque obituary, The Guardian, December 17, 2004.

SaveNetRadio Announcements, by Dave Solomon.

Schulberg, Pete. (July 15, 1994) The Oregonian *Fox is a business, if not artistic, success*. Section: Televison; p. E1.

"Scott, Cohn": *CNBC*. Retrieved on 2007-11-14.
Scott, Leith (August 1, 2006): "CNN welcoming citizen journalists", Milwaukee Journal-Sentinel. Retrieved on 2007-11-14.
Shah, Saeed. (September 24, 2002): The Independent *Business Analysis: Unstoppable Sky machine rolls on as ITV troubles worsen Dawn Airey's free-to-air television experience will be invaluable to BSkyB as it moves beyond its pay-TV model.* Section: Business; p. 21.
Siklos, Richard (2007-06-10): "What Murdoch's Paper Chase Means for Business TV", *The New York Times*. Retrieved on 2007-07-17.
Smith, Mike: "UK Radio, A Brief History—Other Media Developments."
Soundtrack Net: News: Legendary Composer John Williams Composes New "NBC Sunday Night Football" Theme.
"Stacking the deck in the CNBC Portfolio Challenge?" *Inside Cable News blog* (March 10, 2007). Retrieved on 2007-07-17.
Stelter, Brian (12 December 2007): "Yahoo Deal Adds Content From CNBC", *The New York Times*. Retrieved on 2008-03-31.
Steve Peha and Margot Carmichael Lester, *Be a Writer: Your Guide to the Writing Life* (2006).
Stout, David (2000-05-17): "Helen Thomas, Washington Fixture, Resigns as U.P.I. Reporter", *The New York Times*. Retrieved on 2008-03-07.
"Strib tells AP: we're canceling." MinnPost (2008-08-26). Retrieved on 2008-08-27.
"Sue Herera." *CNBC*. Retrieved on 2007-11-14.
Sutel, Seth (June 20, 2008): "AP, blogger resolve dispute over copyright", *Yahoo News (AP)*. Retrieved on 2008-06-20.
Sweney, Mark (8 January 2008): "New York Times and CNBC in Alliance", *guardian.co.uk*. Retrieved on 2008-03-31.
Ted, Turner: Global warming could lead to cannibalism | ajc.com
"The AP rift". Still a Newspaperman (2008-08-19): Retrieved on 2008-08-27.
"The BBC pro-Israeli? Is the Pope Jewish?-Comment-Columnists-Guest contributors-TimesOnline." Retrieved on 2007-04-11.
The BBC's Editorial Values www.bbc.co.uk/Retrieved 25 November 2006.
"The BBC's Royal Charter and the BBC Agreement." Retrieved on 2007-04-03.
The BBC's success story has a public service plot, Mark Thompson, Financial Times, June 21, 2006
"The Five W's of Online Help" by *Geoff Hart, TECHWR-L*. Retrieved on September 12, 2008.
"The Media Business; NBC to Buy Cable Service", *The New York Times* (May 3, 1988): Retrieved on 2007-07-16.
"The Media Business; New CNBC President", *The New York Times* (July 27, 1990). Retrieved on 2007-07-16.

The most popular sentence in China: "Don't be so CNN!"
The New York City Transit Authority in the 1980s.
"The State of the News Media 2007: Audience." Project for Excellence in Journalism. Retrieved on 2007-03-11.
"The State of the News Media 2008." Project for Excellence in Journalism (2008-04-27).
The Wall Street Journal Online—Best of the Web Today.
"The Wall Street Journal Report with Maria Bartiromo," *CNBC*. Retrieved on 2008-03-29.
The worst reported war since the Crimean: Julian Barnes 25 February 2002, Guardian Unlimited.
Thomas, H. White: "UNITED STATES EARLY RADIO HISTORY."
Thompson, John: The Media and Modernity. Cambridge, Polity Press.
Timothy, Noah: Fox News admits bias!, *Slate*, May 31, 2005, accessed September 26, 2006.
Tom, Aspell: Nightly News with Brian Williams—MSNBC.com
Tom, Brokaw: Nightly News with Brian Williams—MSNBC.com
Topcik, Joel (2006-09-18): "Wald Boosts Business at CNBC", *Broadcasting and Cable*. Retrieved on 2007-07-17.
"Totem Column," *Time*, November 10, 1941.
TQM Communications—AM/FM newsletter number one—Spring 1990.
T-RackS. "Willie Wilcox." Retrieved on 2007-07-17.
Transcript of Friday, July 25, 2008 Hardball with Chris Matthews.
Travel Editor Peter Greenberg—MSNBC.com
TV & Radio Bits—BBC NEWS Changes.
"TV Ark: BBC News Report: Zeebrugge ferry disaster from 6 March 1987." Retrieved on 2007-10-01.
"U.P.I.: Look Back in Sorrow" (book review of *Down to the Wire: UPI's Fight for Survival*), The New York Times, December 24, 1989.
UNESCO. "How to Do Community Radio: A Primer."
"UPI Staff Cuts Include White House Correspondent", Editor and Publisher, July 11, 2007.
Varaždinska televizija: 35 sati talk showa za Guinnessa—Sarajevo-x.com
"VOA: First on the Internet," by Chris Kern (2006).
VTV televizija: Vijesti—Usprkos kiÅ¡i Kiky i Drele i dalje u talk-showu
"War coverage lifts News Corp." The British Broadcasting Corporation. Retrieved on November 29, 2005.
Web Radio: Radio Production for Internet Streaming, by Chris Priestman, January 2002, Focal Press.
WHERE WENT THE 5 Ws?" *The Marcus Letter*. Retrieved on September 12, 2008.
Why are so Many Internet Radio Stations still on the Air?", by Doc Searls, July 17, 2002, Linux Journal.

Wighton, David (2006-05-12): "Lunch with the FT: She's the one", *Financial Times*. Retrieved on 2007-11-14.

"Will NPR's podcasts birth a new business model for public radio?", by Mark Glaser, November 29, 2005, USC Annenberg Online Journalism Review, Annenberg Center for Communication at USC.

Williams, Scott (January 31, 1996): Associated Press *Murdoch taps Ailes for new network; Former CNBC chief set to direct 24-hour news channel, take on CNN.*

Index